A BIT OF
THIS AND THAT

A family history and memoir

Chris McRae

Published in Australia by Silverbird Publishing Pty Ltd.
First published in Australia in 2020

Copyright © Chris McRae, 2020

Cover design: Rebecca McCaig Graphic Design
Typesetting, layout: WorkingType Studio

The right of Chris McRae to be identified as the Author of the Work has been asserted in accordance with the Copyright, Designs and Patents Act 1988. All rights reserved. No part of this publication may be reproduced, stored in a retrieval system, or transmitted, in any form or by any means without the prior written permission of the publisher, nor be otherwise circulated in any form of binding or cover other than that in which it is published and without a similar condition being imposed on the subsequent purchaser.

All efforts have been made to contact holders of copyright. Any infringement of copyright is unintentional. Please contact the author if any information needs to be updated.

National Library of Australia Cataloguing-in-Publication Entry:
Creator: McRae, Chris, author

 A catalogue record for this work is available from the National Library of Australia

A bit of this and that
ISBN: 978-0-6488533-9-8

This book is available for purchase online at Amazon, Booktopia, Book Depository, Dymocks and other online booksellers.
Please search by ISBN.

*To my wife Tricia and children
Ewen, Hannah and Ellen*

BOOK COVER DESIGN CONCEPT

The cover design is an illustrative approach intended to capture broader agricultural landscapes, and in particular the topography of East Gippsland.

A sense of place is an important theme throughout this book and sets the scene for many of the stories that unfold through it.

Considering the title and the fact that the book is a collection of elements brought together — a family history, war letters, poems, memoir — it reminded me of a patchwork quilt and how agricultural landscapes can reflect this when viewed from above. This patchwork effect is included in the illustration of the hills, together with the cleared and uncleared farmland, with a road snaking its way through the middle representing a journey.

The back cover continues this patchwork theme, overlain with various images relevant to the book and in a more earthy tone, designed to be reminiscent of a sepia toned photograph or leather-bound journal.

Rebecca McCaig
Graphic Design

CONTENTS

PRELUDE	 1	
CHAPTER 1	*Beginnings* 7	
CHAPTER 2	*For God, king and country* 21	
CHAPTER 3	*Early days*............................. 71	
CHAPTER 4	*A developing interest*................... 97	
CHAPTER 5	*Times of change*........................ 103	
CHAPTER 6	*College life* 119	
CHAPTER 7	*Commencing a career* 131	
CHAPTER 8	*Consolidation*.......................... 141	
CHAPTER 9	*A consequential time*................... 149	
INTERLUDES		
INTERLUDE A	*Some poems* 171	
INTERLUDE B	*A few kicks* 190	
INTERLUDE C	*Faith*.................................. 222	
INTERLUDE D	*An amazing match* 233	
INTERLUDE E	*Rolling the arm over* 242	
INTERLUDE F	*Some more poems* 258	
CHAPTER 10	*On the move*........................... 289	
CHAPTER 11	*Time in the west* 297	
CHAPTER 12	*Back to Victoria* 305	

CHAPTER 13	*More change*	320
CHAPTER 14	*Dry times*	331
CHAPTER 15	*An unexpected move*	344
CHAPTER 16	*A national initiative*	365

POSTLUDE	375
ACKNOWLEDGEMENTS	386
BIBLIOGRAPHY	388

MAP OF THE BUCHAN AREA

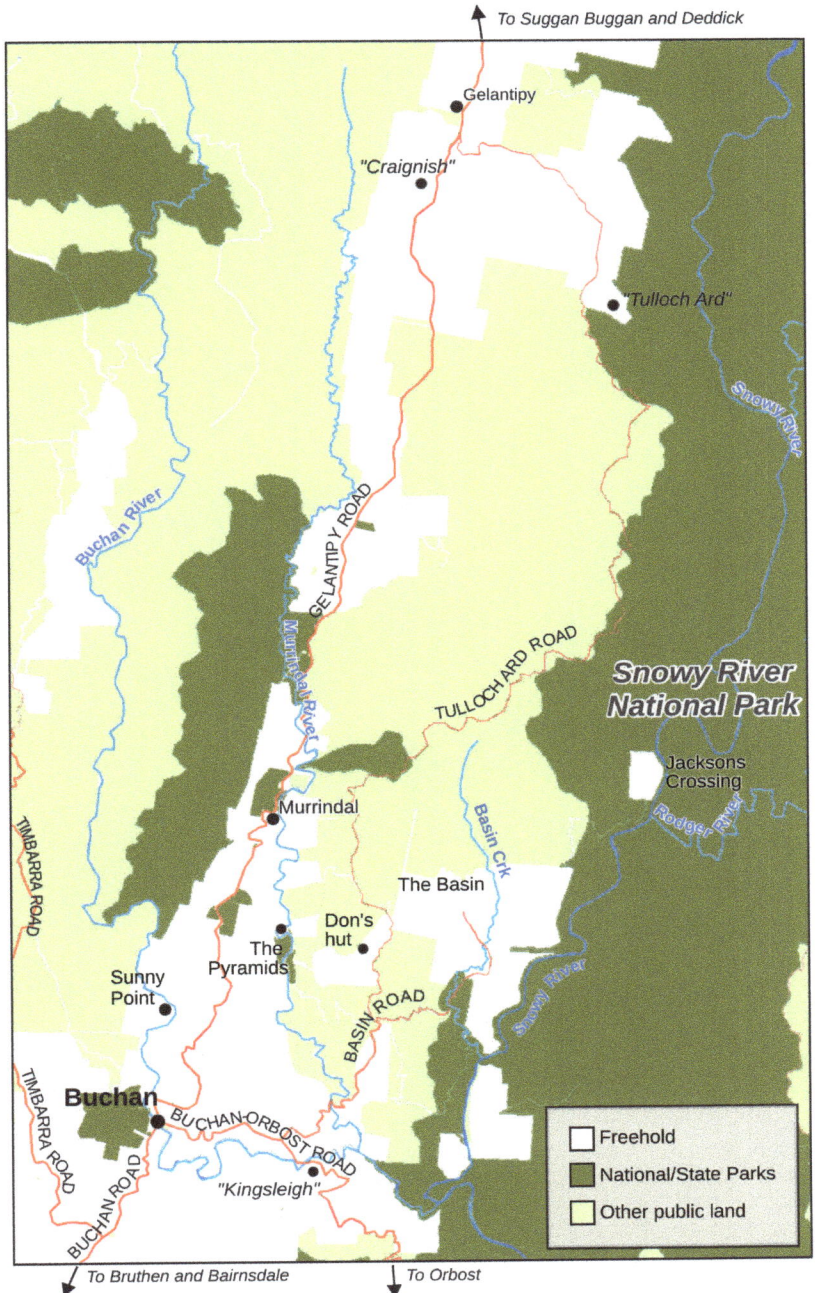

Showing location of properties and areas
referred to in this book

PRELUDE

I lang hae thought, my youthfu' friend,
A something to have sent you,
Tho' it should serve nae ither end
Than just a kind memento:
But how the subject-theme may gang,
Let time and chance determine;
Perhaps it may turn out a sang,
Perhaps turn out a sermon.

First stanza of 'Epistle to a young friend' — Robert Burns

Each of us naturally finds our own life to be particularly interesting, but it is perhaps genuinely interesting to only a relatively small group of extended family, friends and acquaintances. Beyond this, a life story may occasionally elicit interest from others ranging from moderate to passing, but in the broader sweep of life it is sobering to reflect that almost all will hardly raise a ripple.

This is not to confuse interest with individual worth, nor to suggest that the life of each of us is not uniquely and wonderfully important, but simply to reflect that in the plethora of matters which compete for our attention and notice, the actions and life experiences of specific individuals are rarely more than a passingly small component of a vast and expanding totality. (The fact that a surprisingly high percentage of Australians at any given time are unable to identify the current prime minister, doesn't bode well for less prominent individuals having much impact beyond a very small circle!)

I am therefore under no illusions regarding the likely level and extent of interest in this compilation of my family background, experiences and thoughts. The exercise is intended simply to be a selective account of what I judge to be the more influential or interesting experiences of my life, a reflection on some of the people and issues that I have found to be important to me, and a description of, and occasional reflection on, the evolution in my outlook and understanding of certain matters.

I have regularly found documenting issues to be a helpful aspect of fully considering them, which encourages greater clarity in my understanding of them. In keeping with the observations above, I therefore expect to be one of the major beneficiaries of this endeavour, although that is not the primary reason for it. It is my children — Ewen, Hannah and Ellen — whom I have had most in mind when putting this document together. At the very least, I trust they will find it interesting and of some value, as it will endure well beyond my time with them.

It is possible that others may find some interest in these notes as well and, if so, I am glad of that. We are inquisitive beings and can find surprising interest in information about those of whom we know nothing, or whose lives have not impacted ours at all. I regularly find this to be true, for example, in reading obituaries in newspapers; irrespective of the life being remembered, the fundamental human interest involved often makes for compelling reading. (Maybe this effort might generate something of the same interest, without having arisen from the usual precursor.)

It is also valuable to have documented records of experiences and views. Even though some may later be disputed or challenged (or even found to contain inaccurate information or recollections, or opinions no longer held), they at least provide a 'hook' to experiences and times which otherwise could be lost. Just as societies evolve and change over time, so too do individuals' opinions and outlooks. I hope to be able to convey some of my experiences with evolving perspectives in this document. To the extent that I am successful in presenting my thoughts clearly, this may also help my children to understand me (and maybe even themselves) more fully.

I am fortunate to have been part of a close family. While growing up, I found this was particularly the case with the connection to the broader McRae family. In fact, in the process of compiling this document, I have become acutely aware of how much greater has been the influence of and interest in my father's family than that of my mother's, even though as an individual it was she who was a far more important influence on my life.

The connection to family has continued and, since marriage, has expanded to closeness with the immediate and extended family of Tricia, my wife. I am grateful that the younger generations of our families continue to place high importance on these connections, as they have been one of the most significant realities of my life.

The greatest parental influence I experienced was that of my mother, Margaret. She died in 2017 and could reasonably be described as the matriarch of the family. She was a strong character with a positive, engaged and pragmatic approach to life, and a person for whom I have deep love and respect. She never left my sisters Elizabeth and Alison, nor me, with any doubt regarding her belief of how life should be lived. Nor were we left without a clear lived example of this from her. Throughout her life, I experienced her as being loving but not effusive, involved but not interfering, supportive but not pushy, strong but not unfair, and absolutely constant in seeking to provide any assistance or guidance she believed she could.

My biological father, Don, died when I was six years old. I have only vague recollections of him, certainly insufficient to have developed any personal understanding of his character. I have gathered some clues as to what this might have been from letters and other documents of his that have been retained, as well as from discussions with some who knew him, but inevitably this gives a limited and largely point-in-time picture. Most importantly, it precludes the iterative influence he would have had on me as I grew and matured.

Mum remarried around two and a half years after Don died, and thus my major experiences of a male parent are of my stepfather, Alf King. He was part of my life for over 40 years prior to his death in 2001. He was one of the gentlest, most inoffensive and most self-effacing people I have known. I have extremely positive recollections of Alf, his example and his influence on me.

As a result of my age when Don died and Mum remarried, I called both Don and Alf 'Dad'; consequently, to avoid confusion in this document, I will refer to each by their name rather than the familiar title.

Most of the writing in this publication is contemporary, but some is not. I have included a chapter containing some of the letters from the uncle I was named after, who was killed in the First World War. These letters home to his family seem to me to give an interesting representation of the circumstances and experiences that would have been common to many young Australian men and their families at that time. Viewing them over a century later and knowing the personal outcome they preceded, makes them even more poignant.

I have also included some poems written by my father, Don McRae, as well as some of mine. Many of them are intended to be rather tongue-in-cheek, and if the sentiments expressed in any are judged not to have aged as well as they might, I hope this intent can be accepted as at least some mitigation.

Some of the information presented on the experiences of my grandparents, particularly Alexander and Bessie McRae, and to an extent those of my father, have been reconstructed using retained documents and letters of theirs or official property and government records. In some cases this has led to a revision of long-held family perspectives. Even now some conclusions arrived at may not be entirely accurate, but they are almost certainly more precise than their largely anecdotal predecessors.

If an individual's character reflects a mixture of nature and nurture, the above gives some insight into the direct parental and family influences that have impacted me. I hope the rest of this document will shed some light on broader experiences and impacts that have added to this.

CHAPTER 1

Beginnings

My father Don's family was from East Gippsland in Victoria, and I spent the first 16 years of my life there. His paternal grandparents had migrated from Kintail in Ross-shire in the Western Highlands of Scotland, coming to Australia via New Zealand. His maternal ancestors, the Grants, had also migrated to New Zealand, in their case from Glenmoriston, also in the Scottish Highlands.

My great grandfather, Christopher McRae, was born at Inverinate, Scotland, in 1821. In the early 1850s, he travelled to the United States to try his luck in the Californian gold rush. He apparently met with some limited success, but in 1854 he returned to Scotland where, in May of that year, he married Margaret Fraser in Edinburgh.

In that same year, Christopher and Margaret sailed for New Zealand on the 'Dolphin' — along with Christopher's brothers, John and Roderick — arriving in Port Chalmers, Dunedin, in November. Christopher is recorded as working as a shepherd in Otago and having moved briefly to Waipu, north of Auckland, before returning to Southland. He is reported as having owned a couple of properties and working as a bootmaker in the Invercargill area, and as a farmer and whisky distiller in Hokanui near Gore.

The four children of Christopher and Margaret were born in New Zealand, the second of whom was my grandfather, Alexander Fraser McRae, born in 1856, probably at Invercargill.

Some time after 1863, Christopher and his family left the South Island and moved to a property at Patea, north-west of Whanganui on the North Island of New Zealand. The timing of this move and the length of stay at Patea is unclear; it is also unclear whether they made any subsequent moves in New Zealand before moving to Victoria in 1874.

Following their move to Victoria, Christopher and Margaret settled initially at Modewarre near Geelong, and subsequently lived in the Melbourne suburb of Hawthorn. Christopher is said to have lost heavily in the Victorian land boom of the 1880s and early 1890s, which appears feasible but has not been able to be verified. Although some versions of family history suggest he assisted Alexander to purchase land in East Gippsland, this appears unlikely, which perhaps gives some credence to the suggestion of earlier financial loss given his one-time ownership of property in suburban Melbourne. He and Margaret spent their final years living with Alexander and his family at East Buchan and died within a few days of each other in November 1907.

Obituary for Christopher and Margaret McRae from an Invercargill newspaper (New Zealand), December 1907.

It is with deep regret we record the demise of Mr. and Mrs. Christopher McRae, early pioneers of this district, who both

CHAPTER 1   *Beginnings*

passed to the great beyond last month at the residence of their son, Alexander, in Gippsland, Victoria.

Mr. McRae was a native of Kintail, Ross-shire. He left his native land early in life for the Californian diggings and after making a competency there returned to his home. Shortly afterward he married Miss Fraser, a native of Rogart, Sutherlandshire, and in the early '50s left for the colonies and took up land about 3 miles from the Invercargill Post Office, on what is called now the Oteramika Road.

They possessed the warm hearts and generous disposition of the Highland people, and their door was always wide open for their friends. Such welcomes are not so common now.

The deceaseds' hospitality knew no bounds, and away in the far south with their home on the fringe of one of their largest forests, family worship was held as regularly by them as if they were living in the heart of the Highlands.

In 1860 Mr. McRae sold his farm to Mr. Vivian and took up property on the north side of the Makarewa bush, where he and his family worked hard, but owing to the want of roads, he had to leave the place. He then migrated with his family to the North Island and took up land at Patea, but on the eve of the Maori war he had to leave his home and he finally left for Victoria.

The deceased leave 2 sons and a daughter[1] to mourn their loss.

Alexander commenced his time in Victoria at Modewarre and subsequently worked on sheep properties in the Riverina district of southern New South Wales. In the mid to late 1880s, he moved

---

1   Christopher and Margaret had four children: sons John and Alexander; daughters Mary and Helen.

to Gelantipy in East Gippsland and the first record of him applying to lease land in the area appears in December 1887.

Initial European settlement at Gelantipy occurred in 1839, although it was not until around forty years later that access to the district improved beyond a rudimentary droving track. During the 1880s and 1890s, despite its remoteness, Gelantipy saw keen interest in settlement, with many of those selecting land there having a strong Scottish heritage. Other McRaes — including Alexander's uncle Roderick, who settled on a property he named 'Tulloch Ard' — had either moved there prior to his arrival or did so soon afterwards.

(As unlikely as it may now seem, for a brief period following Federation in 1901, there was a chance that Gelantipy's remoteness may have been mitigated to a degree by the placement of Australia's capital city. In the lead up to Federation the location of the nation's capital became a point of contention, particularly between New South Welsh and Victorian politicians. Agreement was eventually reached that it be in New South Wales, but not less than 100 miles (161 kilometres) from Sydney. In the ensuing process to define a suitable location, the towns of Bombala and Dalgety in 1899 and 1904, respectively, were officially nominated as sites for the capital. Both were in southern New South Wales, around three times the necessary distance from Sydney, but less than 200 kilometres north east of Gelantipy. However, both they and other options were rejected prior to Canberra being chosen by Federal Parliament in 1908.)

Perhaps the family connection to the area, the Scottish background of some existing settlers, or both, led Alexander to decide to settle in Gelantipy. Whatever the driver, between 1887 and 1901

CHAPTER 1   *Beginnings*

he selected or took over existing leases for more than 1300 acres of land in the area, in four separate allotments, calling the property 'Craignish'.

My paternal grandmother was Bessie, daughter of Alexander Grant and his wife Mary (nee Cameron), who had both arrived in New Zealand from Scotland in 1840 aboard the 'Blenheim', and married in 1841. By 1850 Alexander and Mary had settled on a property they called 'Tullochgorum' at Turakina between Whanganui and Marton, north of Wellington. It remains as a Grant family farm to this day and is a property with one of the longest histories of uninterrupted family ownership in New Zealand. Bessie was born on the property in 1857, the youngest of seven children.

The basis for the connection between the McRae and Grant families is unknown. They had both journeyed from Scotland and settled in New Zealand, but in quite different parts of the country, some years apart. However, at some stage after 1863, Christopher and Margaret had moved to Patea, approximately 80 kilometres north-west of Turakina, and lived there for a number of years.

When they migrated to Victoria in 1874, it is not clear whether they did so from Patea, or if they had moved elsewhere in New Zealand prior to departing. It is possible that contact between the families first occurred during the period the McRaes were at Patea, although there is also information suggesting Alexander returned to New Zealand for a celebration around 1890, with this possibly being the time of his contact with the Grant family.

Whatever the basis for the connection, Alexander had been in Australia since his late teens and was almost 35 years old when he travelled to New Zealand and married Bessie[2], almost 34 years old, on the Grant family property at Turakina in January 1891.

Alexander returned with his bride to Gelantipy in February 1891, and they lived on Craignish until around 1902. Their family of five was born during this time: Alexander, known as Alistair/Alister (born at Hawthorn in 1891); Christopher (1893); Ewen (1894); Margaret (1896); and my father, Donald Cameron McRae (1898) — the latter four born at Gelantipy.

Bessie kept a diary from 1898 until 1901. Two of the more striking aspects of it are the frequency of visitors to Craignish from within and outside the district, and the extent of Alexander's travel and time absent from the home.

Many of those visiting — close or more distant relatives, as well as others from the district and beyond — remained for meals or overnight, and the sense of pleasure at receiving visitors, open hospitality, and support for others is a strong theme of the records. Such was the frequency of this theme that mention is made in the diary on the rare days that it *did not* occur. As well as locals or visitors doing business, Rev Alexander Morton — the Presbyterian minister who served in Orbost from 1893 until 1903 and regularly visited the district to conduct church services — frequently received hospitality at Craignish.

Alexander ran some beef cattle on the property, but his main business was sheep farming. Bessie's diary records 4,500 sheep

---

2 Bessie was officially known as 'Betsy' and her marriage certificate records her name in this manner. For an unknown reason, from shortly after her marriage, she began being known as 'Bessie' and at least by 1893 was signing her name as such. She appears not to have formally changed her name, because in election rolls of 1905 she is still recorded as 'Betsy'.

CHAPTER 1   *Beginnings*

arriving on one occasion in 1899 and 3,000 on another in 1900. There are other regular references to sheep being bought or sold.

Travel was on horseback or by buggy and Alexander was frequently absent for days at a time. Because of the distances involved and the modes of transport, it was difficult, time-consuming and tiring work, on top of that required to clear and develop his property. Bessie regularly reports in her diary 'Alexander arrived home late, very tired,' or similar, with absences frequently being days or more than a week.

In 1896 Alexander was elected to the Tambo Shire Council, a role which included attending council meetings each month at Bruthen, around 95 kilometres south of Gelantipy. Travel was again by horse, with most meetings requiring three days — one to travel each way and one for the meeting. On occasions Alexander took the opportunity to travel around 30 kilometres further to Bairnsdale for business, which extended his time away.

There was regular correspondence between Alexander and the Department of Lands and Survey. Many letters requested lease payments to be made on his selected land, occasionally accompanied by threats of the land being resumed by the government. Mostly these payment requests were met, albeit sometimes late or in instalments, as means allowed. The formality and civility of both sides is a striking feature of the correspondence, although there is no mistaking the intent with which both represent their positions.

The area is remote from cities, services and markets, the impact even more pronounced with the rudimentary transport facilities and roads of that time than is the case today. When Bessie's father Alexander Grant visited from New Zealand for three months in

1894, he is reputed to have said to Alexander, 'Well, you certainly couldn't have taken her much further away, could you?'

It was not an easy time to begin a farming operation. Apart from the remoteness of the area and the physical challenges of clearing land largely by hand, two other events would have impacted adversely. A major economic depression occurred in Australia in the early 1890s, reaching its peak in 1893. Additionally, what came to be known as the Federation Drought impacted most of eastern Australia from 1895 to 1903.

Both these events would have been detrimental to Alexander's fledgling enterprise, perhaps significantly so. In addition, at some stage early in his venture, likely around the turn of the century, he suffered the theft of a significant number of sheep, which added to the challenges of developing his farming operation. The only hint to the timing of this in Bessie's diary is a reference in April 1899 of men having returned to Craignish when they '…did not find (the) sheep', although it is not certain that the two are linked.

At the time Alexander and neighbour Henry Biggs, who operated a property called 'Glenmore' about 25 kilometres west of Gelantipy, were in a form of partnership in their sheep-trading ventures. The Biggs family left their property in 1902, probably at least in part because of the financial impact of the loss of the sheep.

This combination of factors obviously also had a major impact on Alexander and Bessie at Craignish. Struggling to establish a financially sound operation, around 1902 they and their family moved from Gelantipy to 'Kingsleigh', a property owned by John Henry King on the Orbost Road at East Buchan, which Alexander then managed. It appears most likely this was a move forced on them by the financial pressures they were under and the need for

Alexander to obtain some additional means to support himself and his family.

John Henry King had extensive landholdings in the Buchan district and was the son of a prominent early settler, also John King, from central Gippsland. His great grandfather was Philip Gidley King, a naval officer who had arrived in Australia with the First Fleet, and later became the third governor of New South Wales.

Three generations of the McRae family at 'Kingsleigh', East Buchan, circa 1906 — my great grandparents, grandparents, and father and his siblings. (Photograph: John Flynn)

Standing: Mary 'Cousie' McRae (Alexander's cousin, daughter of his uncle John from NZ), Alexander McRae (grandfather)

Seated: Margaret, Bessie McRae (grandmother), Alistair, Christopher and Margaret McRae (great grandparents)

Front: Christopher, Donald (father) and Ewen

The McRae family was closely involved with the Presbyterian Church and when a young John Flynn, training as a minister, was appointed to Buchan as the first resident home missionary in the district in 1905, he initially stayed with them at Kingsleigh. When his sister, a music teacher, arrived he relocated and shared accommodation with her in Buchan. Flynn left Buchan at the end of 1906 and subsequently became well known as 'Flynn of the Inland' and for founding the Royal Flying Doctor Service. As a keen amateur photographer, he also played an important role in promoting the development of the Buchan Caves as a tourist destination.

One memento I have of Flynn's time in Buchan is a book given as a prize to my uncle, inscribed and signed by Flynn as the: *'Home Sunday Study Scheme Prize, Awarded to Christopher McRae (78%), Presbyterian Mission, Buchan District, 29/10/06.'* Chris was 13 years old at the time and the book — *The Popular Elocutionist and Reciter* — is over 600 pages of text set in approximately 10-point font, which seems to be a rather challenging tome to expect a lad of that age to tackle.

The family continued to live on properties Alexander was managing or on leased land in the Buchan area — initially Kingsleigh, then at South Buchan, and finally Sunny Point just north of Buchan — from 1902 until December 1926.

During this time Alexander remained active in public affairs. His role on the local council continued and he served as shire president in 1918–19. He and Bessie were members of the original Buchan Bush Nursing Association, which in 1911 were the second such association in Victoria to appoint a bush nurse. In 1919 he was president of the Buchan District Peace Committee, formed to arrange local celebrations to mark the 'Victory of Great Britain and her Allies in the Great War'. Given the impact of that event on his family, he would likely have had mixed feelings while doing so.

The property at Gelantipy was retained and the family continued to run it, but Alexander and Bessie never returned to live on it. The circumstances that originally led to them leaving it were apparently never overcome to the extent they could do so.

The property was sold progressively by mortgagees between 1920 and 1926. Over half of it reverted to the Crown rather than being sold at the time for farming purposes. Although this land was subsequently re-surveyed and again transferred for private use, its initial reversion to the Crown indicated Alexander's inability to develop a profitable enterprise on it. Property records reveal that when disposal of the property was completed in December 1926, Alexander and Bessie were left with little or no financial benefit from over 30 years of endeavour on Craignish.

When they left the district following the sale of their property, they were both around 70 years old. They moved initially to rented accommodation at Dandenong where Alistair was located, with Margaret and Don accompanying them on their move. Alexander applied for a job managing a property in New South Wales but was unsuccessful.

After a few months they moved again, this time to a property named 'Riverton' on the Westernport Road at Heath Hill, between Lang Lang and Drouin in West Gippsland. Alexander may have initially had a managerial role on this property, but it appears that from the time of their move to Heath Hill he had effectively ceased active farming. He and Bessie spent the next 11 years living in Heath Hill, during which time they moved from Riverton to housing rented from the government in the small settlement.

Subsequent correspondence remarks on the cramped nature of this accommodation. Margaret ran the local post office and Don worked predominantly as a labourer on district farms.

Late in 1938 they purchased a modest house in Drouin and retired there, both over 80 years old. The purchase was made possible by an inheritance received by Bessie from one of her brothers in New Zealand.

Numerous letters to family members from Alexander and Bessie during their twenty years at Heath Hill and Drouin have been retained. As with Bessie's earlier diary, they provide a rich insight into their activities and those of a range of family members, as well as of the impact of external events on their lives and perspectives.

The most constant features of this correspondence are the strong connection to family, the frequency of hospitality dispensed and pleasure in having the opportunity to do so, and the absolute centrality of Christian faith in their outlook on life.

Many of Alexander's letters have an overt, conservative Christian theme, and they frequently detail what to him were obvious linkages between world events leading up to the Second World War and his interpretation of Biblical prophecy. Bessie also placed great emphasis in her letters on her faith, but was more expansive in the news she provided, particularly regarding the family and, in the precarious economic times of the 1930s, the regularly changing work arrangements for Don and especially Alistair, who by that stage was married with a young daughter.

Drouin is located on the main Gippsland rail line, and following Alexander and Bessie's move to the town, they very frequently had family or other visitors staying or calling in on their way between

Melbourne and East Gippsland. They clearly derived great pleasure from this and it appears as though this and the activities of their immediate family were the main source of external stimulus for them, apart from their continued connection to the local church.

The retained letters describe very few occasions that Alexander or Bessie ventured away from their houses at Heath Hill or Drouin, particularly from the mid 1930s onwards. Financial considerations are either given directly or inferred as the reason for their inability to attend events such as their son Ewen's wedding in late 1934, or the opening of McKillop's Bridge over the Snowy River at Deddick in late 1935 to which Alexander, as a long-time former councillor representing the area, had been invited. One of Bessie's letters describes her severe embarrassment at having left a bedroom light on all night, because of the impact it would have on their electricity bill.

Despite the generally positive or at least accepting tone of correspondence, it appears that the 20 years Alexander and Bessie spent at Heath Hill and Drouin were strongly circumscribed by their financial circumstances. This was probably the case generally from when they left Gelantipy shortly after the turn of the century, although it appears to have become more acute following the loss of their property and their subsequent move from Buchan.

Their straitened financial circumstances appear not to have changed their positive and contented perspective on their lives, however. They regularly express thanks to God for their lot, and strong confidence that all their circumstances and those of their loved ones are in His sound keeping. When difficulties are referenced, they are seldom accompanied by negativity regarding them.

Bessie died at Drouin in February 1947, and Alexander in July 1948. Notes on their deaths in the respective Drouin Presbyterian Church newsletters describe Bessie as 'A good wife, a wise mother, a lovely Christian woman (who) had the spirit and ideals of the great pioneers,' and Alexander as 'That fine old Scot … who had come from New Zealand as a pioneer to the rugged Buchan district … who loved his Bible and the worship of the Sanctuary.' Despite the challenges they endured, it is likely that both, with their dignity and faith still strong, would have deemed their lives well lived for them to be summarised in that manner.

CHAPTER 2

For God, king and country

'So soon the child a youth, the youth a man,
Eager to run the race his fathers ran.'

Lines by English poet Samuel Rogers, inscribed in a book *The poetical works of James Montgomery*, a 21st birthday present from a family member to Chris McRae, 21 May 1914.

My uncle Christopher Fraser McRae was born at Gelantipy on 21 May 1893, the second of Alexander and Bessie's five children. He worked as a farm labourer prior to enlisting in the Australian Imperial Force (AIF) in Melbourne on 28 July 1915. His enlistment record shows him as being 5 feet 8 ½ inches (174 centimetres) tall and 10 stone 10 pounds (68 kilograms). His brother Ewen, 17 months younger, had enlisted earlier the same month.

As was common at the time, Chris was a regular letter writer and many of his letters and cards to his family from his time in the AIF were retained. These, as well as one from Bessie to him, are reproduced in the following pages. Although minor spelling adjustments have been made in some cases, they are otherwise

Studio photo of Privates Ewen McRae (standing) and Chris McRae, Egypt, early 1916

presented as they were written, complete with expressions and terminology used at the time. All have been typed to assist in reading them. Many were written on plain writing paper or cards, but those that were written on various letterheads or particular postcards have had these reproduced, with the text presented beneath them. Most of Chris's correspondence was to his mother, but some also to his brothers and his sister Margaret.

They provide an interesting insight into the experiences of an individual engaged in the First World War. More particularly, they reflect an understandably evolving perspective on his experiences and attitude as a member of the AIF, and the positivity or otherwise with which he views this involvement.

Early correspondence appears much like any that might be received from an absent family member, almost as if on holiday, describing new experiences and the acquaintances he has met. This progressively changes as time goes on, his time away from home extends, and Chris experiences more of the impacts of the war on himself and others.

Some of the later correspondence is clearly constrained by regulations on what can be included. Comments on the weather feature regularly, as do references to individuals from the Buchan district. He reports briefly on his time in France and Belgium, but there are limited descriptions of his experiences at the front and minimal comment on the circumstances faced by him and fellow soldiers. Some correspondence appears, as much as anything, intended largely to assure his family that he is still alive and getting along more or less satisfactorily.

Chris regularly refers to contact with his brother Ewen, but is not keen for his other brothers, Alistair and Don, to join them.

He expresses pleasure that Alistair was not accepted when he attempted to enlist, and urges his mother, if possible, to prevent his younger brother Don from doing so.

Following a period in England in late 1916 recuperating from injury, Chris enjoys a trip to Scotland on furlough, sightseeing and visiting his mother's (Grant) family connections. Returning to England just prior to Christmas, in early 1917 he appears ambivalent but resigned regarding a return to France.

CHAPTER 2 *For God, king and country*

Chris enlisted in Melbourne on 28 July 1915, then on 11 August he moved into a military training camp at Castlemaine in central Victoria.

Presbyterian Church of Victoria.
PRESBYTERY OF BENDIGO.
Castlemaine
August 16th 1915

Dear Maggie,

Just a few lines to let you know how I am getting on. I have been having a jolly good time. We get steak for breakfast, bread and jam for dinner and stew for tea. I have got my overcoat dungaree rig-out, 1 pair of socks and boots. I wrote to mother a few days ago. I suppose she got the letter. Castlemaine is a very nice town. The hills all round are all trenched and scratched about where people have been looking for gold. There is very good grass about here. The crops along the line between here and Melbourne are looking splendid. We had church parade last Sunday afternoon. There were hundreds of people there besides the soldiers.

I'm dashed if I can think of anything to write. George Huxford has been promoted to corporal and he is drilling our section. Jack Woodhouse is a real blob at drill. I don't know how long we will be camped in the market building where we are at present. I think if it keeps fine we will be shifted out to camp pretty soon. When you write let me know Ewen's address. Harold Slocombe had a letter from him the day before we came up here. How is Alister getting on at the quarry? There are an awful lot of young fellows up here tonight. There is a piano and a couple of organs and also a ping pong table. There is some boxing going on in the next room and I am anxious to have a look at it and as I cannot think of any more news I think I will close now. Hoping this finds you all well as it leaves me.

I remain
Your loving brother
C.F. McRae

CITIZENS' DEFENCE LEAGUE.

SOLDIERS' READING AND WRITING ROOMS.

CASTLEMAINE *August 21st*

Dear Don,

I received your letter and was pleased to hear from you. I also received a letter from Maggie today. Tell her I will write to her another time. I was sorry to hear that Alister was crook but hope he will be right again by the time this letter reaches you. I have been keeping first rate since I came here. A good many fellows have got colds but that is the only kind of sickness there is in the camp. The place we are camped in is swept out and disinfected every day and we are all paraded up to the town hall to get our throats sprayed. We have not been vaccinated or inoculated yet but I suppose that is to come. Every night some of the officers come round with small pieces of bread with eucalyptus on them and we have to eat one. So they seem to be pretty careful about trying to keep down any sickness. I think we will be shifted out to tents on Tuesday or Wednesday. It is about a mile out of the town where they are making us camp. We were marched out and shown the place this morning before breakfast. Jack Woodhouse wrote to Alister a few days ago, but he addressed the letter to South Buchan so I don't suppose he got it.

I have been having a good time. I think I will begin to get fat soon. I had my photo taken today but I can't get them for about a week. I will send some home when I get them.

How are you enjoying the ploughing? I suppose you are in pretty bad humour sometimes. How are you getting on with the bagpipes? I am sorry I didn't bring them with me now but I suppose they would only be a nuisance to me. There is no music in the camp except a mouth organ and Jack Mitchell bought a Jews harp. Jack could not get off to attend his court case. I think he wrote to Thompson and told him to stop it.

I am about stuck for news so I think I will have to cut this letter short. I have been making a brave attempt to fill this page but I am afraid I can't. We got our pay on Thursday and some of the fellows have been pretty lively since. We had an open air concert last night on the parade ground. There was some pretty good singing. Dash it I can't think of any more news anyhow. If I give you any more now I will have none left for the next letter I write so I must close now. Hoping this finds you all well.

I remain

Your loving brother

C.F. McRae

P.S. Jack Woodhouse and Jack Mitchell wish to be remembered to you all.

C.F.M.
Military Camp
Castlemaine
August 26th 15

Dear Mother,

I suppose you are wondering that you have not received a letter from me the last few days. Well I have not had a chance to write as we were shifted out to camp last Monday and as I had no writing material I could not write. We arrived here about 4 o'clock and it was raining and the tents were not up. It was fairly cold standing about while the tents were being rigged. We have a good camp. It is on the side of a hill and the ground is pretty gravelly and so we have not much mud. We have pine floors on the tents and there are drains down each side of the tent so we are pretty right if we do have rain. I received Maggie's letter yesterday and was pleased to hear that Alister was getting pretty right. I did not do any visiting in Melbourne as I had no time. I will have to bring this to a close now as I have no time to write more.

I remain your loving Son
C.F. McRae

CHAPTER 2 *For God, king and country*

> **CITIZENS' DEFENCE LEAGUE.**
>
> **SOLDIERS' READING AND WRITING ROOMS.**
>
> CASTLEMAINE *August 30th* 191 5

Dear Ewen,

I received your welcome letter today and was pleased to hear that you were well. I wrote home and told them to send me your address but I have not got it yet. It was a bit of a surprise to me when I got your letter. We have a splendid camp here and there is no sickness much, only a couple of cases of measles I think. I was enjoying myself all right but I would like it better if we were together. There was a football match between A & B Company today and B Company had an easy win. The camp have challenged the Castlemaine team and the match is to come off on Saturday. The stadium was opened today. There was one fight but it was a real pussy of a fight. It only lasted one round. I would have sent your razor before but I didn't know your address. We have been having a pretty good time but the tucker is not kept up too flash but it is improving. Huxford is a corporal but he is nothing flash. He had a ... (ripped paper) ... MacPherson the other night. Mac said in the letter that ... (ripped paper) ... had broken down and was back in Buchan. Well I am ... (ripped paper) ... writing so I will have to bring this to a close. Hope you are well as it leaves me.

> I remain your loving brother
> C.F. McRae
> Address
> B Company
> 8th Platoon
> Castlemaine
> p.s. sending along your razor

CITIZENS' DEFENCE LEAGUE.

SOLDIERS' READING AND WRITING ROOMS.

CASTLEMAINE 1915

Dear Alister,

Just a few lines to answer your letter. We have just come home from a good long march and I am feeling a trifle tired. I have just been down to a pie shop and had a devil of a feed so I am not feeling too bad now. We had a pretty heavy shower of rain last night but it has been a fine day today. The camp is still isolated but as there has been no fresh cases of meningitis, I think the isolation will soon be over. About twenty fellows were caught taking French leave last night and I think they were fined £1 so it doesn't pay to break camp. We have a very fine lot of officers here and I think they will treat us well if we treat them well. The officer of our platoon is an exceptionally nice fellow. Our platoon was marched up to a big dam the other day for a swim. I dived in and had a job to get my breath when I came up. The water was that cold but it made a fellow feel splendid afterwards. I was surprised to hear that Ewen was going so soon. I would have liked to have seen him before he left. Tell Don he can give the bike lamp to Percy Kenney if he likes but it is absolutely no good.

Tell Maggie I will write to her next time. I have been writing a good many letters so I am getting jack of writing. I wrote to Mary some time ago but I have not heard from her yet. It was sad about Jim Cameron being killed, he will be very much missed in Orbost. How are the quarries going? We went up to an old slate quarry today. There are great heaps of slate all around the quarry. The quarry is about half full of water. I suppose there is about 60 feet of water in it. Well I think I will bring this to a close as I am only writing a lot of tommy rot.

CHAPTER 2 *For God, king and country*

Hoping this finds all well at home as it leaves me.

I remain

Your loving brother

C. F. McRae

Castlemaine

Sept 21st 15

Dear Don,

Just a few lines to let you know how I am getting on. I received a letter from Maggie today. Tell her I will answer it next time. We have been having very heavy rain. It rained Saturday night, Sunday and Sunday night with hardly a stop. It was also very windy and we had a lively time keeping the tent from being blown over. The rain made the ground very soft and the tent pegs kept pulling out. We must have had over two inches of rain. Harold Slocombe is back again. He has been away in Melbourne in the hospital with the influenza but he is better now. Jack has not left yet but I think he will be leaving sometime this week. The two big writing tents were blown down on Sunday.

Well news is scarce and I will have to leave some for another time. Hoping this finds all well at home as it leaves me.

I remain

Your loving brother

C.F. McRae

I hope the new house will be finished when we get home on leave. I don't think we will get leave for a while yet. One of the officers told us that when we get leave we will have 4 clear days at home. C. F. M.

Castlemaine
Nov 12th 15

Pte. C. F. McRae
9th Platoon
D Company
Castlemaine

Dear Ewen,

Just a few lines to let you know how I am getting along. I received your letter and was very pleased to hear from you. I would have written to you before you left but I lost the card you sent me from Freemantle [sic] so I didn't know your address. I have had hard luck not getting away before now as I have tried twice to get away with reinforcements. The first time they had enough before they came to me and the second time I got in but had the misfortune to get the measles about a week before they left for Broadmeadows. I had to put in three weeks in isolation. I will try and get away with the next lot. I have not been home since I came into camp as they only give country leave from Friday night till Monday night. But I will have a hard try to get home for Xmas. All my mates got away with reinforcements. I am getting sick of being in camp here. The sooner I get aboard ship the better pleased I will be.

I suppose you won't be sorry when you land after being so seasick. I suppose I can look forward to getting seasick. I had a letter from home today but there was not much news in it. They said they hadn't heard from you since you left Freemantle [sic]. There are two or three returned soldiers in camp here now. I have not been vaccinated yet as I was in the hospital when the others were done. Some of them had very bad arms. There are only about seven hundred in camp now. We went for a route march yesterday evening. I suppose we went about 13 or 14 miles. We got back to camp about half past nine at night. Well I will have to bring this to a close now as news is scarce. All the Buchan and Gelantipy people are well as far as I know. Did you hear about Donald McRae's[3] death? Arch Gillies met with an accident, a big log rolled on him and crushed him rather badly but I think he is all right again.

Hoping this finds you well as it leaves me and wishing you all sorts of good luck.

I remain

Your loving brother

C. F. McRae

On 25 November 1915 Chris transferred to 13th Infantry Reinforcements 5th Battalion at Broadmeadows, just north of Melbourne.

---

3 Not an immediate relative.

A bit of this and that

Broadmeadows
Dec 5th 15

Dear Mother,

Just a few lines to let you know how I am getting on. We are getting our final leave Tuesday so I suppose I will be home Wednesday. We were told that we were only getting four days but I am going to see the OC and try and get more but I don't think I can get more as we will most likely be sailing before the 15th. I have been having a rotten time since I left Castlemaine as I have been on duty every weekend and so I haven't had a chance to get into Melbourne. I had 24 hours on duty from 6 o'clock Friday night till 6 on Saturday night and now I have to go on from 6 tonight to 6 tomorrow night. Our company has been falling in for all the jobs. I was very hot yesterday and it is very close and windy today. I was going in to town today but this fatigue duty has put the kybosh on it as we can't leave our lines. Well I will bring this to a close now hoping this finds you all well as it leaves me.

   I remain

   Your loving son

   C. F. McRae

CHAPTER 2   *For God, king and country*

Dear Mother,

Just a few lines to let you know how I am getting along. I intended writing before but kept putting it off and last night I was collared for Officers mess orderly and I just got off a while ago, so I didn't get a chance to write last night. I have only slept in camp 3 nights since I came back from my final leave so I have been having a good time. I never missed a role [sic] call until last night but I don't know how I will get on but I don't think they will say anything as nearly everybody was out last night. We will be leaving on Wednesday. I went down to Port Melbourne and I had a look at the boat we are going on (The Demosthenes). She is a bonzer big boat and a fast traveller. I have nothing but the clothes I have on as they put all our things away while we were on Xmas leave and I can't find out where they put them as all our officers are away on leave. I am dossing in with a cobber. I was down to St Kilda last night, there was a fearful crowd at Luna Park. We had to go up to near Collins St to get on a bus. Well I will have to bring this to a close now. Hoping you are all well as this leaves me.

I remain

Your loving Son

C.F. McRae

I think I forgot to put in a Xmas Card to Cousie so I will put it in here. Better late than never.

On 29 December 1915 Chris left Australia on the T.S.S. Demosthenes. After he sent a postcard to his mother advising he had embarked, Bessie wrote a letter which appears to be the only one of hers to him that has been retained, and which Chris mentions in a subsequent letter. It expresses her love as a mother as well as her pride, hopes and expectations for her son as he sails to face a future of war and other potential pitfalls.

T.S.S. "DEMOSTHENES."

29/12/15

Mrs A. F. McRae

Buchan

Via Bairnsdale

East Gippsland

"On Active Service"

Embarked today but will be in the bay for a few days I think. There's between 1400-1500 men on board. We get bonzer tucker. For dinner we had soup, beef, potatoes and beans. For tea bread and butter and jam and milk in our tea. We have hammocks to sleep in so we are

CHAPTER 2 *For God, king and country*

pretty comfortable. This is the boat we are on. Hoping you are all well as this leaves me.

    C. McRae

Sunny Point

Sunday January 2nd, 1916

Dear Chris,

I am writing to you my first letter this year and I will write you the first day of each week while you are away. That is if I am spared and able to do so. I was pleased to get your postcard last evening. I hope to get a long letter from you from Freemantle [sic]. I wished to send you a farewell telegram but it was supposed to be too late when we got your letter saying that you were embarking on the 29th and it was then the 28th and too late for the mail. However, as you say that you do not expect to sail for a few days I might have sent it but it is too late now.

    I hope dear boy that you will not be too sick and have a good trip over the water. We had letters and cards from Ewen last night from Heliopolis dated 26 November. He had not been getting our letters and we had sent letters and papers every week to him. He was sick when he wrote and longing for you to come before he would leave. He expected to be sent to Suez. He is having a pleasant time with his cousins. They are settled about a mile from his camp so he sees them often and they are good to him. I hope that you will find them when you arrive. It will mean much to you having some of your own folk to go to. Whenever you receive this letter write to your cousin Lizzie, address Miss Macdonald,

    Matron

New Zealand Convalescent Home

Heliopolis

I think that this address will be right. I expect a letter from her as Ewen said that she had written to me.

We missed our two dear boys sadly at Christmas and New Year but perhaps we may be together next. We hope that soon this awful war will be over. We are proud of our soldier boys away and we will be doubly proud to have them home again knowing that they have done their duty by going. That is your duty to your Country but my dear boy you must never forget your duty to your God. Abstain from everything that savours of evil. There is much of it where you are going but I feel my boys will be kept from it all. I trust them, for I know that their minds are pure and their desires are not for that which is not clean.

We all went with the Bowies yesterday for a picnic to Scrubby Creek[4]. All were fishing but did not get a great catch — too much noise. Frank is thinking of enlisting. Don got a card from Jack; he is at Suez.

Now dear I will finish for this time, hoping that you will arrive safe and meet Ewen. Fond love from all at home and God bless and keep my dear boy.

Mother

Be sure to write often — I will be longing to hear from you.

---

4   Bowies were neighbours, and Scrubby Creek a tributary of the Buchan River north of Sunny Point.

CHAPTER 2 *For God, king and country*

After leaving Australia the "Demosthenes" stopped briefly at Colombo, in current-day Sri Lanka, before continuing its journey. The first location overseas where Chris spent an extended period was Heliopolis, north of Cairo in Egypt, where he met up with Ewen and his cousins from New Zealand.

At Sea
Jan 20 '16

Dear Maggie,

Just a few lines to let you know how I am getting on. I have been having a real good time as I was only sick for a few days and it has been nice and calm. We called at Colombo for coal and we were allowed ashore for about 2½ hours. I was pleased we were allowed ashore as I wanted to have a look at the place. It was very interesting to see the natives and their habits. I only saw a few Europeans. The natives are great at trying to get money. When we came up the harbour (about an hour after dark) the niggers were all round us in boats singing for pennies and the next day they were diving for money — trying to sell all sorts of things. They would start at about 4/- and come down to about 1/-. We stayed a day and a half at Colombo. I suppose we will be on land within a week. I got my photo taken before I left and paid for them and told them to forward them to you (12). I also sent my portmanteau and Ewen's violin. Well I will have to bring this to a close now. Hoping you are all well.

    I remain

    Your loving brother

    C.F. McRae

Aerodrome Camp

Feb 14th '16

4245

13th Reinforcement

5th Battalion

Aerodrome Camp

Heliopolis

Dear Maggie,

Just a few lines to let you know how I am getting on. I am enjoying myself fairly well but we are kept drilling pretty solid but we are allowed to go into Heliopolis every night. I was out to see the Pyramids about a week ago. They are simply wonderful. I climbed about 3 parts of the way up one of them but it was too much like hard work so I came down again. It was about 400 feet high and very wide. There is an awful lot to be seen about here. I have met several fellows I know. I went to see J. Woodhouse. He is looking very well. He is able to get out of bed now. Bill Slocombe is in hospital with chickenpox and J Johnstone was there too with the dipptheria [sic] but he is right again. I often see him as he is just a few lines away from our hut. Hughie McNaughton that used to be knocking about Gelantipy is here also. I sent a telegram to say that I had arrived safely. I suppose you got it? Well I will bring this to a close now. Hoping you are all well as this leaves me.

   I remain

   Your loving brother

   C.F. McRae

   P.S. Ewen is well. I am getting him transferred into this company.

CHAPTER 2 *For God, king and country*

Feby. 18 1916

Dear Mother,

Just a few lines to let you know I received your letter dated Jan 2nd. I was very pleased to get it. I wasn't expecting one so soon. I wrote you a letter after we landed and I also wrote to Maggie a few days ago. I am having a good time. Plenty to see. It is very interesting to go about and see all the sights. A fellow sees a lot of things here that he never dreampt [sic] of in Australia. I was at the Palace Hospital the other day getting some teeth out. It is a most magnificent building. There is some beautiful marble in it. Ewen and I were over to see the Macdonald girls[5] last night but we didn't see them. Lizzie has gone

---

5   'The Macdonald girls' refers to Elizabeth (Betty/Lizzie) and Wilhelmina (Mina), daughters of one of Bessie's older sisters, Mary, from New Zealand. They and other New Zealanders set up the 'Aotea' Convalescent Home near Heliopolis late in 1915, as described in the following section of a report on the Home prepared in 2011 by Claire Macdonald, great niece of Betty and Mina. These notes include excerpts from earlier commentary on the sisters and the Home.

The idea of establishing the convalescent home in Egypt was first thought of by the two Macdonald sisters, Elizabeth (Betty) M.A., B.Com. F.I.A.N.Z., and Wilhelmina (Mina). Mina was nursing in Wanganui Hospital and Betty had spent many years travelling the world prior to the outbreak of WW1. They, along with Mysie McDonnell, Ruth Cameron (a niece of Mysie) and Lena McLaren (from Masterton) began to formulate the idea of the home and it was very quickly taken up and committees were formed.

(The nine staff) arrived in Egypt on the 20th October and on the 25th November were ensconced in the private residence of Turkish Prince Ibrahim Halim in Heliopolis.

The palace had been loaned to the British Army at the outbreak of the war by the Prince. Before long the home was over filled with convalescing soldiers who were too well for hospital but not fit enough for combat. The home offered the boys everything from hot scones to tennis.

It has been said 'that within its four walls the trenches are forgotten, there is

away for a holiday as she has not been too well. We have spent some very good evenings there.

Mr Gearing[6] is in this camp somewhere. I intend hunting him up. I think he is in the light horse. I intend going to have a look through the museum tomorrow if I have some time. The climate here is all right just now but I suppose it will be getting very hot soon. It is warm through the day but it gets pretty cold at night. A good many of our fellows have had the influenza but so far I have escaped it all right. Well I must bring this to a close now. Hoping you are all well as this leaves me.

I remain

your loving Son

C.F. McRae

4245

13 Reinforcements

5 Battalion, Aerodrome camp, Heliopolis, Egypt

---

no parade ground, no bully beef and biscuits and no red tape.' 'Aotea' is a home in every sense of the word, and the only unhappy moment a patient knows is when the word discharge appears after his name in the roll book.

The Aotea home was privately funded during its entire duration and was considered 'the best convalescent home in the British Empire'.

The two Macdonald sisters had adventures that sent them into the field hospitals. Being amidst the fighting during a malaria outbreak in Ismailia, they did all the cooking in the 300 bed camp, organised beds, medicine, care and orderlies as the Turks and Germans were shooting around them.

Mina Macdonald was seen daringly clad in split riding pants, galloping through the desert with the legendary Australian icon 'Banjo' Paterson, who penned 'The Man from Snowy River'.

These women who put their lives on the line to establish and run the home were remarkable women; they went on an adventure into the unknown and enriched the lives of many.

6   Buchan Anglican minister.

CHAPTER 2   *For God, king and country*

9/3/16

4245

13th of 5th Aerodrome Heliopolis

(I am not among the lot that are going so I may be here for a while yet)

Dear Ewen,

Just a few lines to let you know that I received your letter. I would have answered it before but I went into Cairo on picket and left your letters in my other tunic so I didn't know your address. We were brought back here this evening and we are going away tomorrow or Saturday. The photos were a complete failure so I only took six as they wouldn't give back the deposit and I wanted something for it. I don't know where we are going, you can address my letters 13th of 5th. I have not heard anything about the transfer yet but I will inquire. I will write later.

   Your loving brother

   C. F. McRae

A bit of this and that

> Heliopolis
> March 13th 16
> No. 1

Dear Mother,

Just a few lines to let you know that I am well. I received a letter from Maggie and also from Cousie. It is the second letter I have received since I arrived here. I have written five or six letters since I came here. The weather is beginning to get pretty warm now. I don't think we will be here much longer as the 14th reinforcements are here. Our company was on picket in Cairo for a few days. I was off for half a day and went to see the Citadel and the blue mosque. They are beautiful. The walls of the mosque on one side are all chipped with cannon balls where Napoleon was trying to destroy it. There is one cannon ball sticking in the wall. I also went to see the museum. It is very interesting. There are a lot of very old curios. The mummies are wonderful. There is one about 3,000 years old and you can see the features on the face yet. Next chance I get I will go to the zoo and the dead city.

Cousie said in her letter that she was giving me her nephew's addresses but she must have forgotten. The New Zealanders are camped quite close to us. I was over to see Mina and Betty, they are both well. Betty has been away for a holiday and she is looking very well. I have a note from Ewen but he could not tell me where he was. All the address he could give was 13 Company, 6th Battalion. I will number all my letters after this one so you will know if you have missed any. I will number this (no. 1). I was glad to hear that you had been up to Gelantipy for a holiday. We don't get much news out of the papers here. But by what we see things are looking better. I am sorry

CHAPTER 2   *For God, king and country*

to hear that Alister is enlisting when there are so many cold footed crawlers that should go. I suppose Bonny was just as pleased that he didn't pass.

Well I will bring this to a close now. Hoping you are all well as this leaves me.

I remain

Your loving Son,

C.F. McRae

4245

13th of 5th

Heliopolis

Egypt

EGYPT. - Sunset on the desert.

26/3/16

No. 2

4245

Aerodrome

Heliopolis

Egypt

Dear Mother,

Just a few lines to let you know that I am well. I got three letters today. One was written on the 26th Dec so it has been a good while reaching here. I went to see Mina and Betty last night. They were both well. They are going away to Ismailia tomorrow as they have started a café there for the soldiers. They have been very good to me. We might be leaving here tomorrow. I have had several letters from Ewen since he left but he can't tell me where he is. The only address he can give is B Company 6th Battalion. Hoping this finds you all well as this leaves me.

I remain your loving son,

C.F. McRae

On 29 March 1916 Chris sailed from Alexandria in Egypt, disembarking at Marseille, France, on 4 April. Early in May he contracted mumps, was in isolation and at base camp for some time, then returned to his battalion in late July.

France
April 10th, 16

Dear Mother,

Just a few lines to let you know that I am well. You will see by my address that I am in France. I can't give you much news but will give you as much as I can. I haven't got to the firing line yet and I don't think we will for a while yet. It is pretty cold here after coming from Egypt where it was so hot. It was very nice to see the green fields after being in the desert for so long. I can't find out where Ewen is but I think he is still in Egypt.

France is a beautiful country, no wonder the Germans wanted it. The only people that you see working in the fields are the women,

CHAPTER 2   *For God, king and country*

children and old men, all those who are fit are at the front. It is just coming spring so the weather will be getting warmer. I don't know how we will get on for letters that have been addressed to Egypt but I think that they will be sent on all right. We have been here for nearly a week now so I'm beginning to get used to the cold. I suppose you will be wondering that I didn't write last week but I didn't know what address to give you. Well I will have to bring this to a close now as I must write to Mina and Betty and give them my address.

Hoping this finds you all well as it leaves me.

I remain your loving son
Pte CF McRae
4245
13th of the 5th
1st Australian Divisional Base depot
France

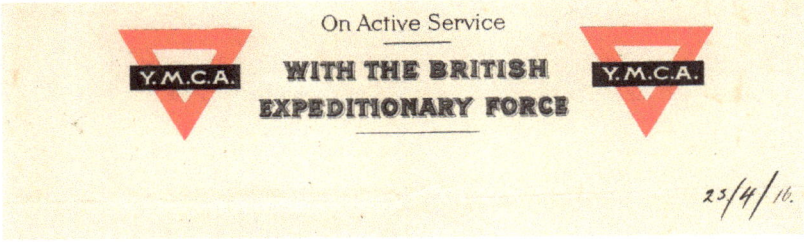

Dear Mother,

Just a few lines to let you know I am well. I haven't seen any fighting yet but I think we will be into it shortly. I have just been on church parade (Presbyterian) and we got a very good address. It was very wet yesterday but it is a beautiful sunny day today. The weather is getting warmer now. I haven't had any letters since I left Egypt. I don't know where Ewen is as it is over a month since I heard from him. There is not very much war news in the papers here. I wrote to Betty and Mina and gave them my address but I haven't heard from them yet. Perhaps they didn't get my letter. Well I will bring this to a close now. Hoping you are all well.

    I remain

    Your loving son, C.F. McRae

4/5/16

Miss M. McRae

Buchan

East Gippsland

Victoria

Australia

Dear Margaret,

Just a few lines to let you know I am well and enjoying myself pretty well. I haven't been in action yet and have no idea when I will. Hoping you are all well.

    I remain, Your loving brother

    C. F. McRae

    4245

    13th of 5th

    1st A. D. B. D

    France

CHAPTER 2   *For God, king and country*

ENVIE.
ENVY.

France

May 13th '16

Dear Don,

Just a few lines to let you know how I am getting on. I have had the misfortune to get the mumps but only a slight attack but I suppose I will have to put in a week or two in isolation.

Trusting you are all well at home.

I remain your loving brother.

C. F. McRae

4245

13th of 5th

2nd Infantry Battalion

1st A. D. B. D

France

France

May 24th, 16

Dear Mother,

Just a few lines to let you know how I'm getting on. I was pretty crook with the mumps for a few days but I'm better now. I suppose I will be getting up in a couple of days. I am just about sick of bed as I have been in 13 days now. The worst part of it is that I will most likely miss my company as some of them have left since I came into hospital.

I had a letter from Betty yesterday. She and Mina were both well. They had been down at Ismailia starting a club for the soldiers. She said they worked pretty hard getting it started but the soldiers appreciated it very much.

Well I must bring this to a close now. Hoping you are all well.

I remain

Your loving son C. F. McRae

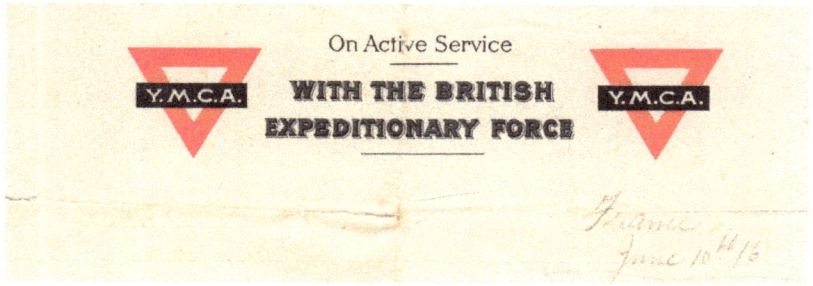

Dear Mother,

Just a few lines to let you know that I am well again and back with my company. Some of them have gone to the trenches so I suppose I will be following shortly. I think my letters are going astray as I get very few and I know you write regularly. I hope you are getting all mine;

though there is no news in them I know you're anxious to hear from me. Well as I have no news I must bring this to a close now.

Hoping you are all well.

I remain your loving son, C.F. McRae

5th Battalion

1st A.D.B.D.

France

France

18/6/16

Dear Mother,

Just a few lines to let you know I am well. I received a long letter from Margaret a few days ago and was pleased to get it as there was a lot of interesting news in it. I was glad to hear that Alistair didn't pass as I don't think it was his place to come. I suppose Don is anxious as ever to come. Margaret said in the letter that she sent some postcards to Ewen and I. I didn't get mine but I got Ewen's by mistake, I'm sending them on to him. Margaret said you were sending me a cake for my birthday. I haven't received it yet and I don't think I am likely to get it. I spent my birthday in hospital. Taffy is the only chap here that I know from about Buchan. There are several Bairnsdale chaps here. I suppose Father will know one chap as he had something to do with the Bairnsdale paper and used to go to the council meetings and get the news etc. His name is Dean.

Well I will close now. Hoping you are all well.

I remain

Your loving son C.F. McRae

5th Battalion

1st A.D.B.D.

France

France

1/7/16

Dear Margaret,

Just a few lines to let you know I am well. I received a long letter from you a few days ago also one from Cousie. I hadn't had a letter for over a fortnight. I get a letter from Ewen occasionally. He was quite well last letter I had but he said he was getting very few letters from home. I was sorry to hear that Archie Gillies was so ill. Tell Cousie I will write to her later on. Well I have no news so must close now.

    Hoping you are all well as this leaves me.

    I remain

    Your loving brother C.F. McRae

France

Sept 5th, 16

Dear Mother,

Just a few lines to let you know I am well. We have been having a fair amount of rain lately but the weather has not been cold. I haven't seen Ewen for about a fortnight as I am on traffic control and I am not near him. I haven't had any letters for over a month now. I got your parcel all right after it had been nearly 4 months on the way. My address is A Coy. 5 battalion. Well I must close now. Hoping you are all well as this leaves me. I remain

    Your loving son C. F. McRae

CHAPTER 2   *For God, king and country*

France
Sept. 26th 16

Dear Mother,

Just a few lines to let you know that I am well. I had a letter from Margaret a few days ago dated 28/6/16. It is the first I've heard from home for some time. I was sorry to hear that the dingoes had been killing the sheep. I've had a good spell for about three weeks as I have been on traffic control but I'm going back to the battalion tomorrow. I just got a letter from Don (28/7/16) since I started writing this one. He sent me two photos, one of himself with the bagpipes. He looks as if he's been having a night out. The other of Margaret is not too bad. We are having nice weather now although at times we get some rain. I saw J Johnston about a week ago. He is in the 14th battalion. He hasn't seen anything of the other Jacks. If you know their address please send it as I don't know where to look for them. Well I must bring this to a close now. Hoping this finds you all well as it leaves me.

   I remain
   Your loving son
   C.F. McRae
   PS I am enclosing a bit of heather that was given to me by a cobber.
   C.F.M.

On 8 October 1916 Chris was injured in the field and on 17 October was transferred to hospital in England for a hernia operation. He remained in various hospitals in England, on furlough in Scotland and at army bases in England until early February 1917.

No. 12 Ward
Norfolk and Norwich Hospital
Norwich
18/10/16

Dear Mother,

Don't be alarmed when you see this address. I have been admitted into hospital for a slight operation. You will see by my address that I am in England. I have been in Belgium for about two months at Ypres. Before that I was at Pozieres on the Somme, we had some very hard fighting there and lost a lot of men but the Huns have been driven back a long way. It is impossible to describe what the artillery fire was like. For ten minutes we had about a thousand guns playing on a front of a few hundred yards of trench, firing at about the rate of one shot every two minutes. That would mean about 5000 shells. When we got to the Hun's trench there was hardly any of it left but he had dugouts about 30 feet underground which the shells could not penetrate. He must have thought he was there for good as it was just like a furnished house inside. Beds, tables, carpet on the floor, shelves around the walls, electric lights etc. I suppose they were the officers. I saw Ewen on his way up to the trenches when I was coming away. He has been very lucky. I can tell you that I'm jolly glad to get away from the trenches for a while. Well I must bring this to a close now hoping you are all well. I remain

    Your loving son

    C.F. McRae

    Don't worry about me as I am in a good hospital with plenty of nice nurses

CHAPTER 2 *For God, king and country*

Norfolk & Norwich Hospital

Oct 27th '16

Dear Mother,

Just a few lines to let you know that I am getting on first class. I wrote to you about a week ago telling you that I was undergoing an operation. Well I have been through it and am getting on fine. This is a photo of part of the hospital. The ward I am in is not showing on this card. I haven't heard from Ewen since I have been in England, but I have hardly had time yet. I saw him and his cobbers going up to the trenches the day I came away.

Don't let Don enlist if you can stop him as he has no idea what it is like and he would never stand the marching with his knee. I can't find out about poor old Jack Mitchell but Ewen had a letter from Jack Woodhouse and from what I can make of it Jack Mitchell has been killed[7]. Well I must bring this to a close now. Hoping this finds you well.

I remain Your loving Son

C. F McRae

---

7   Jack Mitchell survived the war.

6/11/16

Dear Margaret,

Just a few lines to let you know how I am getting on. I will be able to get up in a few days. I have just received the parcel containing socks, handkerchiefs and soap that Mother sent me. The weather is beginning to get a bit cold now. I will work my head and keep from going back to France before Xmas (getting cold-footed!) The Presbyterian minister's wife often comes to see me, she gave me this card. It's a very old church built 1096. I haven't heard from Ewen since

CHAPTER 2   *For God, king and country*

I have been in hospital. If I get long enough furlough I intend going up to Scotland. Well I have no more so I must close now. Wishing you all a merry Xmas.

I remain, Your loving brother

C. F. McRae

Norfolk and Norwich Hospital

Norwich

Nov. 14th 16

Dear Mother,

Just a few lines to let you know how I'm getting on. I have been out of bed now for three days and I am feeling pretty well. I was very weak for the first day. I had to sit down nearly all the time but I can get about fine now. I was out and had a look around the town yesterday. It is a very nice town. There are some very old buildings in it. I may be going away from here to a convalescent hospital any day now. I have some souvenirs that I will try and send home when I get out of hospital, a clip of German bullets, a nose cap of a small German shell. I don't know if I will be allowed to send them but I will have a try. I am enclosing a French paper half franc (5 pence). I had a lot of souvenirs from Egypt but I lost them all. I will send you some French postcards (views of Boulogne), we were not allowed to send any views from France. I haven't had a letter for over a month. The weather here is beginning to get fairly cold. I don't think the war is going to finish for some time yet as it is very difficult to advance when the weather is wet, the ground is very boggy. Well I must bring this to a close now as I am going out and the other lads are waiting for me.

Hoping you are all well in wishing you a Merry Xmas and Happy New Year.

I remain

Your loving son

C.F. McRae

No 1 Australian Auxiliary Hospital

Harefield

Nov. 24th 16

Dear Mother,

Just a few lines to let you know how I'm getting on. You will see that I have been shifted from the hospital I was in as they shifted all the Australians to Australian hospitals. I haven't had any letters since I've been in hospital except one from William Grant. I am quite right now so I suppose I will be heading back to France soon. I don't like the idea much as it is getting pretty cold now. We had some snow last week but it only lay on the ground for a few hours. I haven't come across anybody I know in this hospital yet. It is only about half an hour in the train from London. We came through London when we were coming here. There are a good many wounded going back to Australia soon. England is not a bad place but there is no place like Australia, but I am afraid that we won't get back for a long time yet as the war is far from finished. I see by the paper that the Austrian emperor is dead. I haven't had a letter from Ewen for some time but perhaps he didn't get my letter with my address. I may be going to a concert in St. Paul's this evening. I think we get 14 days furlough when we are convalesced, if so I will go and see Willie Grant. I wrote to him and told him I would

CHAPTER 2   *For God, king and country*

try and get up to see him. Well I must close now as I have several more letters to write.

Hoping you are all well as this leaves me.

I remain

Your loving son

C. F. McRae

4/12/16

Weymouth

Dear Margaret,

Just a line to let you know that I am well. I have been shifted to Weymouth. I will be getting furlough any day now. We get fourteen days. I haven't heard from Ewen since I left France though I have written him several letters but I saw one of his mates at Harefield and he told me Ewen was in hospital in France with boils. I am quite right now so I suppose I will be getting back to France before long. It is pretty cold here now. We are just alongside the sea. England would be a pretty place in the spring and summer but I don't think much of it in the winter (too cold). We get pretty good tucker here, better than in the hospitals. We got a good bit of red-cross stuff in the hospitals. Harefield is an Australian hospital and the sisters are Australian. Hoping you are all well.

I remain, Your loving brother

C. F. McRae

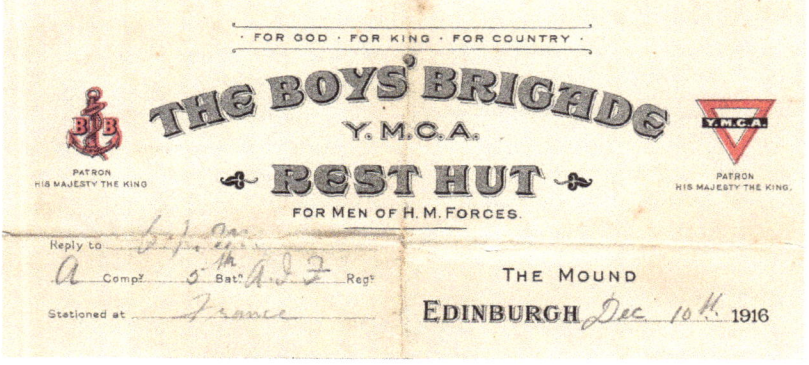

Dear Mother,

Just a few lines to let you know how I'm getting on. I am quite right now and I'm on my furlough 14 days. I left London yesterday morning 10 o'clock and arrived here about 8 last night. I am going on to The Mound tomorrow. I have been having a bit of a look around Edinburgh today. I went and had a look at the castle but could not get inside as it was Sunday but I will put in a day or two on my way back. It is a wonderful old castle. It is built right on top of a big rock. I was up on top and had a look at all the cannons etc. but could not get into the rooms where all the old relics are kept.

I think I will put in a day in Inverness on my way back. I had a letter from Ewen two days ago saying that he was in a hospital at Boulogne

CHAPTER 2 *For God, king and country*

with pneumonia but was getting better. I suppose I will be back to France soon. I have 14 days leave and three of them have gone already. I have £17 coming to me in my pay books and £1/2/4 ration money so I don't think I will run short of cash. Well I think I had better close now as I have not much news. Hoping you are all well as this leaves me.

I remain

Your loving son C.F. McRae

Wareham

Dec. 23rd 16

Dear Mother,

Just a few lines to let you know how I'm getting on. I have just come back from my furlough. I had a very good time. I put in two days in Edinburgh and the rest at The Mound and Dornoch. They were very pleased to see me at Torboll and I had a real job to get away. I also put in some time at Evelix in Dornoch, Alex Grant's place. Willie Grant plays the pipes very well, he was in a pipe band. Mrs Grant is a very good piano player and singer but she won't open the piano till the war is over. George Grant (Alex Grant's son) is married. His sister Kitty is also married, she plays Highland music beautifully and the piano and George's wife is also a splendid player. I would have had more of a tour but I couldn't get away from Torboll, but I was quite satisfied with what I had. Malcolm and George Fraser, Grandma's nephews, also live at The Mound. I went to see Ewen the day before yesterday. He is in a hospital in Camberwell (London). He is getting all right now but has been pretty ill and looks very thin. I liked Edinburgh very much. I had a look through the Castle but there was not much to see as all the old relics had been removed on account of the bombing raids. I also saw John Knox's house, the Heart of Midlothian, and Hollyrood Palace and the old Scottish House of Parliament. Well I must bring this to a close now. Hoping you are all well.

I remain

Your loving son

C.F. McRae

Dear Margaret,

Just a few lines to let you know that I am well. I am still at Wareham and think I will be here for some time yet. I have not been getting letters for a good while now as I have been shifting about so much but I think I will get them all right now as I got a few old ones today. I wrote to Mother last week and told her all the news so this is only going to be a short letter. I haven't seen any of the Buchan boys since being in England but I think J Mitchell is over here somewhere. I don't know what sort of a day we are going to have tomorrow, but I think it will be very tame. The weather has not been too good as it rains nearly every day and it is pretty cold. The only snow I saw was when I was coming away from Scotland. It was snowing very heavy between Inverness and Perth. I have been for a good tour since leaving France.

CHAPTER 2   *For God, king and country*

From Dover to Norwich (East Coast) then to Weymouth (SW Coast) then London to Edinburgh, from there to The Mound and Dornoch then to Wareham (SW Coast, England) and I suppose I will see a bit more before going back to France. Well I must close now, hoping this finds you all well and wishing you a Happy New Year. I remain

Your loving brother

C.F. McRae

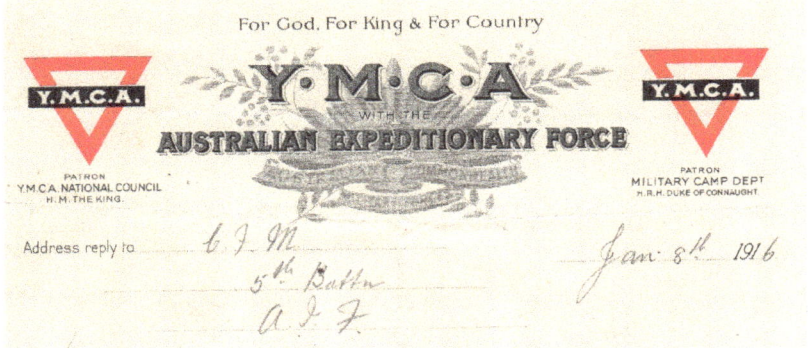

Address reply to C.F.M., 5th Batt'n, A.I.F.[8]

Dear Mother,

Just a few lines to let you know how I am getting on. I am still at Wareham. It has been a very nasty day. It was snowing this morning and it came on to rain about 12 o'clock and it has been raining ever since so we have had no parade today. We have a good fire in the hut so we are pretty comfortable. I had a letter from Ewen yesterday, he was still in bed. He will be pretty weak when he gets up. I don't think he will see France again as he won't be fit to go back for a good while and I don't think the war is going to last much longer. I am hoping that I will not have to go back. The troops must be having a very bad

---

8   Although this letter is dated January 8 1916, its correct date is January 8 1917.

time in France now as the weather is so cold. I have a bad cold but it is getting better. Well I must bring this to a close now.

    Hoping you are all well.

    I remain

    Your loving son

    C.F. McRae

Perham Downs

Feby 6th, 17

Dear Margaret,

Just a few lines to let you know that I am well. I have not gone to France yet but we have been warned we are leaving tonight, but I don't think we will go till tomorrow night. I thought we were going about a week ago. I got some old letters (June 18th, 16) from you and Mother. I haven't heard from Ewen for about a fortnight. He was getting on well the last I heard from him. We had a fall of snow two days ago (about 6 ins), it is still on the ground. The weather is a bit warmer now than it was last week. I haven't been able to get any leave from here or I might have been able to see some of the Buchan lads as I think some of them will most likely still be at Salisbury. Most of my mates have been killed since I left the Battalion so I don't care what Battalion I go to. Well I must bring this to a close now. Hoping this finds you all well as it leaves me.

    I remain

    Your loving brother

    C. F. McRae

CHAPTER 2   *For God, king and country*

Private Chris McRae, studio photo while on furlough in Scotland, December 1916

Chris returned to France on 8 February 1917, re-joined his Battalion on 14 February and was wounded (severe gunshot wounds to the face) the following day. He was admitted to a field hospital then on 21 February was transferred to the 5th General Hospital at Rouen, France, where he died on 4 March. His family was notified on 12 March, with official details provided in September.

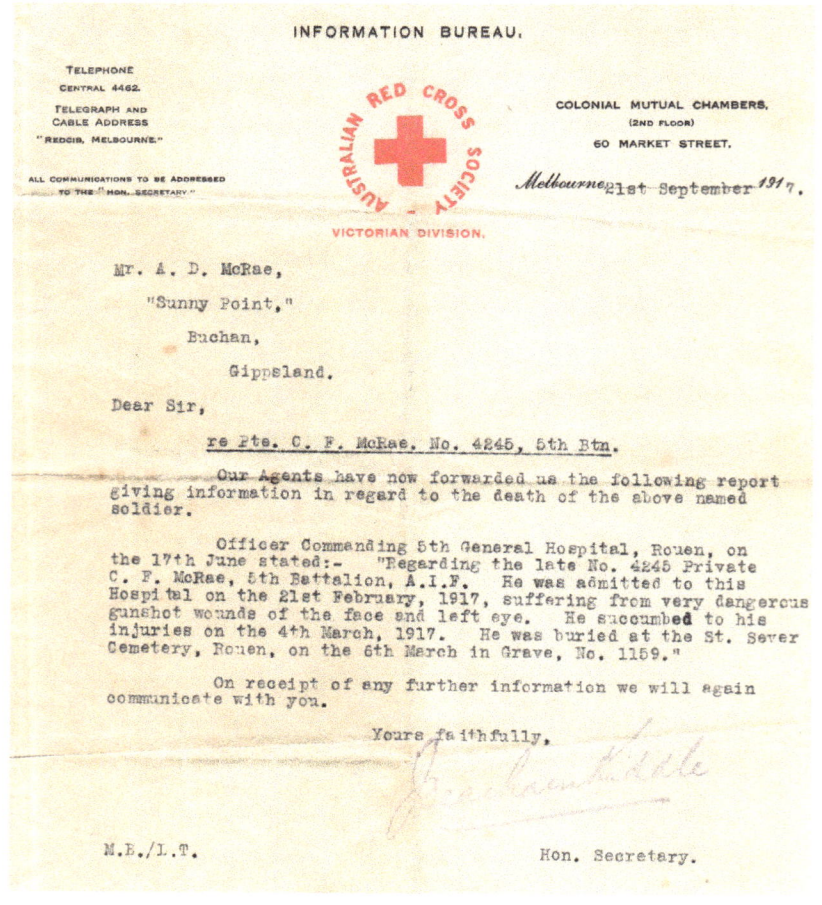

CHAPTER 2   *For God, king and country*

Reflection

I never met the uncle I was named after; he was killed over 30 years before I was born. I have had some of the artefacts of his life for many years — a couple of war medals, a South Buchan Football Club cap, a book he received as a Sunday school prize and a framed memorial gratefully presented to his family in 1920 by the community of Buchan — but it is only in the last year or so that I have been aware of and had access to his wartime letters to his family.

I have frequently found myself becoming strangely emotional when looking through them and reflecting on the circumstances of their writing and the outcome — both for him and the millions of soldiers and civilians impacted — of the endeavour he was engaged in at the time. This experience of belated personal grief — insignificant, distant in time and minor as it is — attests to the pervasive and ongoing impact of that war. Perhaps more than anything this has caused me to reflect on issues of militarism, its place in my experience of life and my views on it.

My generation has not faced a World War so it can be said that we have reaped the benefits of the efforts of former generations who endured these events and were 'successful' in them. This is a matter for appropriate and great thankfulness to those who served Australia militarily. It is important that we continue to acknowledge and honour the individuals who were involved and the sacrifices they made, although I don't believe this should prevent us from questioning the sense of our involvement in war, our willingness to use it as a means of resolving differences, or the inference that support for militaristic posturing is a prerequisite for demonstrating pride in one's country.

On that basis, and from an observation point afforded by geographic distance and the passage of time, it seems that Australia had reasonable cause to become involved in the Second World War, but that the First was predominantly a wasteful exercise of nationalism and destructive patriotism, largely senseless even for those in Europe. For Australia I can understand the ties to Britain and the Empire which made our involvement highly likely, although the racially based justifications supporting this, which were influential at the time, do us no credit. Neither presents a compelling logical, as distinct from emotional, reason for our involvement.

In Australia there is a rather confused relationship between politics and military matters, where rhetoric and reality appear almost transposed.

Leaders from the conservative side of politics have been most active over the last 20 years or so in promoting the increased prominence of military and patriotic matters, such as the focus on commemorating ANZAC Day and on the Australian flag. They have also been inclined to link the nebulous concept of 'Australian values' to matters associated with military activity and to conflate this with the projection of strength regarding our dealings with other countries and new arrivals to this country, particularly those from non-European nations.

The appropriate commemoration of service to or defence of the country has become confused, maybe deliberately so, with a partisan political perspective on our national character. Many conservative leaders have inferred, if not stated directly, that those who don't share their outlook on the country's culture are morally suspect, less individually worthy, and reflect less these ill-defined 'Australian values' than those who do. They have frequently displayed an inability to distinguish between national pride and jingoism, confused the latter with leadership, and appeared to portray sentiments such as concern and compassion as being 'un-Australian'.

In my lifetime conservative leaders have also been more inclined than those from the progressive side of politics to lead Australia into wars. The two most lauded conservative leaders of that period — Robert Menzies and John Howard — both led governments which took Australia into wars to which there was significant political and public opposition and where subsequent events overwhelmingly proved this opposition to be valid. Neither appears to have suffered much in the estimation of their supporters as a result of these misjudgements, although I suspect there are many thousands of individuals and families in Australia, and millions more in Vietnam, Iraq and elsewhere who have very personal cause to hold a different view.

Conversely, the person widely regarded most highly as a wartime leader of Australia when there was a real need for such leadership was John Curtin, a leader from the left of politics. Coincidence? Perhaps, but it does demonstrate that those who beat the drum loudest on some matters are not always those who have most earned the right to do so.

What to take from all of this? Probably not much, except to say that I have a deep and abiding disregard for any politician who stands in front of a phalanx of Australian flags and uses terms such as 'defending Australian values', 'standing up for Australia' or 'un-Australian'. Few things so starkly call to mind Samuel Johnson's aphorism 'Patriotism is the last refuge of the scoundrel,' nor more clearly suggest candidates for it to be applied to.

This is not because the terms themselves or the sentiments they evoke are intrinsically inappropriate or unworthy of support or respect. It is because the partisan use of them by politicians is most often mere cant.

This seldom ends well for Australia's role as a principled global citizen, nor for the cohesion of our society, whatever short-term political benefit some may seek, or even appear to gain.

CHAPTER 3

Early days

Don went to school in Buchan and subsequently worked as a labourer on the family farm, and probably for others in the Buchan and Gelantipy district as well. He lived with his parents during their time in the Buchan district and moved to Dandenong and Heath Hill when they relocated there around the beginning of 1927. He remained in that district working predominantly as a farm labourer until his parents moved to Drouin late in 1938.

He had no regular job during his time at Heath Hill, although he was seldom unable to find some form of work. Even during the Depression it appears he was most commonly engaged in fencing, working on sheep properties, or growing potatoes on leased land. Trapping rabbits and foxes then selling their skins also featured in his activities, as did regular trips back to Buchan.

He was a keen cricketer, playing with Yannathan Cricket Club, which was part of the Pakenham and Kooweerup District Cricket Association between 1926 and World War 2, and won the club bowling average in 1934–35.

From letters he wrote, it is obvious he had an interest in

literature, perhaps to a degree beyond that which was common among those of his schooling and occupation. This correspondence also includes irregular reference to national economic events, where his sympathies appear to have favoured the political left. He was a regular writer of poetry, frequently with a humorous slant and usually inspired by an event he wished to comment on.

Don returned to the Buchan district to live after Alexander and Bessie moved to Drouin. He initially continued to work as a farm labourer with no consistent place of employment, and appears to have spent considerable periods of time with his brother Ewen and his family at the Pyramids — a property on the Murrindal River north of Buchan that Ewen had moved to prior to his marriage to Jessie Hicks late in 1934. This property was adjacent to a site where a massacre of Aborigines occurred in 1850[9].

Don had never owned property and his working life had resulted in him having few financial resources, so it was a significant step when in April 1943 he took out a lease on 300 acres of uncleared Crown land near Mount McLeod, between Murrindal and the Basin, on the Tulloch Ard Road. The rent was set at five pounds six shillings and six pence per annum and in the lease documents he is described as a 'farm labourer' of Murrindal, via Buchan.

It was a condition of such leases that the property be fenced

---

9   There is strong local folklore regarding this event, despite there being some variations in the details surrounding it. The associated written and oral histories indicate that the massacre, involving between 15 and 20 Aborigines, was most likely in reprisal for spearing of cattle. The Aborigines were thought to have been trapped against a bluff and shot. Their bodies were disposed of, possibly by being thrown into a hole or cave where the Murrindal River takes an underground course beneath the Pyramids.

within six years, vermin controlled and that 'substantial and permanent improvements' to the value of five shillings per acre be made to the property by the end of the third year of the lease, and to the value of ten shillings per acre by the end of the sixth year. A note dated September 1949 on the lease documents indicated that all conditions had been met to that stage.

Don built a bark hut on the leased block and that became his home for the next few years, although he continued to spend considerable amounts of time with Ewen and his family, who relocated from the Pyramids to the Murrindal property of Jessie McRae's parents, Walter and Alice Hicks, when Walter died in 1945.

This had a pivotal impact on the family as it was to Murrindal Primary School that Mum, then Margaret Knox, was appointed in 1946 as a 21-year-old on her second teaching placement.

Mum's family were from the Numurkah district in northern Victoria. My Knox great grandparents William and Elizabeth (nee Penman) had both emigrated from Scotland — Elizabeth as a three-year-old with her parents from Fifeshire, just north of Edinburgh, on the 'Marco Polo' in 1862, and William from Kilmarnock, south of Glasgow, on the 'Great Britain' as a 20-year-old in 1869. William and Elizabeth married in Ballarat in 1875, with Elizabeth a few months short of her 16th birthday (!). Their first child was born three months later in June 1875 (!) and in August of that year they took up residence on a block of land at Drumanure, south-east of Numurkah. William had been granted a licence on the block, adjacent to one taken up by his brother Robert, the previous November. They called their property 'Doonside'. My grandfather Christopher William Knox, one of seven children, was born there in 1885.

Family of great grandparents William and Elizabeth Knox, circa 1903.
Likely taken shortly after the death in 1903 of eldest son,
Alexander (28 years old), as the result of a farm accident.
A fifth son had died in infancy.
Back: Christopher (grandfather), John, Margaret, Jane
Front: William, Archibald, Elizabeth

Records of the Presbyterian church at Drumanure reveal that services were originally held in the houses of parishioners, with William and Elizabeth's home listed as being one of those used in 1882 or 1883. In 1885 William received the Crown grant for 319 acres of land he had selected, the same year that the family are recorded as being one of the originals attending services when a church was built at Drumanure.

Christopher Knox lived with his family and worked on their farm. He was a keen sportsman and in 1907 had the distinction of winning the Stawell Gift, which was then and remains Australia's premier professional foot race. It is run at Easter, at the time over 130 yards.

CHAPTER 3 *Early days*

Christopher ran off 12½ yards and started as the 6/4 second favourite behind the 2/1-on favourite W.A. Hill, from Moonta in South Australia who ran off 9½ yards. He started a half yard behind the out-marker J. King (12/1), with F.S. Jones (10/1) from Hobart off 11 yards, being the fourth runner.

The summary of the race reports:

King broke away before the pistol went off and he was put back a yard. He repeated the effort to anticipate the starter and was penalised a further two yards. Hill made a hot run to try and gain the lead, but just failed to do so by a foot, Knox striking the tape in front of him. King was only about three yards away from the first man, so that he must have been nearly a winner had he not incurred a penalty just before being sent away. Time 11⅖ sec.

Finalists in the 1907 Stawell Gift
Christopher Knox (grandfather), the winner in 11⅖ seconds running off 12½ yards, is on the left

Knox family at time of the marriage of grandparents
Christopher Knox and Frances Danson, March 1916
Back: Margaret, Elizabeth (nee Ritchie) and John,
Christopher and Frances (nee Danson), Jane
Front: William (son of John and Elizabeth), Elizabeth (great grandmother),
Archibald, William (great grandfather), Angus (son of John and Elizabeth)

Chris's win was very well received in his home district. The train he arrived home to Numurkah on was met by a host of admirers, and steamed in to the strains of *See the Conquering Hero Comes* played by the town band. He and his trainer were carried from the platform on the shoulders of admirers and supporters. It appears, though, that Chris had no particular love of running and, with the exception of winning a comparatively few races at district sports meetings, did not capitalise on his prowess. The same was the case with his football involvement, where he is said to have continued playing longer than he was inclined to only because of the 'earnest solicitations of club members'.

It is likely that the prize money from the win (£75, equivalent to

CHAPTER 3   *Early days*

just over $11,000 in today's money) provided a short-term fillip to the family's farming operations, struggling on an area proving too small, in the pre-irrigation era for that district, to make a satisfactory living from. It eventually proved insufficient to overcome this fundamental difficulty and, when William died early in 1920, the property at Drumanure passed to Christopher and his mother, then was sold soon afterwards.

In 1916 Christopher had married Frances Kate Danson, the youngest daughter and one of ten children of William Danson and Margaret Smeaton. William and Margaret had married at Creswick, near Ballarat, in 1867, having both arrived in Victoria some years previously, he as a 21 year old in 1854 from Cumberland in north-west England and she as a 6 year old from Tillicoultry, Scotland, in 1855. Christopher and Frances continued to run the family property until its sale in March 1921. They then moved into Numurkah where their two children were born, William (Bill) in 1922, and my mother, Margaret Frances Knox, in 1924. Christopher purchased and ran a butcher's shop in the town and died in 1938.

Following her father's death, Mum moved in early 1940 from Numurkah to Melbourne. With the aid of a scholarship apparently arranged by a family friend, she attended Presbyterian Ladies College (PLC), at the time located in East Melbourne. After completing her schooling at PLC, she began teacher training. Because of the shortage of teachers during the war, she was appointed after one year's training to Gould, a small school between Moe and Walhalla in central Gippsland, now submerged beneath the Moondarra Reservoir. After two years at Gould she was transferred to Murrindal.

In rural areas at the time, the teacher most commonly boarded with a local family, usually one with children at the school. This was the case with Mum when she moved to Murrindal, where she had among her students Ewen and Jessie McRae's three children — Alice, Alex and Jessie — and boarded with their family.

This obviously brought her into contact with Don, who continued his practice of visiting from his hut in the bush a few miles distant. Despite the difference in ages — she turned 22 during the year and he 48 — a relationship developed between them and they were married in December of that year. It was an uncommon match and would no doubt have been seen as such by many at the time. Discussing this in later years, Mum reflected that it was one she was entirely content with, based strongly on mutual love, and over which she never had regrets.

Following marriage, Mum and Don settled into life on a property at the Basin to the east of Don's block, which they initially leased from Henry Hodge. It was a major change in circumstances for them both.

The Basin was a small settlement where three families at that time lived on a small area of cleared land approximately 20 kilometres east of Buchan. The southern property was owned by Angus Armstrong and his wife Maisie, that in the middle by Rob and Gwen Hodge, with we McRaes at the northern end of the clearing. There was a small, unpainted four room house of rough sawn weatherboards on the highest point of our property[10]

In a small hut just north of our house lived Alec Fraser. Alec had grown up at Gelantipy and married a cousin of Jessie McRae. He

---

10   The houses and farm buildings on all three properties were destroyed by bushfires in 2019-20.

and his wife lived separate lives and Alec, an alcoholic World War 1 pensioner, had lived in the house at the Pyramids following the move of Ewen and Jessie McRae to Murrindal. Following further health problems, he moved to a small hut built for him by Don on the Basin property.

The property was originally a Crown grant of roughly 500 acres (200 hectares), granted late in 1941 to Henry Hodge for seventeen shillings per acre. Henry Hodge split the property in 1942, retaining 300 acres and selling 200 acres, known as the 'Lightwood paddock'.

In 1950 Don, by now listed on title documents as 'grazier, Buchan', purchased the 300 acres from Henry Hodge at £7 per acre to add to the 300 acres he leased near Mount McLeod. Over the next few years, he split the 300 acres at the Basin, selling half to neighbour Rob Hodge and retaining the remainder, as well as re-purchasing the Lightwood paddock.

In 1956, when forced by ill health to leave the property, he sold this paddock to Angus Armstrong and the 150 acres of the home property to 'Mick' and Vere Moon[11]. The lease on the Mount McLeod block was taken over by John Gillan, son of a Presbyterian minister whom the McRae family had become closely associated with during their time at Drouin in the 1940s.

In July 1947 my older sister Elizabeth was born. The timing of

---

11   Vere Moon was also an artist, originally from suburban Melbourne. During the Second World War she had worked as a draughtswoman in the Military Intelligence and Operations Unit of the Army, in St Kilda Road. In the early 1950s, following her marriage to Rayford 'Mick' Moon, a member of one of the pioneer families of the district, she moved to Buchan. In 1975, Mum arranged for Vere to paint three scenes from the area and gave one to each of Elizabeth, Alison and me as a present that Christmas. The paintings are reproduced in this book.

**Wedding photo
— Mum and Don McRae (1946);**

this event would no doubt have had some district tongues wagging, maybe more than usual given the age difference between Mum and Don.

Family reactions varied. Despite the conservative Christian and moral perspectives of many in the McRae family, they remained strongly supportive and continued to be so in future years. Such was not the case with Mum's mother who had considerable difficulty in accepting the turn of events, in much the same way as she had some years previously when she discovered one of Mum's closest friends at Teachers College was a Catholic!

In 1950 I was born and younger sister Alison followed in 1951. The Hodge boys, Neil and Colin, were a little older than Elizabeth.

CHAPTER 3   *Early days*

'Mount McLeod at sunrise' — painting by Vere Moon.
Shed and stockyards at the Basin, East Buchan,
with Mount McLeod in the background

Tony Brownlow was around their age and being raised by the Armstrongs. There was therefore some contact with a small number of other children at the Basin. There was a primary school operating at East Buchan but given the distance and transport conditions at the time neither we nor the Hodge boys attended it.

Correspondence school was thus the order of the time. Elizabeth had more than two years of this under Mum's tuition, and I had commenced at the beginning of 1956, prior to our move to Bairnsdale in the middle of that year. I recall 'Kindergarten of the Air' being a regular morning activity in the room where the large valve radio stood.

With prevailing road and vehicle conditions, the Basin was

***'The Lightwood paddock'** — painting by Vere Moon.*
View east across Basin Creek to the Lightwood paddock.

quite remote. Trips to Buchan for us occurred relatively commonly, perhaps every two or three weeks. But a trip to Bairnsdale, a further 75 kilometres beyond Buchan, was a big and irregular event. Neither Mum nor Don had a driver's licence when they arrived at the Basin. Both were taught to drive by Rob Hodge, obtained their licences and purchased a late 1920s-era Dodge utility, which gave them a bit more flexibility. Trips along the winding gravel road through the bush to and from Buchan would always require some of us to ride in the back of the ute, as there was not enough room in the cabin for all family members.

The road from Buchan was reasonably well formed to Hodge's property, but for the final few hundred metres from there up to our house it was little more than a roughly defined track across the paddock, its location varying over time. As there was also quite a rise to our house from Hodge's, it was not uncommon to have to walk some of this distance because the track was too wet for the ute to get up the hill.

Conditions were difficult, with no telephone or electricity (mains power did not arrive at the Basin until 1968). Lighting was provided by kerosene lamps and hurricane lanterns. The families set up a communication link between themselves using an ex-army field telephone, and collaborated with each other where possible in collecting items for others if one family happened to be in Buchan or Bairnsdale for any purpose.

Mum was a keen reader and maintained this interest through

'The Basin in autumn' — painting by Vere Moon.
View north on the Basin Road, across Basin Creek and former Hodge property to former McRae property, with house on the cleared hill.

Mum and Elizabeth, circa 1949, at Don's bark hut near the Basin, East Buchan, in which he lived prior to marriage

membership of the postal library service run by the Athenaeum Library in Melbourne. She also had a piano which she played intermittently.

With no electricity, all clothes washing was done manually in a copper and troughs out the back of the house. Water was obtained from a tank on the side of the house, but needed to be used judiciously. I don't have a clear recollection of how often we children had baths, but only one lot of bathwater was ever used for all of us. There was no plumbing, with water being heated on the wood stove in kerosene tins repurposed as water buckets. Even after a well was sunk near the house and a manual pump installed, water was used very carefully.

Sheep were killed for meat, occasionally supplemented by rabbits. A house cow provided milk and butter and any of the chooks that dropped off in egg production also found their way onto the table. There was a vegetable patch and an orchard, from

CHAPTER 3   *Early days*

*McRae children — Chris, Alison and Elizabeth
— at the Basin, East Buchan, circa 1953*

which fruit was preserved and jams made. A few fruit trees were in place when Mum and Don moved to the property, and Mum had added additional trees in a small orchard following her arrival.

There was initially no refrigerator, with any food to be kept relying on either a Coolgardie safe, a meat safe or salting — depending on what it was and how long it was to be kept. A small kerosene refrigerator arrived probably around 1954 or 1955, a gift from Ewen and Jessie, and this seemed to be a wonderful leap forward. I am sure Mum found it to be so.

I recall reasonably regular interactions between the neighbouring families. Visits to one place or another for us kids to play, or the parents to meet for a cup of tea or evenings playing cards were quite common. Events such as Guy Fawkes night around a bonfire at Hodge's have stuck in my memory.

The remoteness of the property and transport conditions meant that visits from those outside the district were not common. Alec Fraser's daughters lived in Sydney and they and their families visited the Basin on one occasion during our time there, as did Mum's brother Bill and his wife and son, and her mother.

Charlie West, a bushman who owned land at Jackson's Crossing, north east of the Basin on the Snowy River, would occasionally call in while riding through leading his pack horse, but by far the most common visits other than by the immediate neighbours came from the McRae family from Murrindal. Even these could not be described as regular and would usually result from one or more of the family riding the approximately 10 kilometres of bush tracks between the properties, rather than driving the 35 kilometres by road through Buchan.

We didn't have a tractor — Rob Hodge owned the only one at the Basin — so farm work was done using draught horses. A sledge was pulled behind a horse to move items such as fencing equipment and posts around the place, and I recall a trip to Timbarra north-west of Buchan on one occasion for Don to purchase another draught horse for use in ploughing the small paddock in which maize was grown. Towards the end of our time at the Basin, there was a move in the direction of mechanisation when a Buchan farmer with a tractor was contracted to do some ploughing for us.

We ran sheep and cattle, and I suspect it was fortunate that the time coincided with historically high wool prices as it would have been a rather precarious existence making ends meet from the farm, as it undoubtedly was for many small landholders in the area. Although I had no concept of this at the time, I have no doubt that we would have derived little more than a subsistence living out of the place, and I know Mum subsequently expressed considerable gratitude for the support received from the extended McRae family and friends over her time at the Basin. This help would certainly not have all been one way, and the mutual support given between families, to the extent each were able to, is probably one of the enduring recollections of many in similar circumstances.

One of our regular excursions was to church in Buchan on a Sunday afternoon. The single Protestant church in the town was shared by the Presbyterians and the Anglicans, who worshipped in it on different Sundays, and I recall trips into the town to attend the monthly Presbyterian service. At that stage it was led by John Paton, who had been born in the New Hebrides (now Vanuatu) to a prominent Scottish Presbyterian mission family and had served as a missionary there himself. By the time of his role at Buchan, he was the home missionary with the Presbyterian church based at Lakes Entrance, where he served between 1947 and 1958.

*McRae children — Elizabeth, Alison and Chris
with family ute at the Basin, circa 1953*

He and his wife Vera would come across from Lakes Entrance in a taxi (he didn't own a car) to conduct the service in the small, single-room church. Mrs Paton would take the kids out for Sunday school part-way through the service and, depending on the weather, this would be held on a rug on the ground in front of the church or, if the weather was cold or wet, we would pile into a parishioner's car in front of the church and have our lesson there.

We were subscribers to a correspondence Sunday school and, even if we had been to church during the day, Sunday evenings often involved a time of family worship at home, where hymns would be sung, the Bible read and prayers offered. Mum played the piano to support our singing. It was a practice I became used to participating in regularly during later years on visits to Murrindal. Recollections of the music played and some of the hymns sung remain most strongly — such as *Shall We Gather at the River* from the Basin and *The Sands of Time are Sinking* from Murrindal.

I have no recollection of Don becoming ill or of understanding its seriousness, although in retrospect there were events which now make this obvious. In late 1954 we travelled to Melbourne — an unheard-of event — for Don to visit a doctor. In 1955 he again travelled to Melbourne for surgery to have a kidney removed; subsequently I can recall him convalescing at home for some time.

The 1954 trip to Melbourne is etched in my mind for another reason: it was my first experience of spending a few days at the cricket. Both Mum and Don were very keen cricket followers and probably the timing of the Melbourne trip had as much to do with the Test cricket itinerary as it had with Don's health. At least all possible efforts would have been made to coincide the timing of medical appointments and the cricket.

CHAPTER 3   *Early days*

**Children at the Basin, East Buchan, circa 1953
(Photo: courtesy Neil Hodge)**
L to R: Elizabeth, Alison and Chris McRae, Neil and Colin Hodge,
Tony Brownlow

I had occasionally been along with Don for short periods at cricket matches in Buchan. Mum played tennis and, as the recreation ground was virtually next door to the tennis courts, Don would go along to watch the cricket if there was a match on at the time. The cricket at the Melbourne Cricket Ground was a totally different matter, though.

Australia was playing England in the third Test match of the 1954/55 series. It turned out to be quite a prominent match in which Frank Tyson tore through Australia in the second innings and won the match for England with figures of 7 for 27. Probably as much as any other match, this one cemented his reputation as 'Typhoon' Tyson.

All of this was of no interest to me. My only positive recollection of the days we spent at the cricket was watching the tractor mowing the ground before play each day. I remember spending extended periods kneeling with my back to the ground and head in my hands on the old wooden bench seats in the Southern Stand, known as 'the Outer', wishing for the day to conclude. At one stage Don attempted to enthuse me by advising that a wicket had fallen, but I could not have cared less. I couldn't imagine a more boring way to spend time.

My perspective changed subsequently. I gradually began to play the game as well as to derive great pleasure from watching and following it. In the 65 years since that inauspicious beginning, I have been to watch all except two or three touring sides who have visited Australia and played Test matches in the state I was in at the time of their visit.

In mid 1956 we left the Basin and purchased a house in East Bairnsdale. Although basic, it had some definite improvements on our Basin accommodation: electricity and basic plumbing being among them. There was still no telephone and initially no hot-water service. We continued to operate with a 'dunny' in the backyard, but at least there was now a regular service to remove and replace the cans.

At the same time we sold the old ute and bought a new Standard 10 car, which seemed to be quite a step-up in vehicle quality. Mum went back to teaching at Bairnsdale Primary School, and we children began attending Lucknow Primary School.

I had not attended a school prior to this, apart from a two-week period at East Buchan when Mum filled in for the usual teacher while he was away. All three of us children attended for that period in 1956, even though Alison had not commenced correspondence school at that stage. We swelled the numbers at the school

CHAPTER 3   *Early days*

Children and mothers at the Basin, East Buchan, circa 1953
(Photo: courtesy Neil Hodge)
Back: Maisie Armstrong, Gwen Hodge, Margaret McRae
Front: Neil Hodge, Tony Armstrong, Alison McRae, Colin Hodge,
Chris McRae, Elizabeth McRae

considerably, and I recall the horses that some of the students rode to school being held in an adjoining paddock during the days.

Lucknow was a school of around 100 students and commencing there was quite a culture shock. I had never seen so many children in one place, let alone been expected to interact with many of them in a planned and ordered manner. There were three classrooms: 'Preps' to Grade 2, Grades 3 and 4, and Grades 5 and 6. Alison and I began in the lower group and Elizabeth in the middle one.

I imagine Lucknow was similar to most country Victorian primary schools at the time — Monday morning assembly to unfurl the flag, recite the Patriotic Declaration ('I love God and my country, I honour the flag and cheerfully obey my parents, teachers and the law') and sing *God Save the Queen*, free milk at morning recess, ink wells in the desks of those from Grade 3 onwards, and male teachers referred to as 'Sir'.

I initially had difficulty adjusting to the new routine and regularly found myself in tears because I 'didn't like school', or in a fight because I was teased about it. In a short while, though, things settled down and from that time on, despite the occasional flurry caused by a dislike of a particular subject or teacher, I found school to be a positive experience.

Don was in and out of hospital in the months following our move to Bairnsdale. He was a smoker and suffering from lung cancer, although for some time it was thought that a heart condition was the cause of his ill health. As had been the case with his health problems while we were at the Basin, I had no concept of what they were, their seriousness, nor of their implications for him and the rest of the family. I was familiar with death and its finality from experiences at the Basin with farm and pest animals, but I had not drawn the link between this understanding and Don's condition. In my mind people, particularly adults, just 'were' and continued to 'be'.

Don died in Bairnsdale Hospital on the evening of 14 November 1956. On the morning following his death, I got out of bed, expecting to go to school, when Mum spoke with Alison and me to tell us the news. She had done the same shortly before with Elizabeth, who had returned to her room. Mum sat on the couch with her arms around Alison and me as the three of us cried.

The funeral was held at St Andrew's Presbyterian Church in Bairnsdale, led by Rev David Hodges. We children attended the church service, but not the subsequent graveside service at the Bairnsdale cemetery. I recall coming to a six-year-old's acceptance,

CHAPTER 3   *Early days*

and being comforted that, once everyone left from the cemetery that afternoon, the angels would come to collect Don and take him to heaven.

Don's death would have placed more pressure on Mum than I was aware of or understood at the time. We were within the first six months of having moved to a new town. As well as the emotional impact of being widowed, she had the practical reality of returning to teaching while supporting three children under the age of ten.

She continued teaching, prioritised our involvement with the church and began playing tennis with the local Howitt Park club. She received great support from family and friends, most notably neighbours Bob and Dulcie Lawson, Ewen and Jessie McRae and their family, and Ewen and Don's unmarried sister Margaret, who lived with the McRaes at Murrindal.

During 1957 Mum's mother Frances came to live with us. She was the only grandparent I knew, as both of Don's parents and Mum's father had died prior to my birth. I recall meeting her on only one prior occasion when she visited us at the Basin, and my memory of her time with us at East Bairnsdale is fragmentary and not very positive. Those recollections I do have are of her being a stern and remote person, certainly not one that I warmed to in the expected way of grandparents. She died the following year and although I had no particular emotional reaction to this, I am sure it provided a further challenge for Mum.

All three of we children regularly spent school holidays with the McRae family at Murrindal, which in many ways became a second home for us. At the time I saw this simply as something which was occurring because we enjoyed going there, but later came to understand that the major reason and benefit was to provide practical support for Mum at a very difficult time. A further example came in late 1957, after I had spent a month in the Bairnsdale hospital suffering from pneumonia — memorable mostly for what seemed to be endless antibiotic injections in my buttocks — and then went to Murrindal for a number of weeks to recuperate.

Our McRae cousins were around 10 to 15 years older than us, and we certainly looked up to them and much enjoyed the opportunity to spend time with them, as we did our uncle and aunts. I think that the positive sentiments were largely reciprocated, although I am sure there were times when having younger relatives 'tagging along' when things needed to be done became a bit of an impost for them.

Over time I came to spend most of my school holidays at Murrindal. I particularly formed a relationship with Alex; he became a hero of mine and I a shadow of his during these visits. As a child I believed there was probably nothing that he was incapable of doing. My opinion was enhanced when he returned from a trip into the bush further north to catch brumbies and, after being successful, broke in one he had caught and gave it to me as a present.

My overly flattering youthful perspective was gradually modified by reality as I matured, but I regularly spent at least some holiday time at Murrindal up until my mid twenties. I enjoyed being involved in farm activities and associated pastimes, such as shooting and trapping rabbits.

CHAPTER 3 *Early days*

A soliloquy

As backward o'er the years my glance I cast,
In meditation I survey the past.
The joys and happiness, the doubts and fears,
The cloud and sunshine mingled with the years.
As from a hilltop we perchance look back
Into the distance, far along the track
We've travelled, and we pause there for a span
And trace our journey whence it was began.
Patches of light and shadow meet the view.
Light, when the sun from broken cloud shines through;
Shadow, where passing cloud obscures the light,
Hiding at times the sunshine from our sight.
Likewise through life, as we the journey run
Through light or darkness, shadow, cloud or sun.
At times though darkening clouds obscure our view,
Somewhere they break and let the sunshine through.

—***Don McRae***

CHAPTER 4

A developing interest

Mum had a keen interest in sport and had followed the local football team with her family as a child in Numurkah, where her father had played in his youth. It was a practice she recommenced in 1957 as she settled into life following Don's death. Living in East Bairnsdale and with we children attending Lucknow State School, it was probably inevitable that we began to follow the Lucknow Football Club. After very little time I was hooked both on the game and the experience of following it.

The decision to follow Lucknow also had a longer-term impact on me. Their jumper was black and white vertical stripes and I was attracted to following the Victorian Football League (VFL) team which played in the same colours: Collingwood. I had no sense at the time of the strong emotional reaction — both positive and negative — that club draws from football supporters and saw it as a clearly inspired decision when Collingwood won the 1958 VFL premiership. Although premierships in subsequent years have been far less frequent for Collingwood, despite participation in numerous grand finals, I have never regretted that early decision.

I suspect Mum, as an Essendon supporter, would have seen it as one of the few downsides of our period supporting Lucknow.

Lucknow played in the Bairnsdale and District Football League (BDFL), a local league stretching from Swan Reach in the east to Lindenow South in the west and Paynesville in the south. Lucknow, Wy Yung and Bairnsdale Rovers (later renamed West Bairnsdale) — clubs based in or very near to Bairnsdale — made up the remainder of the league.

There were a number of other football leagues in the area at that time. The Omeo and District Football League — Ensay, Swifts Creek, Omeo and Benambra — took in the Tambo valley and the area above the Tongio Gap. The Snowy Valley Football League was still in existence, comprised of Buchan, Nowa Nowa, Newmerella and Marlo. Bairnsdale played in the Gippsland Football League, which was made up of clubs from Orbost to Heyfield, although in the 1960 season they, as well as Maffra and Heyfield, moved to the stronger Latrobe Valley League. This league then stretched as far west as Drouin when that club also joined the league that year.

As has been the case throughout Victoria, in the years since there has been considerable change in leagues and the teams in them. Some of the above leagues now don't exist and all leagues in the area are now more geographically spread and comprised of different clubs to what they were in the late 1950s. The Snowy Valley League folded in 1959, the Bairnsdale District League at the end of 1972, as did the Gippsland League in 1973 (although that name now applies to the league broadly containing the teams which made up the Latrobe Valley League in the 1960s, with the addition of Leongatha and Wonthaggi from South Gippsland). A

CHAPTER 4   *A developing interest*

number of the above clubs no longer exist and some neighbouring clubs, fierce rivals as separate entities, have amalgamated.

For me, following football as a young child was a particularly local pursuit. We didn't have to travel far even to 'away' games — less than 20 kilometres. The Saturday outing to watch the football, buy a pie or hot dog from the canteen, and perhaps even spend time helping to look after the scoreboard at home games was something I eagerly looked forward to. It was always good to go onto the ground for a kick of the football with others before the game or at half-time. Going into the rooms, knowing who the players were (and even sometimes having them know who you were!), going onto the ground at three-quarter-time to be around the players' huddle and listening to the pep talk from the coach was all part of the weekly ritual.

There was no junior football on offer in Bairnsdale at the time. The BDFL reserves was the earliest competition to aspire to play in. This was an Under 18 competition and it was unrealistic for anyone of my age at the time to expect to participate, although one or two of the older boys from Lucknow school played on rare occasions. I recall significant excitement one Friday at school when we found out that one of the boys who had been in Grade 6 the previous year had been selected to play in the Lucknow senior team the following day.

For the 1957 and 1958 seasons, I attended most Lucknow games. I didn't go to Bairnsdale games until we returned from Orbost at the beginning of 1961, and even then only to home games. All the while, though, Bairnsdale loomed large in my consciousness. They were the team that the better players from the BDFL went to play for, or 'had a run with' on permit if they were unsure whether they were good enough or wished to commit to the extra travel involved in playing in the larger league. They were the club where most of the captain-coaches in the BDFL came from.

This focus on Bairnsdale made following football in the time we were in Orbost — mid 1959 until the end of 1960 — a slightly different experience. Because Bairnsdale played in the same league as Orbost in 1959, prior to their move to the Latrobe Valley League, I found it hard to get too excited about supporting Orbost in the two football seasons we were there, despite the fervour of my friends for doing so. I even admit to a degree of quiet satisfaction when Orbost lost a close grand final to Stratford in 1960.

Maybe because of my ambivalence towards supporting Orbost, during this time I became increasingly interested in Collingwood. This included being given a hand-knitted Collingwood jumper for my tenth birthday, complete with a plastic patch sown on the back bearing the number of my favourite player, Ray Gabelich. I took considerable pride in wearing the jumper with 'Gabbo's' number on it.

Disaster struck once when we were away for the day and the jumper was left on the floor near my bed. At the time I slept in a bedroom which was effectively a portion of the back verandah enclosed with some sheets of canvas. It was therefore quite accessible, and during our absence our recently acquired pup got in and chewed the number off the back of my jumper. The patch and number were wrecked, although the jumper itself suffered only minor damage, which attachment of a replacement plastic patch and number would satisfactorily hide.

The trauma continued, though, as the local stores didn't have any more of 'Gabbo's' number in stock. In the end I was begrudgingly

CHAPTER 4   *A developing interest*

mollified by the attachment of Ray Willett's number; at the time he appeared to be an up-and-coming Collingwood player, but eventually played only a few games before becoming a prominent country footballer in the Bendigo and Goulburn Valley Leagues. I particularly recalled my Orbost experience when we moved to Rutherglen in 1994 and Ray was a teacher at the primary school our children attended.

As a child my information on football beyond the small local area came largely from listening to the scores from the VFL, Amateurs and local leagues on the ABC Radio Sporting Roundup at 6.30 each Saturday evening. This program was required listening. Local results were given in some detail, including the names of goal kickers and best players, and I became familiar with the names of prominent footballers and their affiliation with the various towns around Gippsland.

Technology and ease of travel make experiences nowadays very different to those of earlier times, and this is as true for following football as it is for many other aspects of life. It is now easier and takes less time to watch a game of football on TV direct from Melbourne, or anywhere else in Australia or the world, than to go along to a local football game. We have access to the actions and thoughts of AFL players via social and other media constantly and virtually instantaneously, and hence they are far more visible and 'real' than they were in the 1950s.

My experience was quite different. We didn't have television (as was the case for many in Bairnsdale at the time) and in country towns the extent of information on and exposure to VFL football and footballers, and probably even interest in them, was far less than what it now is.

As a result my understanding of footballers and their capabilities had a very local and constrained focus. In my mind at the time there was a clear line of progression in capability, and hence realistic attainment, that any footballer could aspire to — commence with BDFL seconds, progress to BDFL firsts or Bairnsdale seconds, then finally move on to Bairnsdale firsts (but only if you were particularly good). In this localised view, playing with Bairnsdale's senior side was the realistic pinnacle of football achievement for me.

In theory there was the VFL beyond this, but that was so remote and being able to play there so unlikely in my mind, that it almost didn't need to be considered. The VFL was seemingly such a distant place that very few locals, even those playing for Bairnsdale, were likely to be good enough to ever play. The most obvious local impact of the VFL for me at that time, and for a number of years later, was through the likes of Eddie Lane and later John McMahon, Bill Thripp and Ian Aston, who all became playing coaches at Bairnsdale after playing VFL football.

The thoughts about the football prominence of Bairnsdale must have been quite strongly ingrained in my young consciousness and to have remained there despite broadening perspectives as I grew older. In later years I played football in a number of towns and for different clubs, but I recall the particular excitement I felt in being selected for and playing my first game for Bairnsdale seniors in 1970, when I returned to the town after completing study at Dookie College. Ten or twelve years earlier I couldn't have imagined ever being able to reach that seemingly dizzy level of achievement!

CHAPTER 5

Times of change

During 1958 we began to be regularly visited by a Mr Alf King, a primary school teacher from Orbost. He was a kind, gentle man who showed great interest in and patience with us children and we all came to very much enjoy spending time with him. That was obviously true for Mum as well, and later that year she and Alf announced that they were to be married the following year.

Alf was a member of a Bairnsdale family and his late father had operated a small joinery business in the town. He and Mum were married in May 1959 and we then moved to Orbost, initially living in the vacant Presbyterian church manse prior to relocating at the end of the year to rent a small Housing Commission house in the north of the town. Alf taught at Orbost Primary School and we set about making friends, getting involved in the life of the town, and becoming used to operating as a recently modified family.

Alison and I attended Orbost Primary School, just across the road from the manse, with Elizabeth attending the High School. I was in the class taught by Alf for the remainder of our first year at Orbost, and early the next I recall receiving a 'Herald

Wedding photo — Mum and Alf King (1959)

Learn-to-swim' certificate for swimming 25 yards in the Snowy River at Marlo. I also began attending Cubs, the initial step in an enjoyable involvement in the Scout movement for many years.

These were among a growing number of personal and organisational involvements that, with the local Presbyterian church, became central. A highlight was the annual Sunday-school picnic, held at the Marlo Racecourse in at least one of the years we were in Orbost, and in particular a long wooden slide constructed by one of the parishioners. Using this required us to sit on heavy hessian bags to avoid getting splinters as we sped down its length, but it was a great attraction and a source of seemingly endless fun.

I recall very few difficulties in settling into our new family arrangements during our time in Orbost or subsequently. Mum remained the organiser and driver within the family, a role she had been forced into following Don's death, but also one with which she was temperamentally comfortable and adept at fulfilling. Alf was far more at ease providing support; he was uncomfortable being the centre of attention or in leadership roles. However, I have encountered few people in my life who were as constant in thinking of others, caring about them and their various needs, and doing what he could to encourage and assist them.

Alf would never have felt at ease in a management position at a school (or in any other situation for that matter), but he was ideally suited to his role as a primary school teacher. I doubt that there would have been any child, no matter how difficult or disruptive, who would not have received a greater sense of support from Alf than they did from other teachers, and probably also from others in their lives. He had the capacity to see some good in all people and circumstances and to highlight this, rather than the more apparent difficulties or challenges for which they may have been more generally known.

His personality and actions later made him a favourite among the children of our wider family and of his grandchildren. Over many years Uncle Alf or 'Pa' spent endless hours with all the family children and was much loved as a result. Spending time with him was undoubtedly the highlight for children on trips to visit him and Mum, and they would revel in the seemingly inexhaustible reserves of patience and interest he would expend on them.

Alf was also heavily involved in the work of the Presbyterian and then Uniting Church, particularly its pastoral care work, as well as that of other caring organisations in the town. He and

Mum formed a strong partnership in this regard, she being to the fore if organisation was required, and he ensuring everything and everyone was thought about, supported and made to feel welcome. In 2002, shortly after Alf's death, Mum was recognised as Bairnsdale's 'Citizen of the Year' for her work supporting a range of local causes, but there is no doubt that the award also owed much to the support and effort of Alf over many years.

He was by no means what may have been described at the time as a 'man's man', and when growing up there were times I felt that it would be preferable if he was more assertive in his actions, particularly when it appeared to me that he was being taken advantage of. I was of the view at the time that this was the appropriate way for 'real men' to respond. This was not his nature, though, and it was an unrealistic expectation to have of him. I eventually came to understand this and received a lived lesson that offence in whatever form is only acute when it is taken, not when it is given, and that each of us has a choice in how we choose to respond to any perception of it.

After a year and a half in Orbost, at the end of 1960, we returned to Bairnsdale and to Alf's family home, which he now owned. He had transferred to a teaching job at Bairnsdale West Primary School, which Alison and I began attending in 1961 while Elizabeth attended Bairnsdale High School.

During our first year back in Bairnsdale, I was faced with a decision on where to move for secondary schooling. I had not thought much about what career I wished to embark on, beyond a vague inclination to become involved in farming in some way. Even that was not based on any logical analysis of the likelihood of being able to do so, but as the Technical School offered a practical rather than academic emphasis it was the school I enrolled in for 1962.

CHAPTER 5   *Times of change*

Coincidentally, Mum later became a staff member at the school. Having not returned to teaching following her marriage to Alf, in the early 1960s she retrained as a librarian through distance education at the Gippsland Institute of Advanced Education, now part of Federation University Australia. In 1965 she commenced as librarian at Bairnsdale Technical School and continued in this role until her retirement in 1989.

The Technical School was located to the east of Bairnsdale township on the embankment above the Mitchell River, between the town's largest caravan park to its east and police station to its west. It was the successor of the Bairnsdale School of Mines, which had commenced on the school's site in the late 19th century. Some of the original buildings were still in use, with transportable classrooms positioned between the main building and the riverbank. An asphalt quadrangle was located in the space between the main school building and the police station. It was here that assemblies were held prior to each class and where students would congregate at the end of the school day to catch school busses to places such as Lakes Entrance, Paynesville, Bruthen, Lindenow, Mount Taylor or Meerlieu.

J.J. (Jack) Hennessy was the school's uncompromising principal. He appeared to students to be a severe and distant man, and it was a line-ball decision on whether the predominant emotion felt towards him was fear or loathing. Occasionally in the playground, theatrically performed excerpts of Ray Charles' recent hit, *Hit the Road Jack*, would be heard, with care taken to ensure that teachers were unlikely to witness the performances. Most students felt more comfortable if required to interact with the upper management of the school, to do so with the more approachable Headmaster Ernie

Illidge — although it was a time when interactions between staff and students were generally quite formal and restrained.

Perhaps because of the times, or maybe as a result of the principal's inclinations, there was a military flavour in many school practices. All students, apart from those in Forms 5 and 6, were required to assemble in their form groups on specific lines in the quadrangle at the start of each day, after lunchtime, and following morning and afternoon recesses. There was an expectation that those assembling would do so quietly and in straight rows, with staff patrolling to ensure this occurred.

There was a raised podium set against the school building at the front of the assembled students, from which a designated staff member would conduct the business of the assembly.

Often there would be information to pass on or instructions to give. Irrespective, at the end of each assembly, all would be required to formally stand 'at ease' and the command 'School, ATTENTION!' would be given. All were expected to snap to attention, and we would march into class to the beat of bass and side drums played by a couple of students.

Marching was prominent in other school activities as well. In preparing for inter-school athletic sports, training for participants to march into place at the final presentation ceremony of the sports seemed to receive almost as much attention as did that for the athletic events themselves. The annual event for schools to commemorate ANZAC Day (held on the afternoon prior) also required us to march for at least the final few hundred metres of the trek from the school to the town cenotaph. I recall preparing for this by groups of us honing our marching skills on the roadways of the caravan park adjacent to the school.

CHAPTER 5 *Times of change*

Corporal punishment, almost exclusively the strap or 'cuts', was much in vogue and was thought by us students to be over-liberally dispensed. It was probably less so than we perceived at the time and, despite some students becoming well known for the frequency and scale of their infractions, the majority remained within the bounds of acceptable behaviour most of the time.

There was a general understanding about the degree of pain likely to be felt by falling foul of those dispensing this punishment. Some teachers were identified as high-frequency/low-impact purveyors, while others were treated more warily because they were known to be the opposite. Mary Martin, the junior school Social Studies teacher was a member of the first group ('I got the cuts from Mary again today — didn't even hurt'), while the Sheetmetal teacher, Harry Elsdon, was an example of the latter ('Tell ya what, ya don't wanna get the cuts from Harry!') I was among those who had limited first-hand experience with which to refine these assessments, but can vouch for the accuracy of them both.

The minimum school leaving age at the time was 15 years and there was a major decline in student numbers once that age was reached. Few attending the Technical School intended to go on to tertiary study, and virtually all who did so progressed to diploma courses at larger institutions such as Yallourn, Footscray or Swinburne, which were all at the time known as Technical Colleges. Anyone who aspired to university would attend the High School.

There were around 90 students in Form 1 when I commenced in 1962; only nine remained in Form 5 in 1966, although class numbers were bolstered to 17 by others who had transferred to the school or had repeated a year. While a small number of those who left in the intervening years had transferred to the High School or left town, most had finished school to commence apprenticeships, return to work on family farms or to take on labouring or retail roles.

During Form 4, I set my sights on moving on to tertiary study in agriculture. For a while I contemplated transferring to the High School, which would have given me the option of completing Form 6 and attending university, but decided to remain at the Technical School and aim to gain entrance to a diploma course at an agricultural college. This happened at the end of Form 5 and, even though I eventually completed a degree as well as a diploma, I don't regret the slightly longer path I took to do so. At the time I thought nothing of the route I had taken, but subsequently found in the roles in which I worked during my career that very few of my contemporaries had undertaken their secondary education at a Technical School.

My bedroom at Bairnsdale was a bungalow behind the house, previously a small workshop for Alf's late father who had run his joinery business from it. When we arrived in early 1961, it was cleaned out and converted from its former role, and its most recent manifestation as a storage area for junk, into a bedroom. With a bit of masonite lining, an extra window and a coat of paint, it became quite a comfortable room, even though the floor mats needed to be judiciously placed in winter to guard against cold winds entering through the worst of the cracks between the unevenly shrunken hardwood floorboards.

Behind the bungalow was the woodheap and beyond that, in the south-east corner of the block, was the chook house containing the ubiquitous peppercorn tree. A laneway ran along the back of all the blocks in the street and between those of the rear neighbours, whose houses faced into the adjoining street.

CHAPTER 5 *Times of change*

The bungalow was raised about 30 centimetres above the ground on stumps and the space underneath it became a very handy place to store extra pieces of timber or other items which 'may come in handy' in the future. The gap caused problems in other ways, though, as it allowed cricket or tennis balls to regularly disappear under the bungalow, which was large enough to make it difficult to locate and extricate them.

The area under the bungalow also appeared to be a favourite meeting (and fighting) place for the neighbourhood cats. There were frequent bursts of growling, high-pitched caterwauling and scrambling around, which were a bit annoying whenever they happened, but particularly so when they woke me before dawn on cold winter mornings. As a result of a seemingly endless sequence of these occasions, when I was around 12 or 13 years old, I decided I would do something about it.

Even a fleeting moment of reflection or common sense would have revealed the stupidity of my plans, but in my enthusiasm to 'teach those cats a lesson' neither occurred. My idea was to set a snare to catch a cat as it moved under the bungalow from the woodheap. In case the deterrent impact of being snared was not enough by itself, I then planned to administer a swift 'clip around the ears' to the animal before releasing it, confident that it would by then have realised the error of its ways and not repeat its disruptive behaviour.

A roughly defined track led under the bungalow from the woodheap and I assessed this as having resulted from cats moving along it. I had some old baler twine (used on rectangular hay bales common at the time), tied one end to the stump nearest to the track and moved some wood into place to further encourage its use. I then formed a slip-noose with the loose end of the twine and set it up directly in line with the track, in the hope that a cat would run into it and the noose would then tighten around it.

It didn't take long for the plan to succeed, and on a crisp winter's morning I was woken by a level of yowling, hissing, scrambling and growling under the floor beneath my bed beyond anything I had previously heard. But it was cold and I was a bit tardy in getting out of bed to sort the matter out. Fortunately (I thought) this didn't matter, as reasonably soon the commotion stopped and that was the last I heard of it.

Shortly afterwards I got out of bed and checked the scene, noting an area of considerable disturbance on the edge of the woodheap and a frayed piece of baler twine still tied to the nearby stump. The action had obviously been so intense that the twine had frayed and snapped and the animal caught in the snare had headed off. I imagined it would thus have been suitably 'deterred', believed therefore that my plans had been successful, and went inside to have breakfast.

The animal didn't get far, though. A short while later, as I went out the back gate to the lane behind our house to ride my bike to school, I was met by a couple of boys from nearby.

'Someone's been hangin' cats around here. We found one strung up on the fence beside your place. We know whose it is, so we've dumped it on his back lawn.' They were referring to a neighbour a few doors down, whose back fence I had to ride past on my way to school. I didn't dare look over the fence as I rode down the lane that morning.

The cat had thrashed around sufficiently to fray and break the twine near to the stump, but a small piece of wood had obviously caught in the end of the remaining twine. The escaping animal, with the snare still around its neck, had frenetically leapt the paling fence between our place and the largely empty double-block backyard of the next-door neighbour. The wood had stayed on one side of the fence while the cat had careered over to the other, with the inevitable outcome.

For some time I lived with the expectation of significant recriminations, but none came. Although we knew and got along very well with the relevant neighbour, I don't recall the issue ever being raised with me or even talked about, and I certainly never felt the desire to check whether any link had been drawn between the deceased cat and me. It didn't seem to impact at all on neighbourly relations, but I did become more accepting of a bit of noise under the bungalow following the experience.

Having commenced attending Cubs in Orbost, I continued doing so when we returned to Bairnsdale. I recall having a disagreement for some reason with Mum and Alf regarding moving on to Scouts when the time came to do so, but they prevailed and I soon became grateful that they did. I very much enjoyed the physical and outdoor activities of Scouts, eventually moving on to Senior Scouts and leaving the movement only when I moved from Bairnsdale to study at Dookie College. The numerous hikes, camps and other activities over the years were a great experience. Most of these were in various locations around East Gippsland, although there were trips to other parts of the state, including Wilsons Promontory and Anglesea, and I also had the good fortune to attend jamborees at Dandenong in December 1964–January 1965, then Wellington, New Zealand, in January 1966.

To earn some money to fund attendance at the New Zealand

jamboree, I stripped wattlebark. Bark from the black wattle had been used in the leather tanning industry for many years, and stripping wattlebark had been a regular undertaking in many areas of central and southern Victoria since the mid to late 1800s. It was a relatively common practice in parts of East Gippsland previously, but was gradually becoming less so, in part because of the increasing availability of synthetic tanning solutions.

As the trees which are stripped of bark die, the introduction of Victoria's native vegetation regulations in the late 1980s made the practice illegal. When I was involved, however, in the mid 1960s to early 1970s, it was still a legitimate means of earning some money. Following my late 1965 efforts, I had two subsequent summers (the last being 1971/72) spending at least some time stripping bark, generally with some project in mind to spend the funds on. It was quite a physically demanding job, but one that I eventually became reasonably proficient at, certainly to the extent of making it worthwhile and (marginally) remunerative.

I was fortunate that an area of private land owned by Alex McRae at Shaw's Gully, between the Basin hut and the Pyramids, was a great spot for black wattle. This became the most common site for my bark-stripping activities and there were always enough suitable trees to make the effort worthwhile.

Stripping wattlebark was a summer job, when the sap in the trees was 'running' and the bark could be most easily removed. Little was needed in the way of equipment. I used a tomahawk to cut and prise off the bark, enabling it to be pulled off by hand, and had two sturdy leather straps to pull the bundles together prior to tying them up with tie-wire.

The process involved making a horizontal cut completely around the base of the tree, around 1 to 1.2 metres above the ground. This base bark was then pulled by hand from the tree in strips as wide as possible; sometimes a further cut was required where the tree met the ground to enable the bark to be removed. This bark was then placed across the two leather straps laid on the ground. Following that the bark was prised from the upper edge of this cut and strips of bark pulled from the tree to as high up the tree as possible. Once that had been completed, I climbed the tree with the tomahawk in my belt then used it as needed to remove as much bark as feasible from the upper branches, again in as long strips as possible.

When the bark had been removed, the long strips of bark were folded to the length of the bark originally removed from the base of the tree and also placed across the straps. When a suitably sized bundle had been formed, the straps were pulled tight and two lengths of tie-wire placed around the bundle near the straps and tied off. The straps were then removed for use on the next bundle and the bundle placed on its end against the tree to dry, prior to being collected a few weeks later for sending off to a buyer.

Most trees were relatively easy to climb with limbs close to the ground, particularly in more open areas. In areas of denser bush they tended to grow taller and more erect, and some didn't have limbs which could be reached from the ground. In these cases a quick mental cost-benefit analysis was required on how to proceed.

If it appeared likely that a good lot of additional bark could be obtained by climbing the tree, strips of bark could be left attached to the tree and used as 'ropes' to climb up to the lowest branches. This was quite an enervating task and would not be undertaken unless the spoils of undertaking it were judged to be adequate. If this was not the case (or if it was late on a particularly hot day!), as much bark as possible would be removed while standing on the ground and that from the higher reaches of the tree would be foregone.

The OH&S implications of the job don't stand up to scrutiny, although that fact didn't enter my head at the time. I was most commonly working alone many kilometres from the nearest house, having ridden a horse or driven to work for the day, with no means of communication. The job involved use of a tomahawk and climbing trees, which were particularly slippery once they had their bark removed. The risk of something going astray was real, although certainly less than was the case in some other rural practices at the time. Thankfully, nothing did.

The job was useful in helping to develop self-discipline. Being a physically demanding task and working alone, the temptation to take extended breaks or to proceed sedately was always there. It is never difficult to convince yourself that there is a good reason not to get fully involved with or continue a difficult task. As well as that there was a degree of comfort in that no-one else was there to observe any slackness, although as the funds earned depended entirely on the output achieved, the consequent poorer financial outcome would also only impact me.

I found I could best handle this by setting myself a reasonably challenging target of bundles to complete in a day and to not leave until the target had been achieved. It was probably only a means of fooling myself but it seemed to work, and I have found the same approach to be useful in other aspects of life since.

The bundles of bark were left to dry for a few weeks then sent off for use in the tanning industry.

Jackson's tannery had stood on the banks of the Mitchell River

CHAPTER 5   *Times of change*

at Bairnsdale, just east of the town, for almost a century since it commenced business in 1876. As a child I recall the smell that was regularly associated with it, as well as once being somewhat disappointed with the returns I got for some rabbit skins I sold there. By the time I was looking to sell the bark I stripped, however, it had ceased operations and I sold the bark to an agent in Melbourne.

CHAPTER 6
College life

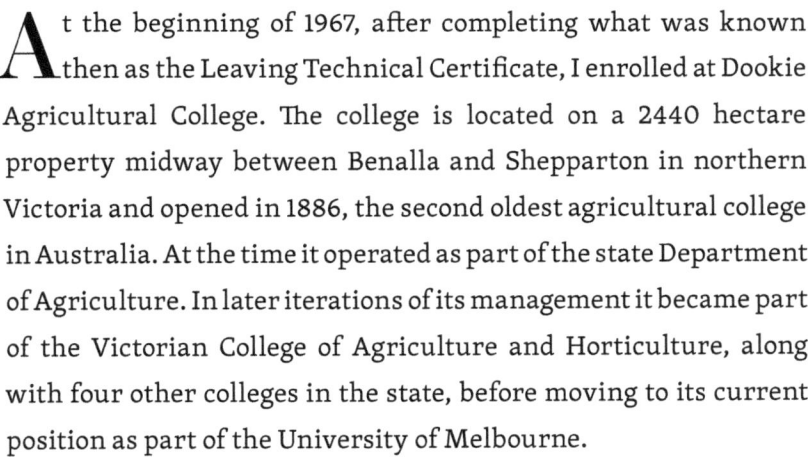

At the beginning of 1967, after completing what was known then as the Leaving Technical Certificate, I enrolled at Dookie Agricultural College. The college is located on a 2440 hectare property midway between Benalla and Shepparton in northern Victoria and opened in 1886, the second oldest agricultural college in Australia. At the time it operated as part of the state Department of Agriculture. In later iterations of its management it became part of the Victorian College of Agriculture and Horticulture, along with four other colleges in the state, before moving to its current position as part of the University of Melbourne.

When I attended Dookie it was in the final year of providing a three-year diploma in agriculture, which had been upgraded to a diploma in agricultural science for students commencing in 1966. At the same time the entrance requirements had been raised from requiring a pass in the Intermediate Certificate (current Year 10) to Leaving Certificate (current Year 11). These increased requirements indicated the beginning of a movement away from primarily training students for farming roles to training agricultural technologists. It offered a single course with virtually no opportunity to specialise in any specific aspect of agriculture, apart from when choices were made on projects that students undertook at various stages throughout the course.

The diploma course at Dookie was more practically oriented than the degree course offered at the University of Melbourne at the time, or at La Trobe University, which began offering degrees in agricultural science in 1968. Some students still went on to careers in farming, but many more went to technically rather than academically oriented careers in state government departments of agriculture or conservation, in agribusiness, or in related fields.

During my time at Dookie there were approximately 240 students enrolled across the three years, all males and all living full-time in dormitories on the campus. The college was effectively a reasonably self-contained small community, with approximately forty houses for married staff, accommodation for single workers, a primary school (Currawa), a small local store/post office with its own postcode and a small medical centre staffed by a resident matron and visiting doctors. It was an operational farm with a dairy herd, cropping operation, sheep flock, beef cattle herd, poultry operation, piggery — 'Home of Australia's first herd of HYPAR (Hysterectomy-Produced, Artificially-Reared) pigs' — an orchard and market garden, mechanical workshop, blacksmith, and had its own slaughterhouse and butchery. Produce was utilised in the kitchen for student meals, sold to staff or sold off-farm.

The annual cycle of activities in all these aspects of agriculture was integrated into the theoretical and practical training provided to students. Structured time involved around 70 per cent lectures and laboratory practicals and 30 per cent farm work,

CHAPTER 6 *College life*

progressively covering all aspects of the college's operations. Each year it was common to be required to return to college to work on the farm for a week during one of the fortnight holiday breaks in May or September, as well as for a week or more during the six-week summer holidays.

Dookie was quite a regimented facility when I arrived but became less so during the three years I spent there. As may be expected, there was often a difference between what was decreed to happen and what actually did happen regarding various matters, but the regulations themselves and the general approach to student oversight gradually become less constraining over time.

The way in which the college operated was beginning to change when we arrived to commence our time there at the start of 1967, although this wasn't initially apparent. For the first couple of weeks only third-year students and we first-years were present. It was a period of what was known at the time as 'orientation', but in today's more enlightened and genteel world would be classified as 'bastardisation'.

Each third-year student was assigned two first-year students to 'instruct'. In some cases, mainly dependent on the character of the third-year instructor, this was carried out reasonably civilly against a general background of denigration, demands to complete menial tasks and regular verbal abuse towards first-years. In others, real or perceived shortcomings or misdemeanours of first-years were punished by public denigration or shaming. Flushes or royal flushes were threatened and perhaps in some cases administered, as were dunkings in the dairy-effluent pond. Late-night hikes and runs around the college or to the top of nearby Mount Major featured on occasions. Some first-years were smeared with molasses and chaff and required to run around the college grounds. Attempts to intimidate were present or never far from the surface during most interactions.

The final event in this process, proclaimed as being necessary to enable we first-year students to become 'real' Dookie boys, was to be a blood drinking ceremony. On the day of the event a vat of blood was obtained from the butchery and displayed in one of the dormitories as the material to be drunk that evening. Some of those deemed in need of punishment during the day were required to put their arms into the vat and stir its contents. Following a long and vigorous march around the college grounds in the evening, we were all lined up outside a building at the Rural Training Centre, a facility away from the main administration area.

We each had a cup and were moved along as blood was ladled from the vat into the cups, then led into a pitch-black building. It was impossible to see anything at all. When all were inside, lofty sentiments regarding the privileged state we were about to enter by drinking the blood and thus becoming Dookie boys were loudly proclaimed out of the blackness by an unseen third-year. We were ordered, on the count of three, to drink the blood with dire consequences promised for those not doing so.

As the emotions and tension rose and the count dramatically reached three, lights were suddenly turned on and shouts of 'Don't drink' rang out. This was unfortunately too late for some, including a colleague standing next to me. As he held the cup to his lips to take his drink, it was rapidly brushed from his hand by one of the third-years standing nearby, but the sight of blood dribbling from his mouth and across his chin stayed with me for some time. I'm not sure how well he enjoyed the food and drink laid on, and the subsequent camaraderie between us and our third-year instructors, to mark the end of our initiation process.

In the following two years Dookie initiations were significantly tamer, even when we were in the position of being third-years ourselves and may have been expected to exact some vicarious revenge for our experiences a couple of years earlier.

For my first two years at Dookie, meals were served in the large dining room, Swinburne Hall, later converted for use as a library and resource centre. All students were required to attend breakfast at one of the two 'sittings' and to occupy a specific allocated spot at the tables so that the attendance roll could be marked. There was also two lunch and dinner sittings, with all required to be present at the designated time. A roster was in place for lecturers and branch managers to preside at meals and say grace, with many appearing quite ill at ease fulfilling the latter task.

Meals were distributed and plates collected by waiters. The meals were distinguished more by their quantity than quality, but overall there was little to complain about. Speed of eating and then getting on to do whatever else was a priority at the time was a feature, as was the range of terms commonly used for various food items. These were passed on from year to year and many obviously reflected their genesis among a group of adolescent males, which could embarrass visitors, however, these terms became second nature to students and were generally ignored by those presiding over the meals.

In my final year a new kitchen and cafeteria-style dining hall was built and accompanied by a move towards self-service and far greater informality around meals.

On the lawn in front of the administration building, just to the south of Swinburne Hall, was a tree of significance. The original tree had been planted some years previously during a visit to the college by the state's governor, but numerous replacements had subsequently been necessary. The original 'Governor's Tree' and its successors had never been able to survive the depredations wrought over the years by students making it their final point of attention after a night out. It was well watered but over fertilised, and the Horticulture Branch were singularly unsuccessful in selecting a tree suitable for such conditions.

Perhaps it was an impossible task, and an indication of the impact of this unwanted attention arose subsequently. In 1970 a student at the college was killed in a car accident. As a memorial a tree was planted in the location of the ill-fated 'Governor's Tree' and treated with far greater respect by students. Almost 50 years after the event, there is a wonderfully formed and robust eucalypt growing in the location of so many prior failures.

Some staff, particularly those in technical or supporting roles, had been at Dookie for many years. There tended to be a more rapid turnover and slower replacement of lecturing staff, commonly leading to a shortage of lecturers, a circumstance which provoked a student protest during a visit by Minister for Agriculture Gilbert Chandler early in 1969.

As might be expected in a reasonably sized but partially isolated community, a degree of familiarity developed between staff and students, characteristics of most staff were well known and many were most commonly identified by their nicknames. Some of these had obvious origins and others less so; some were endearing and others more pointed.

While more common among staff other than lecturers, the trend started at the top with the principal, Les 'Droppo' Provan,

CHAPTER 6   *College life*

so nicknamed because of a facial scar in the shape of a tear drop. Droppo's passion for roses also saw the rose garden at the top of the driveway in front of the administration building colloquially called the 'Tear Drop' because of its shape.

There was also Droppo's brother Mac 'Buzzie' Provan (the Building Instructor), 'Greaser' Borthwick (assistant in the Building Branch, named for his demeanour with students), Bob 'Piggy' Grey (no prizes for guessing the branch he managed), 'Chookie' Callander (previously Poultry Branch manager, but at the time Farm Branch manager), and 'Spy' Scott (Poultry Branch manager, whose nickname arose from a perceived likeness to characters in the 'Spy versus Spy' cartoon strip of *Mad* magazine).

'Chuckles' McKenzie was the Dairy Branch manager, 'Snow' Amor the Stock Branch manager, 'Ned' Brooke the farm supervisor and 'McBook' Allan the Scottish botany lecturer. Others included 'Tex' Hart (tractor driver), 'Charlie Chaps' Freeman (wool-classing instructor — 'You've been a bit hard on them, have you chaps?' he'd say, if students visually assessed wool samples as being 64s quality rather than his preferred 70s), 'Doc Death' Young (the general administration assistant whose nickname dated from his time providing basic first aid to students, prior to a nurse being appointed to the medical centre), 'Sharse' Ennor (the vertically challenged House Supervisor), 'You Know' Randell (the farm economics lecturer with a habit of using the term 'you know' to overcome a speech impediment) and a number of others. Barry 'Whipper' Croke (short for whippersnapper — a young, confident person), prominent in later years at Dookie and a future principal, arrived in 1969 subsequent to, and perhaps as a result of, the student protest early that year.

Alec 'Chuckles' McKenzie had been at Dookie as Dairy Branch manager since the late 1940s, his nickname probably an affectionate reference to his usual solemnity as well as his habit of standing back and chuckling at students when they made a mistake. He had a range of memorable sayings and traits, not least of which was his love of the Ayrshire breed of dairy cattle which the college ran. He was a taciturn character with a habit of using particular words or phrases such as 'however' or 'in fairness to yourself' in his speech, which led to him being regularly mimicked by students.

If he thought a student's work performance had been below par, he would likely say something such as, 'I don't think you have done as well as you could have today — however.' Anyone reporting this assessment to his fellow students would do so word for word, and others would immediately know who had given it.

In his lectures he spoke affectionately of the genetic worth of particular families of Ayrshire cattle, most notably those of his revered 'Silky' family. He tended to view human traits in animal breeding terms as well. I grew considerably during my first year at the college, and Chuckles enquired late in the year on the physical stature of my parents. Not finding my answer a satisfactory explanation for my growth, he surmised that I 'must be a throwback'.

While the college dairy at that stage was far less modern than many in the industry, the training and attention to detail instilled by Chuckles were of a high standard, and students came to appreciate the integrity and thoroughness of his approach.

Geoff 'Ned' Brooke had also had a long association with the college, again dating back to the 1940s. He had been prominent in implementing major soil and water conservation works on the

CHAPTER 6 *College life*

college farm, with the largest of the resulting dams, colloquially known as 'Lake Brooke', proposed for irrigation. A miscalculation in the water-harvesting capacity of the farm left Lake Brooke with insufficient water to irrigate even the smallest paddocks for much of our time at the college. The large laneway leading from the farmyard to the paddocks on the south of the property was known as the 'Ned Number 1 Highway'. As with a number of others, Ned's wife also worked at the college, in her case as an assistant in the chemistry laboratory, and they suffered the unspeakable tragedy of losing a teenaged son in a shooting accident while he was spotlighting during my time at the college.

Some of the less prominent characters on the college were nonetheless memorable because of their idiosyncrasies. Morrie Wolfe, the college fencer, had a seemingly endless array of shirts, jumpers, vests and coats that he regularly wore. He was also particularly responsive to changes affecting his bodily comfort. While working throughout the day, he would progressively remove or replace items of clothing in response to changes in his level of exertion, wind speed or direction, drizzle or, seemingly, even events as minor as a cloud passing in front of the sun! It became a diversion for students working with him to note the number of wardrobe adjustments Morrie made throughout the day.

Bruno Serek was the college groundsman. College sporting teams were well served by his efforts over the years. He displayed little interest in viewing the outcome of his work during the cricket season, but during the football season he would stand behind the goals at the college end of the ground and yell, "Tis bewdee for college!' in his excited Italian accent whenever the locals scored a goal.

Students were not permitted to have cars at the college until late in 1967. Many did though, and the various spots just off the college property where they were kept were well known to both students and staff. I recall walking around the dairy paddocks one Sunday morning in mid 1967 with Chuckles McKenzie. As we came over a rise and looked into a neighbouring farmer's paddock, we saw about 10 or 12 cars not very well hidden in a small gully. Chuckles remarked drily, 'Hmm, must be a field day here today,' as we kept walking.

I obtained my driver's licence during my second year at Dookie. As I didn't have a car, a fellow student allowed me to use his, and we drove into the nearby Dookie township to visit the local policeman 'Big Jim' Williamson for the test. After a few basic questions on road rules at the police station, Jim asked me to drive down to the main street for the parallel parking test.

There was only one other vehicle in the street at the time, so Jim told me to assume the position of a second vehicle and park behind the lone car. With that task safely completed, he got out of the car and went to post his mail for the day. He then asked me to drive a short distance out of town, perform a handbrake start and execute a three-point turn on a slight rise near the Catholic church, then return to the police station. That was it!

I was pleased to face nothing more arduous than this in gaining my licence, but the experience was one symptom of a road safety system in need of significant improvement. The road toll the following year was of such magnitude that the 'Declare War on 1034' campaign was begun in the *Sun News Pictorial* newspaper based on the number of road fatalities that year. Victoria commenced decades of high-profile public policy changes and education, which have now collectively reduced the road toll to around a quarter of that in 1969, despite a massive increase in vehicles using the roads. There is no doubt that the increased rigour around granting licences, along with many other features, is much more appropriate today.

The size and diversity of the student group had positive effects quite apart from issues relating to the course being studied. Fellow students with similar interests could be found in most cases, and the confined living arrangements assisted in learning to live in close quarters with those of different interests, inclinations or personal approaches. They also assisted to broaden and enrich the life experiences of all students. A significant range of interests, social gregariousness, attention to study and personal involvements co-existed largely harmoniously. I was probably among the quieter students throughout my time at Dookie, but never found this an impediment to participating in and enjoying any activity I wished to become involved in, or to not doing so with those I was not inclined to indulge in.

At the time I didn't perceive any difficulty in the way in which I settled into the college, dealt emotionally with the impact of living away from home for the first time for an extended period, or in how I tackled the work required of me. Looking back at mid-year and end-of-year reports reveals some telling observations, however, particularly regarding my first year. This year apparently started off well academically, but it was observed at mid-year that I 'should display more interest in the livestock branches'. The final report for the year was by far the worst I received, with my academic results diminished and the concern regarding livestock branches having expanded to a need to 'adopt a more energetic approach to his practical work'.

That apparently occurred, as the mid-year assessment for second year revealed me as having 'worked very well' and shown 'a pleasing improvement'. The report at the end of that year described me as 'a steady, reliable and conscientious student', 'a good influence in the College' and 'most capable at practical farm work'. Third year continued the positive trend and I was awarded my diploma in agricultural science at the end of it.

I arrived at Dookie as a naïve 16-year-old, one of the youngest in the intake of that year. Perhaps in keeping with many of that age at the time, I was comfortable that — apart from a few minor loose ends which could be tidied up when time permitted — I had life fairly well sorted out. My experiences there progressively helped me realise, firmly but comparatively painlessly, that this was far from the case. It was one of the more important formative experiences of my life. I learned quite a bit about agriculture over the three years there, but much more about myself and about life generally.

Coming to understand the pleasure and importance of learning in all aspects of life, both professional and personal, was at least as valuable as any technical benefit I gained. Living and interacting closely with a wide range of other students and staff, forming opinions and making personal decisions on an increasing number of issues was necessary.

Reflecting subsequently, I came to understand and appreciate more fully the immense value of my time at Dookie. It came at a time when I was chronologically nearing adulthood and contributed significantly in guiding me towards that stage emotionally as well.

CHAPTER 7

Commencing a career

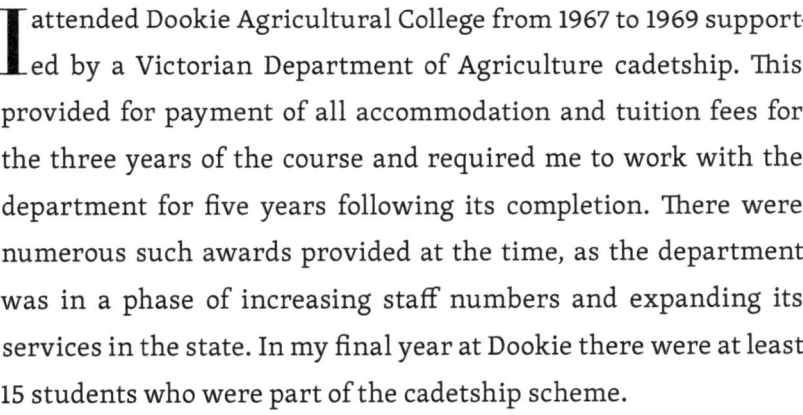

I attended Dookie Agricultural College from 1967 to 1969 supported by a Victorian Department of Agriculture cadetship. This provided for payment of all accommodation and tuition fees for the three years of the course and required me to work with the department for five years following its completion. There were numerous such awards provided at the time, as the department was in a phase of increasing staff numbers and expanding its services in the state. In my final year at Dookie there were at least 15 students who were part of the cadetship scheme.

In a scenario very different to today's job market, towards the end of our final year all cadets were provided with a list of more than 30 possible departmental jobs to express interest in. The range of choices was wide, from regulatory roles in livestock or plant industries, research support, through to advisory roles based in district offices across the state. I was keen to become involved in district advisory rather than research or regulatory work and expressed interest in a job at Bairnsdale, working in the beef industry. I was successful and commenced an involvement with agriculture in regional areas which lasted for the next 30 years, apart from three years studying at Melbourne University.

The state government at the time was placing increased resources into farm advisory or extension services, sometimes supported by Commonwealth government funding. Their aim was to assist the agricultural industry to become more productive and for farmers to implement and benefit from the advances being made possible by agricultural research. They largely justified their expenditure in doing this by reference to the importance of agriculture to the economy and the benefits to the state derived from increased production and efficiency of their agricultural industries. Victoria provides just less than 25 per cent of Australia's value of agricultural production from 3 per cent of the country's land mass, and agriculture is an important domestic and export industry for the state.

Over time the focus and means of providing these services has evolved as agriculture has changed, governments' perspectives on their role in assisting industries have been redefined, and other sectors have seen value in providing some of the services previously provided by governments. It is possible to examine this evolution through the prism of changes that have occurred in the economy, society and agricultural industry over the same period.

Agriculture is commonly a larger component of less-developed economies than it is of more diverse and mature ones. Individuals and populations initially prioritise obtaining the essential products of agriculture, such as food and clothing, above more discretionary items. As wealth and economic maturity develops, the need for these staples continues, but other sought-after yet less essential items progressively become those on which additional wealth is spent. Even though the size and value of the agricultural industry may expand, it commonly becomes a smaller proportion of more mature economies, as the range and importance of other sectors in the economy expand at a comparatively greater rate. This generalisation tends to hold even when exports are a major focus of agricultural production.

As a sector in a developing economy, agriculture also tends to go through a sequence of phases over time, where the primary focus of activity of the industry evolves in response to changes in the social and economic conditions of the society in which it operates and of markets being supplied. As the primary focus moves from one phase to the next, some features of previous phases continue to a greater or lesser extent, resulting in the management demands on producers and industries becoming more complex and sophisticated over time. In practice most phases tend to co-exist in mature industries and may not always arrive for all industries or regions in the usual sequence or at the same time. But the generalisation is useful in looking at what advisory services are provided and how they are delivered.

The first of these phases is 'production', where increasing demand for product by consumers and economic return to producers is met by increasing the area of land used for agriculture. A point is eventually reached where additional land becomes either unavailable or not economic to develop, and the focus evolves to 'productivity', or increasing the level of production from the existing land area. This phase intensifies as eventually the area of land being used for agriculture declines, when competing uses become comparatively more valuable and land transitions to these higher value uses.

As productivity intensity rises, the pressures on the

natural resource base supporting the increasing level of productivity become more apparent and pressing, and hence 'sustainability' increases in importance. Finally, as economies mature and diversify, their sophistication, buying power and range of markets increase, greater levels of product specificity and differentiation are demanded and paid for by consumers, and 'marketing' increasingly becomes a focus for agriculture. The industry in effect transitions from being a producer of commodities to a supplier of products.

When I commenced work in 1970 Victoria was far from an immature economy but, examining agriculture in the state over the years of my working life, each of these general changes is apparent, albeit with regional and industry differences in some cases in their extent and timing.

In 1970 agriculture accounted for more than 10 per cent of the value of Victoria's economy. Since then the value of agricultural production has increased in real terms but the prices farmers have received for their products have consistently risen more slowly than the costs of this production. Farmers have responded to this continuing cost-price squeeze in a range of ways, often influenced by their geographic location and personal circumstances. Farm productivity has risen, but farms have also been consolidated and farmers have left the industry. In many areas competing land uses have become more attractive, for a range of reasons, and land has gradually transferred from agriculture to these alternative uses.

Compared to 1970 there is now approximately 25 per cent less land being used for agriculture and around a third the number of farms. The average area of each farm in Victoria is now over double what it was in 1970. The value of production from each hectare used for agriculture, and from each farm, have both risen significantly as these changes have occurred.

The economy of the state has also diversified and expanded, more rapidly than has agriculture. Despite the increase in its real value of production, agriculture now contributes less than three per cent of the total value of Victoria's significantly larger and more diverse economy. The number of people engaged in it has declined slightly, but the aggregate number in other industries has expanded comparatively more. As a result, the proportion of the workforce engaged in agriculture has declined from around nine per cent in 1970 to less than three per cent now.

All of this has occurred as the focus on natural resource management has increased, perhaps most visibly evidenced by the growth of environmental awareness and accompanying legislation, together with the development of movements such as Landcare. Natural resource management has become institutionalised through national and state approaches to catchment and water management, and most local action and government support is now coordinated through these arrangements.

As this change has occurred, the economic evolution of individual industries has continued and agriculture has responded to changed demands and expectations from society and the broader economy. Scale of operations, levels of mechanisation and labour efficiency have all increased. Markets in water and carbon have been established to join those of other agricultural inputs, and market-based approaches to promoting native vegetation conservation and biodiversity management have been trialled. Issues driven by consumers or community groups on matters such as farm animal welfare, ethics, live animal exports, environmental management, the social licence to farm and genetic modification are increasingly impacting agriculture. The industry operates under national and international challenges which include increasing population and food demand, water scarcity, biosecurity pressures and climate change. As a strongly export-oriented industry, agriculture is impacted by global economic and trade issues to a greater extent than more domestically focused industries.

While the statistics above, regarding agriculture's development over the last 50 years, present a positive overall picture of the ability of an industry to evolve in the face of changing circumstances, they also mask a wide range of smaller changes impacting individuals, families and communities. Some of these have been positive but difficult outcomes of business failure, personal and family trauma and the decline of communities have also occurred.

As with other areas of society, the impact of change in agriculture and rural communities has not been uniform. Individuals and families have varied in the success with which they have managed these changes. Some towns and districts have had more success than others in maintaining their strength as agricultural fortunes have changed, or in diversifying their focus in response to this occurring. On occasions the changes have provided fertile ground for populist politicians and others to either rail against or to claim they can prevent.

Governments have provided advisory, regulatory and research services to the agricultural industry as these changes have occurred. Consequently, the perspectives on what levels and types of support governments should provide, and how, have also changed.

When I began work in the Bairnsdale office in 1970, the district was largely in the 'productivity' phase, but with remnants of the 'production' phase remaining. Although alienation of land from the Crown to freehold had largely ceased and most farms had been cleared of vegetation to the extent they were likely to be, there were still some areas where land clearing and initial sowing of pasture was a focus, most notably in the more remote mountainous areas of the district.

Advisory services to farmers were predominantly provided by the government and focused on individual producers. In many respects it was a form of personal farm advisory service provided and funded by the state government. Few private agricultural consultants operated in Victoria, and none that I recall were based in East Gippsland. Some groups, such as the Gippsland Sheep Breeders' Association, existed and were an effective means of demonstrating and providing management advice. The major growth in group-based advisory services had not yet begun, despite some early forays into that area in the dairy industry.

Department services were structured along discipline and industry lines. While there was a position of District Agricultural Officer in place, with Barrie Bardsley filling that role, this was effectively a coordination role, with all staff formally reporting to a state-wide manager of their discipline, usually based in Melbourne. Gerry Vivian was the district Beef Industry Officer with whom I worked, and Bob Carraill was the Senior Beef Industry Officer for the state, based at Werribee. In subsequent years this role was capably filled first by Peter Bailey and then by Geoff Kroker.

The beef work at Bairnsdale was mainly directed towards the improvement of genetic and management techniques applied to herds (productivity) where individual producers sought assistance. Although I was not at a level in the organisation to be impacted, I perceived there to be a high degree of autonomy given to local managers and senior staff to decide on the focus of programs and how they were run.

While the extent of differentiation in roles and the potential for career advancement between departmental staff with degrees and those with diplomas (such as awarded at Dookie) was decreasing, it was still evident. This didn't impact me during my year at Bairnsdale, but its likely future impact was the basis for my decision early in 1970 to seek to return to study and obtain a degree. It appeared likely to offer more scope for future opportunities, and this subsequently proved to be the case.

A personal issue I faced during my year of working at Bairnsdale was military conscription. This had been introduced by the federal government in 1964 as a consequence of Australia's involvement in the Vietnam War. It was implemented by way of ballots held in the first and second half of each year, in which those males turning 20 years old within the six months of the ballot were eligible to be 'called up'. Birth dates within the six-month period were selected at random, with those born on the balloted dates required to do two years of national military service, known colloquially as 'nasho'.

During my time at Dookie, the biannual ballot and subsequent letters to impacted individuals were a source of great interest. Being a small community, we had a reasonably accurate idea of who was facing the ballot at any time. On the days that notices arrived in the mail, news spread around the college quickly as to who was in and who had missed out. While other tertiary institutions were the focus of considerable public opposition to conscription and the war, I don't recall any great level of this among students at Dookie,

CHAPTER 7   *Commencing a career*

even though we all were or had been faced with the prospect of being directly impacted by it.

While initially it was policy for those conscripted not to be sent to war zones, in 1966 this had changed and, by the time I was old enough to be part of the ballot in the first half of 1970, there was a reasonable chance of conscripts being required to serve in Vietnam. Australia's losses of volunteer and conscripted soldiers continued to grow, even if at a reduced rate to previous years, and domestic opposition to the war continued strongly.

Against this background and also because I was just beginning my working career, I was certainly not keen to be conscripted, but didn't feel strongly enough on the matter to contemplate doing anything other than what the ballot determined.

Early in March 1970 I received notification that I had been called up. After initial disappointment, I began to look at what impact this was going to have. Ostensibly the outcome was that I was required to commence 'nasho' in the second half of the year. However, I had failed what was then known as Matriculation English in my first year at Dookie. A pass in this subject was mandatory if I intended to move on to university studies, so early in 1970 I had enrolled in a night class at Bairnsdale High School to achieve this.

As a result of being enrolled in a course that would be completed before the end of the year, I was able to defer national service until the first half of 1971. I had sought to defer it to beyond the completion of my hoped-for university study, but understandably this request was denied, as at that stage I had no surety that I would be successful in gaining entry to university.

During the year, I played football for Bairnsdale and in an early game injured my knee. I had previously had some difficulty with a similar injury. I wasn't badly inconvenienced but it was a bit painful and appeared as though it may cause me to miss a few games, so I visited a doctor at the local clinic who I had been told by those around the club was 'good with knees'. The prognosis was positive, I was prescribed some anti-inflammatory pills and exercises, and as a result missed only one game of football.

Later in 1970 I attended an army medical examination at the same local clinic. Coincidentally, although I was examined by another, the doctor I had consulted earlier in the year was also conducting army medicals at the same time. Having been required to detail any recent medical treatments, I referenced the one from earlier in the year. The examining doctor asked whom I had visited for that treatment, and when he had finished his examination went and had a chat with him, returned, then advised I was free to go.

A short while later, I received notification from the government that I had failed the medical examination but was provided with no reasons why. The note simply advised that 'The medical professional who examined you has recommended you seek further treatment for the ailment identified' (or words to that effect). I wasn't sure what the ailment was.

On revisiting the examining doctor, I was told the failure was because of the injured knee and the risk that the army would have ongoing liability for medical expenses if I had further problems with it during my time doing 'nasho'. A strongly risk-averse approach had been taken.

I was certainly delighted with this outcome, but felt a little sheepish about it. I had experienced no further knee problems during the year, nor have I since. The outcome was one that I accepted gratefully, but was happy not to discuss too broadly, even though I really had no cause to feel personal embarrassment regarding it.

An interesting postscript to this was a discussion I overheard between my parents shortly after the outcome had been received. While also being relieved, Mum expressed the concern, 'How will I be able to tell people that he's failed?' I imagine it was mainly concern about me as a fit and robust person appearing to avoid responsibility, and the fear that others may infer it resulted from deceit, rather than the legitimate failing of the medical that was behind the comment.

CHAPTER 8

Consolidation

I attended the University of Melbourne from 1971 to 1973 and obtained an honours degree in agricultural science, again on a cadetship provided by the Department of Agriculture. During this period I lived in a boarding house in East St Kilda, run by a family we had known in Orbost, mostly memorable because of the number and range of personalities who passed through it during my time there.

Although the degree course was for four years, those holding a diploma were given credit for the second year, which at the time was held at the university's Mount Derrimut Field Station to the west of the city. I therefore completed the course in three years. Despite the degree course being academically more rigorous and demanding than the Dookie diploma, I found it overall to be less challenging. At the time I put this down to me being older and more mature, as well as being better able to place in context some of the topics being studied, particularly the more applied ones.

All graduate cadets with the Department of Agriculture were required to undertake further on-the-job training following

CHAPTER 8 *Consolidation*

university. This was nominally an 18-month period at a research institute conducting a research project, followed by a similar period in a district office. At the conclusion of this time, a decision was made jointly between the staff member and department on where and in what role an ongoing placement would be made.

In my case it was agreed that I would re-join the Beef Branch, however, I would first be posted to the district office at Warragul, carry out a research project from there, then transfer to Leongatha for my ongoing appointment. Steve Walsh and Stewart Anderson were the Beef Branch members based at Warragul, so I joined them in the programs they had running in the district. Barrie Bardsley, who I had previously worked with at Bairnsdale, was Regional Officer at the time, before leaving early in the year to another role and being replaced by Andrew Volum. Peter Medling commenced as Senior District Officer at the same time as me.

I commenced working at Warragul in January 1974, then shortly afterwards the global oil shock caused a major reduction in the prices of beef cattle, particularly impacting the Japanese beef market. The Japanese were increasingly major importers of meat from heavy bullocks, a market that many producers in West and South Gippsland targeted.

For my research project, I conducted a face-to-face survey of producers to discover how they were responding to the major changes in the market, with the aim of being able to identify what advisory programs may be most beneficial to implement.

During the conduct of this survey in 1975, I also took on a role editing a book on agriculture in East Gippsland. It was being produced as a memorial to Frank Drake, a long-serving and highly regarded Bairnsdale officer who had been killed in a car accident in 1968. A group of farmers from throughout East Gippsland, along with agriculture department staff, had commenced the task, but it had floundered for want of someone being available to concentrate on completing it. Given my background in East Gippsland and current training program, it was determined I should take the task on.

I found this to be a very enjoyable and fulfilling role and was pleased in early 1976 when *Land to Pasture — Environment, Land Use and Primary Production in East Gippsland* was launched by a former colleague of Frank Drake, Professor Lionel Stubbs, at a Gippsland Sheep Breeders' Association dinner.

During my time at Warragul the focus on 'production' was effectively a thing of the past. Programs supporting 'productivity' and 'marketing' were conducted, with attention to increasing herd performance through genetic improvement, increasing the efficiency of pasture utilisation, and producing cattle to meet defined carcass and market specifications. Using demonstrations and discussion groups, rather than advice to individual producers, which by that stage was well established in the dairy industry, became increasingly common.

Of all the staff at the Warragul office, perhaps the typist/receptionist Miss Lewis was the most notorious. She did have a first name — Flossie, presumably a derivative of Florence — but first names had no currency in the office world of Miss Lewis. She was to be addressed as 'Miss' and all male staff, however junior, were addressed by her as 'Mister'.

When I worked at Warragul, Miss Lewis was, I guessed, in her forties and had been in her position at the office for many years. She lived with her parents and I was told by someone else in the

CHAPTER 8 *Consolidation*

town that her father was 'a difficult man'. She appeared to have few interests outside of work and seldom, if ever, indulged in small talk. Personal interactions with her were marked by her diffidence. I don't recall having any conversation with her in the office other than those concerning work or related to a polite greeting, and I was not alone in that experience.

It was a rare occurrence for anyone to elicit a smile or casual comment from her. She had a club foot and walked with a decided limp, which was in evidence when she patrolled the corridor of the office or walked the block or so into town to buy an ice-cream cone, which was her regular lunchtime practice.

It was said that she did things 'by the book' which, if true, meant that the book she relied on was a very early edition of a much updated one. She didn't necessarily see it as her role to be helpful, if doing so meant a deviation from her current practice or in a direction she believed should not be taken. Staff got used to adjusting their expectations regarding the likely outcome of any discussion seeking changes or improvements to office practice or protocol.

The quality of her work, as the only typist in the office when I commenced there, was cause for ongoing angst and frustration. Staff would receive their work back in duplicate or triplicate, from the mechanical typewriter and carbon paper she used at the time, almost invariably with spelling mistakes, smudges or liquid paper corrections spread liberally through it.

However, life's lessons can come from unexpected sources. Miss Lewis was a regular attender at the Warragul Presbyterian Church. One Sunday the minister Rev Malcolm Williams asked some congregational members to speak during a service regarding their faith. Miss Lewis was one of them and she spoke clearly, confidently and with obvious conviction. Given my experiences from the office, I was both surprised and delighted with her contribution.

A few days later, I met her in the street as she was returning from her lunchtime trek into town for an ice cream. Almost apologetically, she indicated she would like to speak briefly with me (if she could). She made it clear I should only answer her question if I felt comfortable doing so, but she was wondering (if I didn't mind), could I let her know my reaction to her words at church the previous Sunday. I was pleased to respond openly and honestly, saying that I had enjoyed them and found them both interesting and useful.

I have never seen a person's demeanour and facial expression change so positively in response to a comment. Miss Lewis almost blushed with delight and her face lit up with a smile I had previously not known she possessed. She thanked me, I suspect almost embarrassed by her reaction, then continued on her way back to the office. It was the most potent example I have had of the capacity of a positive comment to impact another person.

Both Miss Lewis and I benefitted from that interaction.

As was common in country agriculture department offices, staff regularly wrote articles on topical issues for the local papers. At Warragul there was a roster for this task with each staff member required to produce an article at least every month or two, and more frequently if desired. In addition to this, Dave McQueen, the long-serving District Veterinary Officer, was in the habit of producing an article each fortnight.

Dave was a very ordered, precise and particular officer, highly regarded for his wide knowledge of veterinary matters as well as the thoroughness, precision and diligence of his approach. Perhaps these personal characteristics had been offended too often by the typographical deficiencies of Miss Lewis, but for whatever reason Dave used to write his articles in longhand, using an impeccable cursive script. Although the topic changed each fortnight, the way in which the article was produced hardly varied.

Dave's articles invariably began with a capital letter, suitably indented, on the top left of the first line of a sheet of foolscap paper and concluded with a full stop on the extreme right of the final line of a second sheet. It was rare for there to be a word added or crossed out throughout the text. Those of his colleagues familiar with his approach vouched that he wrote only one version of each article. It demonstrated the level of discipline, skill and attention Dave brought to his role.

Two further recollections I have of my time at Warragul involve Lardner Park, a property south-west of Warragul, and Prime Minister Gough Whitlam. Late in 1973 the Whitlam government had reduced tariffs on farm equipment imports and scrapped the superphosphate bounty. The former was designed to lower costs of purchasing imported agricultural equipment and the latter removed a direct subsidy paid to farmers on the fertiliser they used, which the government believed was no longer justified.

The main event at Lardner Park was an annual, multi-day activity called Gippsland Field Days (now Farm World), featuring machinery and other agricultural exhibits. The Department of Agriculture always had a display at the Field Days, and in February 1974 we were looking forward to a visit from the prime minister, who was to open them that year. It was not the natural environment for a Labor leader, particularly so soon after the removal of an item as much prized by farmers as the super bounty, and a lively exchange with the crowd was expected.

When Gough rose to speak, a crowd estimated at 8,000 gave him a noisy reception, regularly interrupting his address with jeers and booing. He appeared to revel in the encounter. He pointed out that it was a Labor government that had originally introduced the super bounty (jeers) and quoted a statement supporting its removal in times of rising rural returns which, unbeknown to virtually all present, had been made some years previously by the current leader of the Country Party (boos).

As the volume of the heckling and jeering increased, Gough drew himself up to his full, imposing height and urged the crowd to show some respect. It was acceptable for them to heckle him, he said — he expected it and was there to defend himself — but, 'I will not have you booing the Country Party in Drouin or Lardner.' He reiterated the benefit to farmers of his government's reduction in farm equipment tariffs, informing them, 'You've never had it so good,' (more boos), then opened the Field Days. The events at Lardner got wide coverage in the national news that day.

In November the following year, Steve Walsh, Stewart Anderson and I were making silage at Lardner Park, preparing for a feeding trial with steers. We stopped for lunch in a paddock early in the afternoon, turned on the radio in the ute and learned that the Governor-General had dismissed Gough Whitlam as prime minister.

CHAPTER 9

A consequential time

I moved to Leongatha late in 1976 and commenced my role as the first Department of Agriculture beef officer located in the district. Leongatha was a smaller office than Warragul and more informal. Dougal Gilmour was Senior District Officer when I commenced there and over subsequent years Matt Boland, Graham Savage, Neil McBeath (briefly) and Kevin Love filled this role, which morphed into that of District Manager over time. Historically, a large part of the advisory services to the area had been provided by staff based at Warragul or Melbourne but, in the years immediately prior to and after my arrival, greater efforts were made to build up local staff numbers.

I spent 13 years working with the Department of Agriculture at Leongatha. The district covered the area south of the Strzelecki Ranges from Yarram in the east to Phillip Island in the west. While predominantly focused on beef industry issues, I also became involved in advisory and field research projects related to sheep, pastures and economics in the district, as well as beef industry projects elsewhere in the state.

Productivity and marketing programs remained the focus, and increasingly industry groups such as the Gippsland Hereford Group and Australian Farm Management Society, or beef management courses run by McMillan Rural Studies Centre, became the vehicles through which they were provided. Collaboration occurred throughout that time with agricultural show societies at Leongatha, Korumburra, Lang Lang, Glengarry and Yarram in running beef or lamb carcass competitions, to increase producer awareness of market requirements for their livestock.

As the role required significant contact with producers and others, I developed strong connections with a number throughout the district. During my time in Leongatha, producers such as Don and Dorothy Fairbrother from Mirboo, Bruce and Di McMicking, John Box, Graeme Box, Lloyd Dixon and Andrew Dowling from Tarwin Lower, Don Cameron from Ventnor, Jim Lane from Walkerville and many others were very cooperative in hosting trials or management demonstrations. These projects complemented the individual and group advisory programs being run.

Having moved into short-term accommodation when I first transferred to Leongatha, I was soon looking for a more permanent arrangement. Late in 1976 I caught up with Howard Stevens, a teacher at the local High School whom I had met during my time at university. He was also seeking accommodation and we decided to share a small house at Leongatha South. It was a decision which had a major impact on my life.

During 1977 Howard began going out with Lucy Bartlett from Melbourne. On an occasion later in the year, when she visited one weekend, Lucy was accompanied by her younger sister, Tricia. It was a mutually uninspiring experience for Tricia and I, and there

CHAPTER 9   *A consequential time*

was certainly no spark of attraction at the time. Nor was there when we were attendants at the wedding of Howard and Lucy late in 1978.

This changed late the following year when Tricia and I began going out with each other for a few months, before she decided it wasn't working for her — a decision which hit me hard.

Tricia worked as a nurse in Papua New Guinea during 1981 and 1982 and we corresponded in the latter year. On her return early in 1983, we tentatively recommenced our relationship, became engaged later in the year and married early the following year.

It was the best decision I have ever made. The emotional and spiritual fulfilment resulting from marriage to Tricia and from the growth and development of our family have been the most enriching experiences of my life.

Wedding, March 1984
L to R: Alf and Margaret King, Chris and Tricia McRae, Jack and Nancy Bartlett

The path from original meeting to marriage was not entirely straightforward, however, and there is one aspect of it which I reflect on without any pride. Living and working in Leongatha, I returned to Bairnsdale to catch up with Mum and Alf irregularly, probably only two or three times each year. With Tricia living in Melbourne, and both of us quietly sorting out what the future of our relationship was after the earlier false start, I hadn't even informed them that we were going out. The first they heard of it was when I rang them to advise that Tricia and I were engaged. Naturally, it caught Mum very much by surprise. In any circumstance, but particularly given the closeness of my relationship with my parents and the support I had always received from them, it was an appallingly insensitive action on my part.

Early in 1977 I went through one of the more challenging experiences of my life. At the time all was going along positively. I had been in Leongatha for a little over six months, had settled in well and had commenced to develop a good range of local friendships and professional connections. I was enjoying life and work in the town, had been part of the team when Nerrena won its first A-Grade cricket premiership, and the football season was about to begin — with reason to expect it would be a positive one for Leongatha. Life was good.

Following the cricket club presentation evening at Nerrena Hall east of Leongatha one Friday early in April, I was returning home to Leongatha South just after 1 a.m. when I was involved in an accident, which resulted in the death of a pedestrian, a young man from the Latrobe valley. He had been hitchhiking from Morwell to Inverloch, a distance of around 85 kilometres, to go surfing. Having left Morwell around 10 p.m., he had apparently received

CHAPTER 9 *A consequential time*

a ride for the 60 kilometres to Leongatha but had been unable to obtain a lift from there to Inverloch, so had walked for a couple of hours from Leongatha towards Inverloch.

The incident occurred on the crest of a slight rise around nine kilometres south of Leongatha. It was a clear, moonlit evening with only occasional wisps of light fog hanging over the flat farmland. Having not seen any traffic on the road travelling in either direction to that point, I reached the crest marginally before a couple of vehicles travelling towards Leongatha. At the same instant I saw what appeared to be a large sack on the road directly in front of me. I passed over this and, feeling a couple of solid thumps in doing so, reversed to check what it was and to remove it from the road. I was dismayed to find it was a young man, dressed in jeans and a dark duffle coat, who had been lying on the road.

Circumstances unfolded and my emotions swirled around, although the ambulance and police officers involved were nothing but efficient and professional in their handling of the situation. Particularly over the following few days, I struggled to reconcile a plethora of emotions — absolute horror at the outcome of the event, inability to discern anything I could have done differently at the time, and an overwhelming desire or wish that I could do something to lessen the trauma of it for the family and friends of the young man, unknown to me, and for myself.

I provided a statement to the Leongatha police. I attended the funeral at Traralgon because I felt a strong need to do so, despite not knowing anything of the young man nor his family. I left the funeral being grateful that I had attended but still emotionally traumatised, even if this was not outwardly obvious. I did not speak with any of the mourners present nor attempt to interact with his family. I don't know what I would have said had I done so, nor whether it would have been received positively. I felt the need to do something but was completely unable to determine what that should be.

I initially found it difficult to work my way through my emotions following the event or, having recently arrived in the district, to find people locally with whom I was comfortable discussing it. Of the few I confided in, some provided helpful guidance or at least a listening ear, while others, including Christian friends, dispensed formulaic prescriptions which I did not find particularly beneficial. Speaking with Mum was useful, but I eventually found the most effective approach for me was to gradually think and work through the trauma and impact personally.

While I was struggling to deal with the impact of the event, obviously my pain would have been minor and short term compared to that of the young man's family. Understanding this amplified my grief. It also highlighted for me the apparent randomness of life and the fact that we can't specifically prepare to deal with such personal challenges, rather that our entire life perspective and experiences are our preparation for doing so.

I found I couldn't follow the well-meaning advice of some and attempt to discover a 'message from God' in this experience, which they assured me I would do if I sought it fervently enough. If anything, it served to support my growing view that personal understanding is more commonly derived when one's experiences and mental and spiritual perspectives are aligned, and that faith needs to encompass a perspective of life as a whole — spiritual, mental and physical — rather than of attempting to divine

CHAPTER 9 A consequential time

specific meaning from individual 'interventions' in our experiences. Progressively over the following months, I was able to move to a level of acceptance and greater comfort on this matter.

A Coroner's Inquest was held and concluded with a hearing at the Leongatha Court House in October of that year. The local JP handling the inquest found that the young man had been lying on the road prior to being struck. The finding was accidental death. The policeman who handled the case wrote in his deposition: 'From my enquiries, I can place no blame whatsoever on McRae.'

I was certainly heartened by this official finding. It coincided with the position I had eventually been able to reach myself over the preceding months, but obviously could do nothing to redress the impacts. Had it differed from this, I believe I would still have been comfortable with the position I had reached — such had been the mental, spiritual and emotional process I had worked through in arriving at it.

I again had the opportunity to speak with members of the young man's family present at the hearing but did not do so. I am still not sure if that was the correct decision on my part, but at the time my uncertainty remained on how best to initiate such contact and their possible reaction.

I reflected on the event and Coroner's findings subsequently. Without any possibility of obtaining more information, understanding why the young man had been lying on the road at the time of the accident was particularly puzzling. The Coroner effectively opted for fatigue as the reason. He proposed that the young man had left his home many kilometres away on a Friday evening following a week's work, been forced to walk late into the night, and had eventually despaired of being able to obtain a lift to his destination. He had stopped for a rest by the side of the road, inadvertently fallen asleep and toppled onto the road.

I had no cause to doubt this proposition, and in the circumstances it is one which could reasonably be proposed. I was also interested in a news report at around the same time from police elsewhere in South Gippsland and wondered if it may have been relevant to my experience. They warned against a growing practice of hitchhikers lying on the road in their attempts to force drivers to stop for them.

A fictitious character became one of the more notorious farmers in the district among Leongatha staff in the early 1980s. Australia Post had a 'To the Farmer' distribution list, which allowed groups such as rural merchandise sellers, stock agents and machinery dealers to distribute material by mail directly to those on the list. The geographic extent of the distribution could be specified, and on occasions we used this approach ourselves as a quick and effective means of getting information on such things as field days around to all farmers in the district.

A number of McRaes were farmers in South Gippsland at the time, and maybe that caused some confusion in the list as, for whatever reason, I was erroneously on it. I didn't alert the post office to this because the service didn't distribute any personal material, and I occasionally found some information that was circulated to be useful in my role working with farmers.

Early in 1981 staff decided that we would put together a brochure to promote the role of the department in the area, to outline the programs we had running, and to seek ideas for others which producers believed would be useful. The brochure

CHAPTER 9 *A consequential time*

encouraged farmers to get in contact on any matters they may wish to raise. We decided to distribute this via the 'To the Farmer' mailing list.

I received a copy in my mailbox and my mind ran through what sort of reactions others who received it may have had. No doubt these would range from keenness through to total non-interest. I could even imagine a response of disgust or anger that a group 'as useless as a government department' should be sending out what could be perceived to be advertising material. I decided to pursue these latter thoughts and drafted a letter purporting to be from such a farmer, who took a very superior tone in his correspondence.

The letter made fulsome use of the derogatory opinions of us that we had heard over the years — 'ridiculous regulations', 'impractical advice', 'no use to farmers', 'overly zealous stock inspectors and dairy supervisors' and the like. It railed against the growing trend of 'commercial organisations filling our mailboxes with unsolicited trivia', and viewed very dimly the apparent move of government departments 'who at the best of times have only a tenuous hold on the tolerance of those they supposedly serve' into this practice. It finished by advising that the offending material was being returned because 'I would rather it is disposed of in your rubbish bin than mine.' The letter was from 'A C Ralston', with an address in the Strzelecki Ranges between Foster and Mirboo.

At that time all typing and incoming phone calls to the office were managed by a single typist/receptionist, Lyn Nash. We had just upgraded from a mechanical to an electronic typewriter, so I arranged with Lyn to resurrect the old typewriter and type up the letter, complete with a few deliberate spelling mistakes and other typing errors. The only other person in the office I alerted to the scam was Ken Laurie, a long-term dairy supervisor, who I thought may be handy later in furthering the subterfuge.

The letter was posted in Mirboo North and sent to Graham Savage, as requested in the brochure. Graham was a quiet, conscientious and effective district manager. He got on well with staff and was well regarded by the farming community in the district. It was a bit harsh for the letter to be sent to him, and he certainly reacted significantly when he received it. I had an office next to his and heard him exclaim loudly after he opened it, before he came in to show it to me. I think he was deciding whether to laugh or to begin to be concerned about its tenor.

I found it extremely difficult to keep a straight face, so diverted the discussion. I said I hadn't heard of the person in question, but that it appeared that he could be a dairy farmer. I suggested that Ken Laurie, having been in the district for many years, might know of him.

Ken took a while to respond. 'Ralston? Ralston?' he pondered. 'Oh, I remember. There's a nutter up in the hills behind Foster by that name. If it's the same bloke, we had him in court a few years ago — he reckoned he had a constitutional right to sell unpasteurised cream. What's he done now?'

This served to both confirm the *bona fides* of the letter-writer and suggest that his letter didn't need to cause as much stress as initially feared, which Graham appeared pleased about.

For the next few weeks the letter became quite a talking point among staff in the district and beyond, and opinions varied on how it should be handled. Some believed that material such as that should go straight into the bin — it was probably a 'rush of blood' letter and in the unlikely event that the writer followed up they

CHAPTER 9 *A consequential time*

could be responded to then. Others felt that all letters should be answered, even if only by a formal acknowledgement of receipt. I wasn't sure how best to bring the scam to a conclusion.

On the evening of 31 March (April Fools' Day the next day), I visited Geoff Cashin, a dairy farmer just south of Leongatha. Geoff was a good friend of Graham's, well known to others in the department and an inveterate practical joker. I gave him a copy of the letter and suggested that the next morning he become 'Arch Ralston' and ring Graham. With the mechanical switchboard in the office, I would arrange for Lyn to switch the call both to Graham and to me, and I would tape it. Geoff could then come to the office for a cup of coffee mid-morning (at that stage all staff who were in the office gathered for morning tea around 10 am) and the tape could be played.

All went to plan, and next morning 'Arch' and Graham had quite a vigorous discussion. Graham handled himself pretty coolly under significant verbal attack, although it was obvious he was feeling the pressure. Arch brought out a range of clichés and stereotypes that befitted a person who felt generally put upon by the world and disgruntled about not having had his letter responded to. They finally agreed to arrange a face-to-face meeting in the near future with Arch advising, 'I tell you what, you'd better be ready, because I'm as savage as a meat axe!' Graham came off the phone quite drained.

Geoff arrived just as all the staff who were in the office, probably around 10 or 12, were gathering for morning tea. With everyone sitting around the table, I provided the surprising news that Graham had received a phone call from the letter-writer Arch Ralston, then played the tape. Most quickly realised that Arch was actually Geoff, but Graham — probably still traumatised by the phone call and obviously bemused as to how a tape of the conversation could have been obtained — remained uncomprehending throughout its playing.

During discussion following the playing of the tape, among much hilarity, Geoff mentioned how he had been forced to respond in certain ways to the things Graham had said and the penny finally dropped for Graham. He was sitting across the table from Geoff, but then virtually levitated from his chair, pointed an accusatory finger at him and shouted, 'It was you, you bastard!' No doubt he was also mightily relieved.

From that time on, Arch Ralston was regularly referred to by staff from the office, and I think Graham eventually came to not hold his 'existence' against me too much.

This period also marked a significant change in the organisational arrangements of the church I attended. In 1977 the Presbyterian, Methodist and Congregational Churches in Australia amalgamated to form the Uniting Church. In Leongatha's case this resulted in a parish that covered a large portion of South Gippsland and numerous congregations, many quite small. Both ministers in Leongatha at the time — Revs Trevor Williams (ex-Presbyterian) and Roy Bowen (ex-Methodist) — initially continued in place.

I remained heavily involved in church activities following the new arrangements, and around 1980 I was encouraged to begin leading some church services. There was a regular demand for lay people to do so, given the number of locations in the parish at which weekly or fortnightly services were conducted. Quite a few others were similarly involved, some having been so for many years.

Over my remaining time at Leongatha, I was involved regularly in leading church services, not only at Leongatha but also

CHAPTER 9 *A consequential time*

at locations such as Boolarra, Mirboo North, Meeniyan, Dollar, Mardan and Tarwin Lower. I enjoyed the times visiting these places and leading services, and the locals were always welcoming and grateful. I understood, though, that this acceptance, while genuine and appreciated, went only so far. For many the presence of 'the ordained man' was vitally important, and rosters for services needed to take this into account and ensure all locations received that benefit as frequently as feasible.

The departmental programs I was involved in during my time at Leongatha reflected developments occurring in the wider beef industry as well as the policies of the government on the services they provided. Most were aimed at improving efficiency of beef production, assisting producers to understand and better meet the demands of markets, and helping them in their constant requirement to improve productivity. Many producers did this independently of any direct contact with the Department of Agriculture, but my role of working with them to demonstrate management approaches, facilitating exchange of information between them and promoting industry developments assisted in encouraging and accelerating change.

Agriculture was expanding the use of objective measurement and more precise information in both the production and marketing of its products, and the impact of this became increasingly apparent in the beef industry. At the time the information flow between producers and final markets was much weaker and less transparent than it is now, but a gradual move away from prioritising aesthetic preferences or prejudices, clearer definition of market demands and greater emphasis on using objective information in both production and marketing, was occurring. These initial changes have been made to appear small by the extent, scale and sophistication of subsequent developments, but at the time their departure from prior practices was significant.

The trend was evidenced by events such as the commencement in 1972 of a National Beef Recording Scheme to encourage greater use of objective measurement in the genetic improvement of beef herds, an increase in the number of saleyards providing live-weight information on cattle being auctioned from 1975 onwards, introduction of a Livestock Market Reporting Service providing objective information on stock sold in 1977, and increasingly specific information being provided by abattoirs on the specifications of stock they required for various markets.

These industry initiatives inevitably resulted in a growing understanding of the links between on-farm practices and the evolving demands of beef markets; while producers were at one end of this chain, their success increasingly depended on them focussing not only on the efficient production of livestock on their properties but also on developments well beyond them.

This connection between farms and markets was starkly highlighted in mid 1987 when residues of organochlorine insecticides such as DDT and dieldrin were detected in Australian beef exported to the USA and Japan, two of Australia's major beef markets. The relevant shipments were rejected and the markets closed immediately. Testing and on-farm management programs were put in place across Australia, advisory and regulatory activities were implemented and a monitoring and assurance program commenced to ensure animals with residues were removed from the supply chain.

Organochlorines had not been registered for agricultural use

CHAPTER 9   *A consequential time*

in Victoria for many years prior to this event. They were effective insecticides, but their persistence and capacity to concentrate in food chains had serious residual side-effects which had led to them being de-registered. Their registered replacements though, such as synthetic pyrethroids, were viewed by some farmers as inferior alternatives. These producers had resented the loss of organochlorines as registered products. Some had kept drums of unregistered product for years and continued to use it, until the events of 1987 forced a change of practice.

Dieldrin had been used to control insect pests in potato crops, and management of its residues in beef cattle grazing pastures following such crops was the most common and highest profile impact of this crisis in Victoria. In South Gippsland beef herds though, DDT residues were the main focus.

Some producers in the district were still using DDT to control pasture pests and consequently faced residue issues in their stock. In developing management plans to respond, they commonly sought to do so as confidentially as possible, given that their problems arose from a non-registered use of the insecticide. Among a number with whom I worked at the time, I recall receiving a phone call at home one Saturday morning from a prominent Australian businessman. He owned a property in the area and was seeking advice both on how to manage the issue on his property and how to minimise the chances of his circumstances becoming public knowledge.

Responding to the residue issue was a challenging and costly experience for all sectors of the beef industry and one which impacted Australia's reputation as a reliable supplier of high-quality agricultural products. Controls on land use remain in place even today in some areas. One enduring consequence of the experience, though, was the introduction or expansion of testing, quality control and certification protocols for agricultural products, from farms to markets, that now provide greatly increased confidence in their quality and integrity.

During my time at Leongatha, changes gradually occurred in how the department's services were provided, what they were and how they were managed. Some of these changes were driven by government policy and others by developing commercial realities.

Projects focussed on productivity and marketing continued, but the means of providing them gradually evolved. Use of groups rather than individual consultations became more important over time, providing the benefit both of a forum for provision of information but more importantly the discussion and refinement of ideas between farmer participants. Some of these were *ad hoc* groups formed for specific short-term purposes, but others such as the Australian Farm Management Society (AFMS), Beef Improvement Association and Gippsland Hereford Group were more enduring, all with a presence beyond the Leongatha district.

One consequence of this connection to industry groups was that I convened the annual AFMS conference held in Leongatha early in 1988. The Society had branches in all states with a number active in Victoria, and Gippsland's branch was centred on Leongatha. It focussed on economic, social and managerial issues rather than technical matters specific to individual industries, and thus brought together participants from across agriculture and beyond. The numbers attending the national conference were greater than the town was used to handling for such events, and certainly put pressure on its conference and accommodation facilities. These and other challenges were overcome though, the conference topics were well received by participants and the event was finally very successful.

Gippsland's agricultural college, McMillan Rural Studies Centre (MRSC), was also an important collaborator. MRSC had commenced operating in 1977. It was a decentralised campus with a head office in Warragul and additional offices at Bairnsdale, Sale and Leongatha. Originally, McMillan staff were co-located at Department of Agriculture offices, prior to purpose-built facilities being provided in all four towns. In the following years I regularly collaborated with local McMillan staff in running short courses, training exercises and longer beef-management courses in what proved to be a very successful model for providing farmer training and education.

In 1986 management responsibility for district programs was transferred from head office to regions, the first time such an arrangement had been in place since the department was formed in 1872. The change was aimed at improving integration of services in rural areas, and Robin (Ras) Lawson became Regional Manager in Gippsland.

The impact of government policy on district programs became more apparent; there began to be greater expectation that programs focused on government priorities would be implemented and coordination of these programs across districts increased. Emphasis on group advisory activities expanded and some individual services such as soil tests, previously provided free of charge, began to be charged for.

Programs to broaden the range of services provided were commenced, as were those to increase the role of women both within the department and as targets of these services. This was most noticeable in the introduction of the Office of Rural Affairs (including some amused comments regarding the name) in 1985. At the same time government and hence departmental financial constraints became more regular and their impacts, including 'staff freezes' and reductions in the numbers of technically-focussed district staff, became more obvious.

Progressively more commercial businesses such as rural merchandise suppliers and milk factories began to employ technical advisory staff and more private agricultural advisors began operating in the district. On occasions there was a degree of co-operation between the commercial and departmental advisors, but most frequently they operated independent of each other. The trend away from the department being the predominant provider of agricultural advisory services to individual farmers in Victoria was clear.

Following marriage, Tricia and I had initially lived in the town, prior to moving in late 1985 to a small property at Fairbank, a few kilometres north of Leongatha. As a hobby we had begun a routine of rearing a few beef-dairy cross calves each year, growing them out and selling them the following year. Our older two children, Ewen and Hannah, were born at the Leongatha hospital where Tricia worked as a nurse, after initially doing so at Wonthaggi.

As time went on, the issue of our plans for the future arose. It was not something which we actively pursued but for me, as changes occurred in departmental arrangements and I became more experienced in my role, I inevitably began to consider this issue. Tricia was comfortable in her role at the Leongatha hospital and had been able to return to it following the birth of both Ewen and Hannah. It was also likely that she would be able to obtain similar work if we moved to another location. At the time though, because we were very settled and happy in Leongatha, our strong

CHAPTER 9 *A consequential time*

preference was to remain there and for me to aim to eventually move into managing the department's office in the town.

Late in 1988 some changes were made in management arrangements for the department in Gippsland, and the opportunity of this preferred outcome being possible in the short-term future was closed off. At the time I was disappointed but, reflecting on this subsequently, it was probably one of the best things to happen in my professional and personal life. It required Tricia and I to actively consider how we saw our future. It was quite possible to continue where we were in a way that was satisfactory, comfortable and enjoyable. Or we could decide to proactively seek a change and be prepared to embrace what this brought. We chose the latter, although we were unsure when a suitable opportunity may arise or where it might be. When it came the following year, even though the first step was a comparatively small one, it did help us to see the opportunities that can flow from such a decision.

INTERLUDES

INTERLUDE A
Some poems

Don was a regular writer of poems. Many were retained and snippets from some were occasionally referred to or quoted by family members when specific events were being remembered. In later years, he occasionally forwarded poems to the 'Letters to the Editor' section of the *Bairnsdale Advertiser,* where they were published. A report in that paper of a concert held as part of 'Back to Buchan' celebrations in 1972 referred to a couple of his poems being recited at the event and of him as being 'remembered with affection for his wit'. A selection of his poems is included here, with brief explanations when necessary to understand their context.

The trapper's lament

By the peaceful Lang Lang River in a garden kept with care,
Where the fragrant scent of roses in sweet springtime fills the air;
And the rippling, murmuring water in the sighing of the trees
Lends enchantment to the music of the humming of the bees,

Dwells a man of reputation; but there's not the slightest doubt,
He's a source of great annoyance to the residents about.
He's an honorary inspector in the Game and Fisheries cause,
And will show no kindly feelings to the breakers of their laws.

All the people in the district, and the camping tourists too,
When those laws they may encroach on are abruptly brought to view
In the light of court proceedings, why those laws they have defied,
And if they pleaded ignorance, our friend would say they lied.

He would tell of how he caught them, "They were easier caught than fish,"
And of how they did abuse him, why they'd throw him in the ditch.
And of how he had informed them that 'twas not his place to fight,
But of course he's not afraid to, still you see it isn't right
That an honorary inspector in the Game and Fisheries cause,
Should stoop so low as fighting with the breakers of their laws.

Says, "We'll fight it through the P'lice Court, that's the safest way for me,
For I have a heap of influence with the PM don't you see;
And it surely is much wiser than to knock a chap about,
Just to take it to the Magistrate and let him thrash it out."

INTERLUDE A   *Some poems*

Well maybe you're not agreeing, but you cannot overlook
That should you chance to knock him you'll be surely brought to book.
So in place of satisfaction got by messing up his face,
You must swallow ill intentions, let sane judgment take their place.

When the autumn days have vanished and cold winter comes along,
He is always bright and happy and you'll always hear his song.
For 'tis in the months of winter there is added to his store,
Wealth obtained from trapping rabbits, for he traps them in galore.

And the farmers, they feel happy and their minds are set at rest
In regard to legal action to eradicate the pest.
And they say we need not worry for there's not the slightest doubt,
That now he's started trapping he will thin the beggars out.

Nature has no doubt endowed him with an enviable gift,
And when he goes a-trapping then you need to make a shift.
For you haven't any prospects, you would never get a catch,
Even though you trapped a lifetime you would never be his match.
He can always catch the rabbits where the other trappers fail,
And reigns King of Rabbit Trappers in this quiet little vale.

But the last time that I saw him he was looking worn and old.
When I asked about his trouble, he to me this story told.
I'll endeavour to relate it, every detail to impart,
And if you've any feeling then I'm sure 'twill break your heart.

It's a somewhat lengthy story and my memory's not too clear,
Still I'm sure that when you've heard it you'll be forced to shed a tear.
It's about a low down Scotsman who deliberately planned
With another stingy Scotsman to trap rabbits on his land.

"Now," said he, "this land I mention I had trapped for 20 years,
And the owner was a digger and I hadn't any fears
That he'd ever let some other darned impostor trap his place.
Still he gave it to a member of that hateful Scottish race.

"There were rabbits on those hillsides, you could count them by the score,
And I counted on the silver they would add unto my store.
On their numbers I would ponder and I'd dream of them by night,
And in daylight I would wander forth and watch them with delight.

"And I watched them grow and fatten." Here his voice began to break,
And his lips began to quiver and his legs they seemed to shake;
But he rallied in a moment while across his face he drew
The lining of his coat sleeve, then continued on anew.

"Yes, those rabbits thrived and fattened, they were raised on English grass,
And I warrant in the market they'd be recognised first class.
All the buyers in the city, how delighted they would be
On receiving each consignment that was forwarded by me.

"But I reckoned without foresight for that mean brute Don McRae
Put his traps into the paddock and he's trapped them all away.
And the only thing remaining, which I truly do abhor,
Is their odour as it's wafted on the breezes to my door."
—*Don McRae*

INTERLUDE A   *Some poems*

The Langview Social Club

Written regarding the commencement of a social club at the Langview Primary School near Heath Hill, sometime during the 1930s. It appears he may have, deliberately or otherwise, misunderstood the meaning of criticism.

Let us bid farewell to dullness, oh, we'll never more feel blue,
On the dreary winter evenings sitting wondering what to do.
For last week they held a meeting in the schoolhouse in the scrub,
And for local entertainments formed the Langview Social Club.

A president's appointed to keep on all a check;
There's a very keen committee and an energetic sec.
And the member's fee's a shilling, if you fail to pay your sub,
You will cease to be a member of the Langview Social Club.

Different forms of entertainment shall be held on different dates,
There will be some social evenings and also be debates.
And some readings from the classics which of learning form the hub
Shall be criticised adversely by the Langview Social Club.

They will criticise Bill Shakespeare and that fellow Walter Scott,
And poor old Charlie Dickens, yes, they'll criticise the lot.
All the works of famous authors who from writing earned their grub,
Shall be badly mutilated by the Langview Social Club.

If you're distant from the city, far removed from all the fun,
With nought for recreation when all your toil is done.
When you're wishing you were closer to a theatre or a pub,
You will find some consolation in the Langview Social Club.
   —Don McRae

A letter to Jessie McRae

Written in reply to a letter from his sister-in-law, Jessie McRae, in which she had 'castigated' him for forgetting her birthday and suggested a contribution of £5 as compensation for the oversight.

In answer to your letter I think Dear Jess I'd better
First apologise to you at any rate,
For failing to remember that the 14th of September
Was an all-important and historic date.

When your letter came to hand and its contents I had scanned,
And your reference to the fiver I did note,
Then I realised too late I had overlooked the date
And my conscience it was most severely smote.

I note what you suggest but I somehow think it best –
(As I fear perhaps ill feeling might arise) –
To send you not one penny, then there won't be cause for any,
'Though what you'll think I only can surmise.

INTERLUDE A *Some poems*

To grant your small request I would gladly do my best,
If I thought that it would do you any good.
I would even make it double and deem it not a trouble,
If I thought that you would spend it as you should.

Perhaps you'll think me funny but I always think with money,
One should be most careful how they give away,
As it sometimes is with folk some are better off when broke,
As riches sometimes sends them all astray.

When you're running short of cash and you're wanting some to splash,
And you think how grand 'twould be to own a pile;
Console yourself with this, there's a mighty lot you'd miss,
And perhaps be happy only for a while.

If it happens that my boat chances still to be afloat –
Though a feeling that she's foundered oft' prevails –
Though it may be just of course she is drifting off her course,
Or is waiting for some wind to fill her sails.

My hopes may not be vain that she'll find her course again,
And come sailing home with riches in her hold.
And if she does, and when, I may think about you then,
When I'm dealing out my surpluses of gold.
  —*Don McRae*

A letter to Charlie Tubb

The Tubb family was from Longwood in north-east Victoria and had a strong military history. Charlie had served in World War 1 prior to being discharged on medical grounds in October 1916. One of his brothers, Fred, had been awarded the Victoria Cross for 'conspicuous bravery and devotion to duty' at Lone Pine, Gallipoli, in August 1915 and was later killed at Ypres, Belgium, in September 1917. Another brother, Frank, had served in the Boer War then, during World War 1, had been awarded a Military Cross for 'conspicuous gallantry' in France in September 1916.

There were a number of connections between the McRae and Tubb families. At least for part of the time the McRaes lived at Sunny Point Charlie owned a property directly across from them, on the east side of the Buchan River. The elder sister of Charlie's wife Ethel was married to John McRae, Alexander's older brother, and in 1928 one of Charlie's younger sisters, Lucy, married Alistair McRae.

After they left Buchan Don and Charlie corresponded reasonably regularly, often in light-hearted, poetical form. The following is an example of this.

INTERLUDE A   *Some poems*

All day I've thought of you dear Charles and so I thought I'd better,
Just take my pen and sit me down and write to you a letter.
It is not news it shall contain but just a brief description,
Of how I witnessed in a dream your premature extinction.

Last night I lay me down to sleep upon my little bed,
And oh! I dreamed a horrid dream, I dreamed that you were dead.
'Twas not from any natural cause, there was a grave suspicion
That you'd been foully done to death by some unknown assassin.

A heading in the press appeared "Mysterious death of Tubby:
Police believe that from a clue they'll soon arrest somebody."
Each day I scanned the papers o'er the culprit's name to see,
But oh, imagine my dismay when they arrested me!

I pleaded of my innocence; it proved to no avail,
They locked the handcuffs on my wrists and marched me off to gaol.
They kept me there for many days, unmindful of my pleading,
'Til up before the magistrate they brought me for a hearing.

The judge read o'er the charge to me and said, "How are you pleading?
I think that from the evidence that you're the man we're needing.
You're charged that by a wilful act you caused poor Tubby's end."
But I replied, "Not me, O judge, he was my dearest friend."

"But we can prove," the judge replied, "that you composed a letter,
And sent it with the earnest hope that you'd receive one better.
We need no other evidence for here's the doctors' version,
The cause of death they all agree was cerebral exertion."

How pleased was I when I awoke and found that I was dreaming,
The perspiration from my brow was absolutely streaming.
But all the day my heart's been filled with very grave misgiving,
And so I send this on to you to ask you, "Are you living?"

PS
I truly hope this dream dear Charles may never prove a true one,
Or that I'd e're be guilty of an action so inhuman.
But if you ever feel inclined and have some inspiration,
Just drop a line or two to me to this here destination.

—**Don McRae**

INTERLUDE A   *Some poems*

A caver's epitath

Don was an early explorer of the caves under the hill at the Pyramids, on the Murrindal River. This poem was written and given to sister-in-law, Jessie McRae, before he commenced this exploration.

Now when this cave hole I descend, should I no more return
I pray you not to grieve for me nor show too much concern;
But leave me there, in peace to rest, way down beneath the hill;
My one request is only this — please execute my will.

To your good man who ceased to smoke, save when he cadged from me,
All my tobacco I bequeath, a full pound there should be.
My boots and socks and pants and shirts, save those that I have on,
My hat and handkerchiefs and ties are his when I am gone.
And all the cash that I possess, you in my pockets find,
Shall all belong to you alone for all your favours kind.
And give my love to all at home and all who called me friend,
And any others whom you'd think would much lament my end.
And tell them that it was my wish and not to take offence,
Because I wished to be left there to minimise expense.

Sometime perhaps you'd feel inclined to take along a tree,
And plant it at the entrance in memory of me.
And on the rock-face you could have inscribed this epitaph,
And placed above it, in a frame, perhaps my photograph.

Epitaph
In memory of poor old Don, who was so full of hope
Of finding something grand down here, descended on a rope.
What happened none shall ever know, he must have struck bad luck,
But as he's not come out again, we think he just got stuck.
 —Don McRae

To Mr V Tuck — from the bark hut at the Basin — 4/6/1943

Written to the storekeeper in Buchan, Vernon Tuck, requesting favourable consideration during war-time rationing.

If you could see me as I am tonight,
You'd witness here a most distressing sight;
A sad, disconsolate, unhappy bloke,
Craving in vain the pleasure of a smoke.

If you have got, as I surmise, a heart,
Could you not once from rigid rules depart,
And from the fountains of your virtuous soul,
Grant a request, my miseries to console.

Send me the fragrant weed that oft' repels
Depressions, gloom and melancholy quells.
That armed against these monsters I may be,
To view all things with equanimity.

Once had I planned indulgence to desist,
And oftentimes the craving did resist;
But ah! methinks the habit has me conquered
Because, without a smoke, I'm fairly stonkered.
  —*Don McRae*

Buchan ugly man contest

Written to describe contestants in an 'ugly man' contest at Buchan, held to raise funds for a local cause. Presumably the three participants willingly took part in the event and the associated public 'denigration'.

Since man was first created and fashioned out of clay,
There's always been the ugly ones since then until today.
But anywhere that you might roam it could be truly stated,
That Buchan claims the ugliest that ever were created.

There's three of them before you here lined up for observation,
Each one a worthy candidate for future coronation.
Yet which one shall be voted in as king of his dominion,
Is just a matter to decide by popular opinion.

Now Douglas Mitton, look at him, his looks portray a dunner;
Yet as a chubby baby boy they say he was a stunner.
To see him you would scarcely think that time would so much change him,
If he has any beauty now it must be all behind him.

Then Harry Cameron, what of him, without exaggeration
If one sees handsomeness in him they've got imagination.
But people say he once was thin until, it has been stated,
His system like the currency became so much inflated.

And what about Bruce Dalley, now you couldn't call him bonnie;
Some people say he never was a really handsome Johnny.
There's really cause for deep regret to think it was so fated
That he and handsomeness should be so distantly related.

* * *

So people now it's up to you to choose from these a victim;
We'll patiently await to hear pronouncement of the dictum.
Then straight henceforth we shall proceed, no penalty omitting,
To crown him king of ugly men in manner most befitting.

* * *

By verdict of the people and by popular decree,
You're selected as the ugliest of all the ugly three.
And it's hereby stipulated that the crown that you must wear
Shall be half a rotten pumpkin stuck with treacle to your hair.
—**Don McRae**

INTERLUDE A   *Some poems*

A letter to Angus Armstrong

Written to a neighbour at the Basin, Angus Armstrong, who had requested Don keep an eye on Armstrong's farm while they were on a holiday, including leaving a couple of old rams to be killed as meat for the dogs.

Dear Angus here I sit me down and take my pen in hand,
To write to you of happenings I can't quite understand;
And just why fate should treat you so is more than I can say,
But things have gone from bad to worse since you have been away.

The first of all the tragedies, poor Bluey died last week;
Then Don committed suicide by falling in the creek.
And Happy tried to jump the fence and fell and broke her neck,
While Twinkle got caught up in wire and she's a total wreck.
And then that last horse that you bought, I just forget her name,
Fell down a hole and broke her leg, I reckon that's a shame.

You'd think that this should be enough but, Lord, 'twould make you weep
To see the havoc that's been caused by dingoes 'mongst your sheep.
There must have been a pack of them the damage that they've done,
They've eaten all that they could eat and killed the rest for fun.

I feel that here I'd like to strike a less discordant note,
Still all your cattle, every hoof, succumbed last week from bloat.
As though to add to this distress the fowls all ceased to lay,
For they, in keeping with the rest, have also passed away.

A bit of this and that

And then from reasons quite obscure as how it did transpire
Your house and contents, every stick, was all destroyed by fire.
In spite of all these tragedies I wouldn't give a damn,
Had not the dogs all died as well through eating too much ram.

It's hard to think the hand of fate should treat you so unkind,
But still it's best to face all this with philosophic mind.
You really couldn't realise the anguish that I feel
When thinking on the tragedies this letter must reveal.

Yet there's some consolation here in thinking on this fact,
That up to date at any rate the farm is still intact.
I trust you won't allow all this to mar your holiday,
And please accept the sympathy of your friend D McRae.
   —Don McRae

INTERLUDE A   *Some poems*

Canberra's orchestra

Written at some stage in the early 1950s, when Robert Menzies was prime minister, Arthur Fadden Treasurer, and Dr HV Evatt Leader of the Opposition.

You can hear it from Canberra, anytime and anywhere,
Strains of melancholy music wafted to you on the air.
Sounding brass and tinkling cymbals fill the portals of the land,
And Robert's now the leader of the great orchestral band.

For Robert plays the fiddle while Arty beats the drum,
And Doc sits in a corner feeling very sad and glum.
His ear is unresponsive both to rhythm and refrain,
And all the serenading only aggravates a pain.

But still the band keeps playing and it's really quite a treat
To see how Arty's drumsticks strike the time with every beat.
The magic of the music is most manifest in those
Who trip a light fantastic to the way the music goes.

While some join in the revels there are others unbeguiled
With the choicest of selections these musicians have compiled.
And Doc keeps on a-hoping, that the time will surely come
When he can play the fiddle and some other chap the drum.
—**Don McRae**

A bit of this and that

Lament to a tin

With his wife Alice and daughter Jessie, Walter Hicks moved from his property on the Rodger River, east of the Snowy River, to Murrindal in 1918. He retained grazing leases on the Rodger River, which he visited intermittently to check his cattle and during which times he camped in the original small homestead.

In 1934 Ewen McRae married Jessie and regularly visited the Rodger River area with his father-in-law.

Walter retained a large jam tin under his bed in the homestead, to avoid having to leave the hut during the night when he visited.

On one occasion Ewen stayed on for some time after Walter had returned to Murrindal. Walter encouraged him to make use of the tin if he wished to. Prior to leaving the Rodger River, Ewen attached this poem (which he had previously requested Don to write) to a stick before poking the stick through the bottom of the jam tin, awaiting Walter's next visit.

INTERLUDE A   *Some poems*

Oh, honest servant, faithful friend,
In praise of you these lines are penned.
Oft' have you served me in the night,
And saved me from the freezing bite.
When bid by nature to obey
Her calls before the break of day,
When chilly winds of winter blew
I feared them not while I had you
Close to my bedside, near at hand,
To serve my needs at my command.
You served me as a faithful friend,
I grieve that this should be your end.

Ah, little know the ones who made
And filled you up with marmalade,
How often you have brought me bliss
And saved me getting up to piss.
'Twas when bequeathe'd to a friend,
You came to an untimely end.
Now sorrowing I fain must seek
Another tin wherein to leak.
Still you I never shall forget,
Oh, dear old friend, I love you yet.
I'll never find another tin,
To serve as well for pissing in.
  —*Don McRae*

INTERLUDE B

A few kicks

Having been a keen attender at local football games, it was a natural progression for me to want to commence playing. I didn't find it easy. The only under-age competition available in Bairnsdale at the time was the BDFL seconds, which was for Under 18s. In 1963, being 12 years old at the start of the season, I began attending training at West Bairnsdale Football Club. Their home ground was not far away, which meant I could quite easily ride my bike to and from training each Tuesday and Thursday evening.

Despite badly wanting to play and believing at the time that I would be able to participate at that level, it was never a realistic option. I was at best of only average capability and the difference in physical size and strength between me and those in the upper end of the age range was too much. Even those of my contemporaries who were generally acknowledged as 'good' footballers seldom played in these matches other than as 19th or 20th man, perhaps with a token period on the ground towards the end of a game.

Resigning myself to not having much chance of getting a game, I took on the job of boundary umpiring for the seconds, which at least meant I had a role other than just watching each week. Even

INTERLUDE B *A few kicks*

then I suspect I struggled to keep up with the game at times, but this didn't seem to cause too many concerns, and I'm sure the club was pleased to have one of the necessary but less glamorous jobs covered each week.

We weren't a 'football family'. Although Mum and Alf gave me all the support I needed, they were not involved with the club at all and didn't attend any games. We had no close social contacts with others involved in football apart from the next-door neighbours, Percy and Marj Edsall, whose son Eddie, three years older than me, had played for the Wy Yung seconds prior to moving to the Bairnsdale thirds (also Under 18), and who were regular attenders at Bairnsdale home matches.

This lack of family involvement didn't impact my keenness, however, and the commitment to bi-weekly attendance at training and of running the boundary eventually payed dividends, albeit by default. Shortly before a match at Swan Reach, it was discovered that the seconds were short of players and all options needed to be exploited. I therefore exchanged my white boundary umpire's tee-shirt for a purple and gold West Bairnsdale jumper, and for the first time joined the team.

All first games, wherever they are played and at whatever level, have something special about them and are memorable because of this. I recollect running down the ramp from the small wooden clubrooms on the Tambo River side of the ground at the start of the match that day and feeling as though I had achieved something wonderful. I was almost flying — when your world is small, it doesn't take much to make you feel on top of it. I recall nothing else from the game and probably hardly touched the ball, but at least I had played and that was enough by itself.

It was also as good as it got for that season, as unfortunately all selected players turned up on time to subsequent matches and I was again relegated to running the boundary.

Prior to the 1964 season, Bairnsdale Football Club commenced a Saturday morning Under 15 competition, the Bairnsdale fourths. This was a very welcome development, as it gave those of us who were too young to get a regular game in the BDFL seconds the chance to play each week against kids about our own age. Some of the older and better players left the fourths during the season to play with BDFL seconds teams, but it served its purpose of giving opportunities to a range of players of disparate capabilities to play each week.

The competition was comprised of four teams — North, South, East and West — formed by zoning the town. I spent the next two seasons as captain of West, which was the first experience I'd had of regularly playing competitive football and feeling part of a team in doing so. West didn't win the competition in either of the years I played (which is really beside the point, even if I didn't see it that way at the time), but the experience served to confirm my enthusiasm for the game and for continuing to be involved with it.

Being too old to continue in the fourths in 1966, I made the decision to return to West Bairnsdale and attempt to play with their seconds team rather than move on to the Bairnsdale thirds. Back at West, I found I could progress from boundary umpire duties and spent the season playing as a permanent back pocket. This was one of the less glamorous positions on the field, but that didn't really concern me if it meant I could get a game each week.

My future in the game didn't appear overly bright, however, for at least two reasons. The first was that I had difficulties at various times during the year with an injured knee, which regularly caused problems and made playing quite painful at times. The second and more pressing challenge was that I was not much good. Although managing to maintain my place in the side each week, it must have been a close-run thing on some occasions, particularly early in the season. Things did gradually improve during the year, though, and in the end I received an award for 'most consistent player', which surprised and pleased me in equal measure.

Everything needed to be kept in perspective, however. At school, despite being one of the 'big kids' in Form 5 (there were only 17 of us in that form in a school of around 400 boys), I was embarrassed and disappointed by not being selected in the school seconds team even though some students from Form 2 were.

I left home to attend Dookie Agricultural College at the beginning of 1967. The college at that stage fielded a team in the Tungamah League and their arch rivals were Dookie, the township a few kilometres to the north. (The clubs amalgamated after the 1976 season to form Dookie United, an outcome difficult to imagine given the rivalry between them at the time.)

Perhaps again unsure about being able to get a game, or maybe concerned about further issues with my knee, I didn't play football in 1967. By the next year I was keen to get back into it, however, and played in the Dookie College seconds, mostly at full back, which was subsequently to become the position I most commonly played.

Mick Morris, the college butchery instructor had been non-playing coach of the college team for a number of years but retired from the role prior to the 1969 season. Alan McNish, a young schoolteacher, was appointed that year to the Currawa Primary School, which was located on the college and which children of the staff and from families in the surrounding districts attended.

After a bit of persuasion, Alan agreed to become playing coach of the college team and it turned out to be both an inspired choice and a very good year for the team.

With students coming and going each year, it was a bit of a lottery as to what standard the college team would be in any year, but 1969 turned out to be one of the better ones in the history of the club. The senior team retained a strong nucleus of the previous year's team, and a number of good footballers arrived as first-year students. (The historical strength of the team that year is illustrated by 11 players from it being named in the 'Best Dookie College Team', selected as part of Dookie United Football Club celebrations in 1995, and a 12th who later played for Dookie being named in their 'Best' side.)

I commenced the year again playing in the seconds, but around three games into the season was promoted to the seniors. The seniors had an established full back, so I was selected in the ruck and played my first senior game against Congupna Road at their ground north of Shepparton. As with my experience at Swan Reach, this was again inauspicious, with my clearest recollection being the marked increase in the speed of the game compared to playing in the seconds, and my frustration in not being able to work out how to play in the unfamiliar ruck position. This latter frustration must have been shared by those on the selection panel, as I exchanged positions with the existing full back for subsequent matches and played the rest of the year in that position. We had a good season and made the finals.

We beat Katandra in the first semi-final and Dookie in the preliminary final but lost to Mulwala in the grand final. With our team's oldest player being 22, and most still teenagers, we led well

INTERLUDE B *A few kicks*

at quarter-time, were a few points behind at half-time, but found the physical approach of our Mulwala opponents (some within the rules and spirit of the game, but much not) too much to withstand in the end.

At the end of the season, we travelled to Adelaide to play against Roseworthy Agricultural College and back via Horsham to play Longerenong Agricultural College. Roseworthy and Dookie travelled for these games in alternate years, with Longerenong playing each on their respective way home.

Given these trips took four or five days in a bus, included a game of football and considerable 'extra-curricular' activities for most at either Roseworthy or Dookie over the weekend, and then

Dookie Agricultural College senior football team, Runners-up, Tungamah Football League, 1969
Back: Daryl Reid, Rod Ackland, Bob Kennedy, Rod Binks, Eric Toose, Chris McRae, Jim Walduck, Wayne Bubb
Middle: John Wain (Trainer), Greg Kotschet, David Leggo, Derek Stabb (Secretary), Trevor Webb, Ian Hollick, Alistair Kensley, Rob Knight (Trainer)
Front: Chas Dickens, Bruce Fry, Nigel Smith, Alan McNish (Captain/Coach), Russell Allison, Rex Pitman, John Chapman, Ken Pullen

another game of football at Longerenong on Monday or Tuesday, Longerenong had a pretty good record in these matches. We managed to win both in 1969, though this did little to erase the disappointment of losing the grand final a few weeks earlier.

Despite losing quite a few players at the end of 1969, the college won the premiership in 1970 when they defeated Katandra. After the disappointment of the previous year, it was great to be at the game to watch that match and see the victory achieved.

Returning to Bairnsdale in 1970 meant making a choice of where to play, realistically either West Bairnsdale or Wy Yung (with whom I played cricket) in the BDFL, or with Bairnsdale in the Latrobe Valley League. After being approached by Bairnsdale, I chose to play there, although I was quite uncertain about whether it may be a step too far for me in standard. Kevin Coverdale, a Bairnsdale local who had played a number of seasons with Hawthorn in the VFL, was coach and I again played most of the season at full back, after playing my first game with them in the ruck (with a similar experience to that at Dookie College).

I particularly recall that season for a few reasons. Most notably it meant that I was playing senior football with a club that as a boy I had seen as being at the peak of local football achievement. It was also the season that I first began to develop a feeling that I was more than just 'making up the numbers', and that gave me a growing sense of confidence. At the other end of the scale, when I retired it was the only one of 16 seasons of senior football with six clubs that the team I played with didn't make the finals. It was disappointing at the time, but in retrospect I can't complain too much about this.

The next season was again going to involve a change of clubs, because I was heading to Melbourne in early March to commence

INTERLUDE B   *A few kicks*

what I hoped to be three years at Melbourne University. I had initially contemplated returning each week to play with Bairnsdale, but soon decided that the travel involved, at the same time as studying, would make this impractical. I therefore faced the question of which football club to join.

I was aware of the Amateurs but had no knowledge or experience of them. My main connection was from hearing scores from Amateur matches reported on the ABC Saturday evening sports programs as a kid, and wondering at names such as Old Paradians, Old Melburnians, Collegians, Old Xaverians and many others — who were they? The university teams — Blacks and Blues — were at least a bit more self-explanatory to me without a private-school background, so soon after arriving at uni I made my way to training at the University Oval.

The Melbourne University Football Club was in many ways unique in that it was comprised of two senior teams, and the club had an aim of maintaining them at more or less the same standard and both playing in the A Section of the Amateur competition. All new players were graded on ability and allocated to either Blacks or Blues depending on the needs of the respective teams. When I arrived, Blues were in the A Section but Blacks were in B, and so there was some effort being made by the club to support the Blacks in their quest to return to the A Section.

I was allocated to the Blacks and commenced a wonderful association with a club and team that has continued to this day. It has been one of the more satisfying involvements that I have had in a sporting club. I look back on my time playing there very fondly and greatly enjoy the continued opportunity to participate in club events and to watch a number of their games each year.

Peter O'Donohue (the 'Silver Fox') was senior coach during the four years I spent playing at the Blacks. He was a former Hawthorn VFL player and coach and had more influence on me as a footballer than any other individual over my career. He appeared to me to have a particular skill in communicating with and helping young men strive to get the best out of themselves and their team-mates. I am sure that many others who were similarly fortunate to play under his guidance felt the same way.

There were others at the club who also had a highly positive influence on me, most notably Brian Costello, the club doctor, and Alex Johnson, the club president, both of whom had one or more sons playing with the Blacks at the time. All three of these men also contributed heavily to amateur football more generally and have been recognised as life members of the Victorian Amateur Football Association.

During the four years I spent with the Blacks, we gradually improved on where we finished at the end of each season, although it was not until my final season there that we played in A Section. The Amateurs run a promotion/relegation system with the top two teams from any section being promoted each year and the bottom two being relegated, so each year we were desperately attempting to at least play in the grand final so that we would be promoted to A Section.

In 1971 we finished fourth in B Section. The next year we lost only three games for the home-and-away season, prior to losing both our finals and thus finishing third. In 1973 we finally reached the grand final in B Section and, although we lost the game at Victoria Park to Reservoir Old Boys, we earned the long sought-for promotion to A Section.

INTERLUDE B   *A few kicks*

I finished my uni course at the end of 1973 and relocated to Warragul, around 100 kilometres east of Melbourne. Having at last reached A Section , I was keen to continue with the Blacks for at least one season, and Warragul was close enough for me to travel back each week to do so. I therefore commenced a routine of training with Warragul during the week and travelling to Melbourne on the weekends, staying at Alex and Val Johnson's place each Friday evening, then playing with the Blacks on Saturday. (Around 25 years later, Alex reminded me of this and asked whether I would mind returning his key!)

We had quite a mixed season in 1974, lost the final game of the season and only slipped into the finals when other results went our way. We then commenced our best run of form for the year, defeating St Bernards then Coburg Amateurs in the first semi and preliminary finals before lining up against Ormond in the grand final.

Ormond had been among the most powerful sides in A Section for some years and had won the previous three premierships. They were widely tipped to make it four in a row, but we continued with our good finals form and had a great win. In successive seasons we had gone from runners-up in B Section to premiers in A Section, which was virtually unheard of and understandably ushered in a significant round of celebrations.

It was a wonderful experience to be part of a premiership team after previously being unsuccessful in two grand finals. I was fortunate to have the experience on further occasions, but a bit like playing a first game for a team, the first one has that special something about it.

There were a few other aspects of my time at the Blacks and the Amateurs that stand out to me. It was where I received the

Victorian Amateur Football Association side, Adelaide, June 1974
(Photo: Frank Boase, Malvern, SA)

Back: Shane Maguire, Chris McRae, Bruce Kefford, Alan Handley,
Roger Wood, Andrew Ireland

Second back: Peter Murnane, Mick O'Donnell, Greg Tootell,
Danny Barklay, Mick Mahoney

Second front: Barry Hibberd, Kevin Grose, Kevin Ladd, Kevin Power,
Ross Duke, Phil Pryor

Front: Bruce Smith, Fred Coldrey (Assistant Manager),
Bruce Bourne (Captain), Laurie Aghan (Coach), John Anderson (Vice-captain),
Lou Zachariah (Manager), Terry Archer

nickname 'Tractor', which has stayed with me ever since. I gather it came about as a reference to the course I was engaged in — agricultural science — and an apparently robust and straight-ahead style of play.

A negative feature was our inability to beat Reservoir Old Boys; they had the 'wood' on us during my time at the Blacks. They had risen through the Amateur ranks year by year following their commencement in the lower grades, until we began playing against

INTERLUDE B *A few kicks*

Australian Amateurs, Section 2 Australian National Football Council Championships, Sydney 1974 (Photo: Melba Studios, Sydney)
Back: Shane Maguire, Chris McRae, Andrew Ireland, Roger Wood, Bruce Kefford, Simon Trumble, Graeme Matcham, Neville Harris
Centre: Gerard Neesham, Kim Underdown, Kevin Grose, Steve Morton, Kevin Griffiths, Stuart Palmer, Mick O'Donnell, Jim Katsaros, Ross Duke, Steve Johnson
Front: Howard Mutton (Coach), Barry Hibberd, Lou Zachariah (Manager), Bruce Bourne (Vice-captain), Paul Rofe (Captain), Keith Sims (Assistant Manager), Danny Barclay, Sandy Cockburn (Trainer)

them in B Section. They had some wonderful footballers, but they also played a physical and aggressive style of game which we obviously didn't handle too well. I played against them on six occasions over two seasons. In 1973 they beat us in all four games — two home-and-away matches and both finals. In 1974, when we had both been promoted to A Section, they beat us in both home-and-away games, even though at the end of the season we were premiers and they didn't make the finals. It was the least successful match-up against another team that I experienced during my career.

Finally, I was fortunate to play a number of games for Victorian Amateur teams against other states and with the Australian Amateur team. In 1972 Victoria lost to South Australia in Adelaide

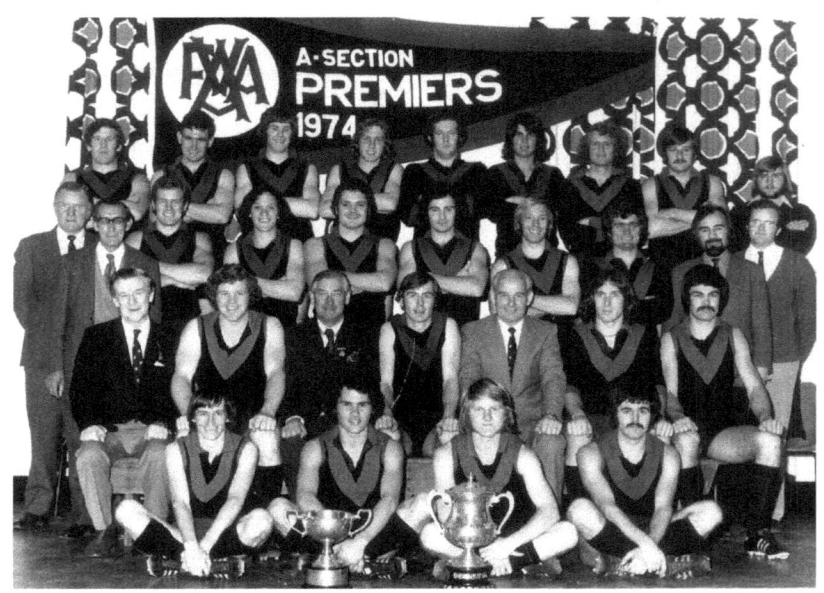

*University Blacks senior team, 'A' Section Premiers,
Victorian Amateur Football Association, 1974*
Back: Tony Costello, Chris McRae, John Larkins, Allan Holmes,
Graeme Matthews, Ian Cordner, Chris Cordner, Graeme Johnson,
Peter Selleck (MUFC Secretary)
Second back: Ernie Cropley (MUFC Vice-president, Curator),
Harry Sharpe (Timekeeper), Russell Bellingham, Andy Johnstone,
Tony King, Jon Webster, Don MacCallum, Dave Pascoe,
Neil Watson (Runner), Leighton Boyd (Team Manager)
Seated: Brian Costello (Doctor), Simon Costello, Alex Johnson (Chairman), Jack
Batten (Captain), Peter O'Donohue (Coach), Tony Moffatt, Rod McLean
Front: Noel Sharpe, Alan Fisher, Ross Perrett, Charlie Kovess

and beat Tasmania in Launceston. In the 1973 Amateur Carnival played on the MCG, we beat both Western Australia and Tasmania, but lost again to South Australia, who won the Carnival. At the end of the week, I was pleased to be selected in the Australian Amateur side, based on performances at the carnival.

In 1974 Victoria defeated South Australia in Adelaide and I was again selected in the Australian Amateur side, this time to play in the Australian National Football Council's Section 2 Carnival in Sydney. It wasn't a successful time for us, as we were beaten by both ACT and New South Wales, but it was a wonderful experience participating in the event with players from Victoria, Tasmania, South Australia and Western Australia.

It was quite a wrench to leave the Blacks and Amateurs at the end of the 1974 season, but having decided to do so, and after training with Warragul for all that year, it was an easy decision to know where to play in 1975. Warragul had won the Latrobe Valley League premiership in 1974 with ex-Richmond player Graham Gahan as captain-coach, but for some reason in 1975 he and the club could not agree on his re-appointment, so he left to coach Yallourn, and Ken Robinson took over at Warragul.

The two years I spent with Warragul were again successful and enjoyable. We had a strong team, as would be expected of a premiership side from the previous year, retained many of the premiership players, and added a few others. After a solid season in 1975, we finally finished runner-up, losing the grand final played at Yallourn to Sale. An interesting aspect of this game was that it was umpired by Ian Robinson, who had a long and successful career as an umpire and officiated in nine VFL grand finals.

The following year we went one better, defeating Traralgon at Yallourn in one of the more free-scoring and higher-standard grand finals I played in.

While moving to Warragul in 1975 had meant I played against some of those I had been team-mates with five years previously at Bairnsdale, moving from Warragul at the end of 1976 to play in 1977 for Leongatha in the same league was a whole new experience. Warragul and Leongatha were not far apart, separated only by the Strzelecki Ranges, and were quite intense rivals. Over recent years that intensity has probably dropped off a bit because of the relative lack of success enjoyed by Warragul, but during the 1970s and early 1980s they were both strong clubs and games between them had a real edge.

Angus Hume was coach of Leongatha in 1976 and 1977 and, while they had finished third in 1976, they were confident of improving on that performance in the coming season.

It didn't take long for a clash between my former and current clubs to occur. In one of the early games of the season, Warragul came over the hills and played at Leongatha and, after a closely fought game, won by a few points. I played a forgettable game and, as I was leaving the ground at its conclusion, I received a reminder of the feeling between the clubs and the fact that I had a way to go before being accepted as a legitimate Leongatha player. One of our female supporters, upset by the loss to the hated Warragul, came up to the players as we neared the rooms and loudly enquired, 'Who were you playing for today, McRae!?'

The season looked up from there, however, and we finished the season playing Traralgon in the grand final at Moe, winning a closely fought match. It was the first of three grand-final clashes between Leongatha and Traralgon over the next four years. Leongatha won again in 1979, with ex-Melbourne player Neville Stone as coach, then Traralgon turned the tables in 1980, when Leongatha was coached by Colin Boyd, who had arrived from Essendon at the start of that season. Traralgon also won the 1978 flag after defeating Yallourn-Yallourn North, with Leongatha finishing third, so the two clubs shared a dominant period in the Latrobe Valley League at that time.

INTERLUDE B *A few kicks*

It was easy to understand why Leongatha was a successful club. They were well led administratively and had numerous clubs in close proximity with whom there was a regular two-way flow of players and coaches. They were at the time the only club in South Gippsland playing in the Latrobe Valley League, which was clearly the highest standard league in Gippsland. At the time the Latrobe Valley League had solid grounds for claiming to be the best in country Victoria, having won the Victorian Country Football Championships in 1979 and 1980. Leongatha was able to attract better players from surrounding leagues to play with them, partly as a result of this. They were also a very keen sporting town and there was strong interest in and support for the club as a result.

I had an amusing experience early in 1980, which had me recalling my own keen interest in local footballers many years earlier, the prominent place they held for me as a young supporter, and the need to keep things in perspective.

Early in a game at Leongatha, I injured a hamstring and came off the ground. After having some ice treatment, I showered and went out to watch the game from a seat just inside the oval's fence. There was a broad gravelled track between the fence and the playing arena on which three or four young boys, around eight or ten years old, were playing with a football near where I went to watch. They were bouncing the ball, doing short handballs to each other, and keeping only a general eye on what was happening in the game.

Bounce, bounce. Handball, handball.

When I arrived, they immediately stopped what they were doing and focused on me — why was I there, rather than out on the ground playing?

One asked, in a very concerned tone, 'What have you done, Tractor?'

'Oh,' I said, 'I've pulled a muscle in my leg.'

'Geeee! Is it your kickin' leg?' he asked.

I assured him it wasn't.

Bounce, bounce.

A small game of one-upmanship then began. Out of the blue, one of the boys said to his mates in a rather superior tone, 'I know Tim Maxwell.' (Tim was a prominent Leongatha footballer at the time.)

Bounce, bounce.

Another, obviously not wanting to let this claim of closeness to a local celebrity stand without testing it, asked, 'Do you know him well?'

The first lad was careful not to overplay his hand, so he replied cautiously but defiantly, 'No, I don't know him well — but I know him!'

Handball, handball.

The next claim of youthful worth resulting from knowledge of a local identity came from another of the boys: 'We live next door to Chris McRae.'

Inwardly my chest swelled; surely, I thought, that claim would match that of knowing Tim Maxwell.

Bounce, bounce.

The youngest lad then piped up quizzically, 'Does he play football?'

In 1980 I was also pleased to be a part of the Latrobe Valley League side which became Victorian Country Football League champions for the second year running. We won matches against the North Central, Bendigo, Wimmera and Western Border Leagues before beating the Ovens and Murray League in the final at Sale. I had played in the first four of these games but missed the final as it was played on a Sunday. It was one of only a few occasions that I missed playing because of my approach to Sunday sport (see Interlude C).

With a number of football clubs in close proximity to each other in country areas, it was common for players from clubs playing in the stronger leagues of the area to be approached to coach neighbouring clubs. I usually experienced a few such contacts at the end of each season and, while I was interested in taking on a coaching role at some stage, I also enjoyed playing in the higher standard Latrobe Valley League, so for some time resisted these overtures.

In the late 1970s Roy Bright was president of Meeniyan Dumbalk United (MDU), a club in the Alberton Football League and he was a regular visitor — 'just to have a chat' — at the end of most seasons. His approach was generally along the lines of, 'We know you won't be wanting to move yet, but I thought I'd come to see you, just in case. Get in touch if you ever decide to change your mind.'

For a number of years, nothing came of this, but Roy's efforts at least sowed a seed in my mind, and at the end of the 1980 season I thought it was time to have a go at a playing-coach role. Roy hadn't visited that year, but I rang him and applied for the advertised MDU coaching job. I was appointed and commenced a tremendously enjoyable period of involvement with the club.

MDU was a successful club. They had won premierships in 1975 and 1976 and had been in or close to the finals in each subsequent year. One year they had the dubious distinction of having gone through the entire season undefeated, only to lose both their finals. They retained the nucleus of a strong team and, from discussions with a few people in the district, I was confident this could be built on to again have them challenging for a premiership.

MDU at that stage was also a very well-run club. Barry Delaney had taken over as president, Allan Herrald was secretary and Merv Bright was chairman of selectors. All did a great job as well as being terrific to work with. There was also always a lot of support for the club from people in the local community and throughout the district.

Having been appointed coach, there was a need to get involved in recruiting new players to come to play for the club, and convincing existing players not to leave. A lot of this involved networks of knowledge and contacts of people associated with the club, particularly those on the committee, and we were quite successful in both areas prior to the 1981 season.

Terry (Tiger) Davey, a wonderful key forward, had played with the club previously and decided to return, bringing with him his mate Ian Baxter, a fine centreman. At the end of the season, these two shared the club's best-and-fairest award, so were tremendous pick-ups. So too was Rod Fox, who was appointed assistant coach and was a top-class and dependable defender. Adding these players, while retaining the bulk of the team from the previous year, certainly set us off on the right track.

Not all was positive, though, and early on we had heard that Paul Heppell, at that stage around 20 years old and developing into a very good forward, was keen to try himself in a higher standard league and was considering a move to play with Leongatha. Barry Delaney and I went to visit him at his parents' home one evening to attempt to convince him to stay with MDU for another season. Thankfully we were successful, and Paul finished up winning the

Alberton League goal-kicking award that year before going to Leongatha in 1982.

I recall another experience on a recruiting visit one evening, where the family had two younger children as well as the target of our interest. The father enjoyed the occasional beer and it was obvious he had done so prior to our arrival.

Following our discussions with him and his son, I was talking to him casually when he said, 'You do a bit of church preaching, don't you? Those two young kids of mine haven't been christened — do you reckon you could do it?'

I quickly said that I couldn't.

'Oh,' he said, 'I didn't have anything flash in mind. I just thought you could come out for lunch on a Sunday and afterwards you could christen the buggers.'

As well as me having to get used to a new club, a new role and attempting to get together the strongest possible playing list, the club and its followers also had to get used to me. I heard a story sometime later (probably apocryphal) that one keen but 'hard-marking' follower of the club commented when he heard of my appointment, 'Whaaat?! He goes to church and doesn't drink piss — how can he be any good at football?'

We had a great season in 1981. We lost only two games for the season — the second of the season to eventual runners-up Foster, and one late in the season to arch rivals Stony Creek at their ground in the centre of the Stony Creek Racecourse. This game was played in very wet conditions and the ground was as deep in mud as any I had ever played on. In covering the game, the local *Leongatha Star* appropriately headlined their report, 'M.D.U. swamped in M.U.D.'

That game proved to be an aberration, though, as we went on to

Meeniyan Dumbalk United (MDU) senior football team, Premiers, Alberton Football League, 1981
Back: Jeff Thomas, Ray Leys, Rod Taylor, Stewart Young, Ross Wise, Paul Heppell, Ian Baxter
Middle: Grant Kuhne, Ian Dunn, Ken Robb, Terry Davey, Owen Lester, Ken Newman
Front: Nick Kelly, John Heppell, Rod Fox (Vice-captain), Barry Delaney (President), Chris McRae (Captain/Coach), Neil Bright, Mick Hanily, (absent: Neville Oldham)

defeat Foster both in the second semi-final at Welshpool and the grand final, played on a very windy day at Yarram.

All premierships are wonderful experiences, but this one was particularly so for me because it was the first (and subsequently proved to be the only) one I had been involved in as captain-coach. The conclusion of that grand final is one of the few times I have felt emotional on the ground at the end of a game, and 1981 remains for me one of the absolute highlights of my football experience.

It turned out that 1981 was also the last year that I played in a football grand final. I had been very fortunate in playing in many senior grand finals, nine in total. In fact, over the nine seasons from 1973 to 1981, I had played in eight grand finals with four different clubs and been a part of five premierships, including one with each club (two with Leongatha) and one as captain-coach. To have been a part of that level of success in a team sport is a great privilege, and I know of many fine footballers who have played many seasons with few, if any, grand-final victories. I look back on each of those experiences with considerable gratitude and satisfaction.

I continued as captain-coach of MDU in 1982, when we lost the preliminary final to Won Wron-Woodside by a few points, and relinquished the role at the end of that season. I continued as a player in 1983, when Peter 'Ziggy' Mabilia took over as captain-coach, and we again finished third after losing the preliminary final to Devon.

In March of 1984 Tricia and I were married, and I was unsure of where I would play in the coming football season. I had strong emotional ties to both Leongatha and MDU, but in the end decided to return to Leongatha, despite the challenge of being older and having to compete again at a higher level. Neville Stone had returned as coach at Leongatha, and I started training and playing a few games into the season. After a couple of 'sighters' in the seconds, I spent the rest of the season in the seniors, although I missed our losing game against Traralgon in the second semi-final because it was played on a Sunday.

I returned to the team the following week for our preliminary final against eventual premiers Warragul, and as a team we were immediately under pressure. I was out-marked on a couple of occasions and taken from the ground. We finished up being very soundly beaten on the day and, although I returned to the field later and played out the match, it was obvious that my time as a senior player in the Latrobe Valley League was over.

It was not difficult to decide to retire from football at that stage. I had no desire to continue as a seconds player at Leongatha, even if this may have involved occasional senior matches. Similarly, I didn't see the point in moving back to MDU or to any other Alberton League club where continuing to play senior football would have been possible. The enjoyment I received from playing the game was heavily tied up with being able to compete effectively at a certain level, and I felt I would likely become increasingly frustrated if I was not able to continue to do that. In my mind it was better to stop before this frustration occurred.

Although I had decided to retire, it wasn't until I cleaned out and disposed of the old Gladstone bag I had used for carrying my gear throughout my career that it became real to me. The bag was in a pretty dilapidated state after all those years of use, and I must admit to not having kept it as clean and tidy as perhaps I should have.

The clean-out was a bit like an archaeological dig with various artefacts from the previous 16 years coming to light — laces of various colours, adhesive tape, sections of elastic bandages, almost-empty tubes of Deep Heat, an old jar of Vaseline, some old screw-in stops and a small spanner, along with sundry other bits and pieces. I didn't quite unearth a pair of Jenkin 'Topliner' ankle-high boots with drive-in leather stops and hard toes, but it wouldn't have surprised me if I had.

I have subsequently not regretted at all the decision to retire at that time. I look back at my experience with playing and being involved with football as having exceeded even my wildest dreams from when I first started to take an interest in the game. I continue to derive immense satisfaction from ongoing contact with teammates and opponents across the state and beyond, sometimes in the most unexpected places. For example, one of the closest friendships our family developed during our time in Moora in WA was with Mike and Gaynor Shallow and their family. Mike was a local veterinarian, and he and I discovered we had played on opposing sides when Dookie played against Roseworthy Agricultural College in South Australia in 1969. That is not an unusual experience and the ubiquity of long-term contact via sport — either planned or serendipitous — is to me one of its most consistent and endearing characteristics.

Looking back, the way in which the game is played now is certainly quite different to what I experienced. It was then far more a series of one-on-one or small group contests in spots across the ground rather than the 'whole of team/whole of ground' approach seen today. The team that won the greater number of these individual contests during the game, largely because the individuals in their team were better players than their direct opponents, usually won the game. It was a more free-flowing spectacle than it is now. The focus on team defence, having large numbers of players around the ball whenever it is being contested, players moving in packs around the ground and the influence of whole-of-ground teamwork, was much less pronounced than it is now.

Probably because of the premium placed on reducing the chance of error and retaining possession of the ball, a far more homogenised style of play occurs now. For example, almost all field kicks in a game now are the standard drop-punt; anyone who executes a torpedo which travels any distance in an AFL game is almost guaranteed to feature in a YouTube clip.

Until well into the 1970s, certainly in country and Amateur football, a mixture of drop-kicks, torpedos, stab-kicks and drop-punts were regularly seen in any game. Full backs kicking in after an opposition behind (and it was very rare for anyone other than the full back to do so) regularly used drop-kicks or torpedos, because they were regarded as being best for gaining distance. For a full back, being able to kick the ball a long distance was seen as being highly desirable. Short kicks from them, certainly when kicking in, were severely frowned upon and thus almost never seen.

There were a number of what were thought to be immutable rules for success in the game which were propounded by coaches almost universally, such as 'punch from behind', 'never short pass on the backline', 'never kick across goal', 'don't overdo handball', 'play on your man', 'don't lead to the dead pocket' and 'kick the ball long'. (The possibility that any player would kick the ball backwards was so remote that there was no need for this practice to be proscribed.) Many (although not all) of these have since been found to be entirely mutable as the game has evolved into the spectacle it is today.

No area illustrates this more than the use of handball, which is now almost as common a disposal method as kicking. During my time at the Blacks, Peter O'Donohue drummed into us his views on handball. While he much preferred a long kick wherever possible, he was accepting of handball providing its use was limited and fitted within his strongly prescribed and loudly proclaimed boundaries: 'One's OK, two's **dangerous**, three's **SUICIDE**!' It became quite a mantra and in subsequent years one of the most frequently recalled aspects of Peter's advice when past Blacks players met and reminisced.

Many years later at a Blacks game, spectators watched as the current team used a seemingly never-ending string of handballs before losing the ball to the opposition. One of those who had been around during Peter's time commented, 'What would O'Donohue call that — genocide?'

Selecting 'Best' teams is always a fraught exercise because there are as many opinions as there are people providing them, and inevitably many of these will differ from each other. Such teams are a great source of debate, with the added benefit of those debating never being able to prove the correctness or otherwise of their opinions or having others disprove them. What better basis for an argument could there be?

I have included here two teams selected by others, which I present for what they are worth. I would obviously like to think they are teams chosen by reasonable judges of the game but make no other comment on them. They consist of 20 players rather than the current 22, as that was the number in teams at the time.

The third team is one I have chosen. I was fortunate to play 16 years of senior football with six clubs, and during that time played with some wonderful footballers. This team is a composite of the best in each position I played with across those six clubs. Mindful of the potential for raised eyebrows from including myself in the team, my only riposte is that I effectively had no competition for the full-back position. When I played in the various teams that was the position I most regularly filled, so almost by default finished up there in this one. (That's my defence, anyway.)

A bit of this and that

Football teams

Best Dookie College team

(Selected in 1995 as part of that year's Dookie United Football Club reunion.)

B: John McArthur (Vice-captain) 1956–58	Chris McRae 1967–69	Bruce Fry 1967–69
HB: Alistair Kensley 1968–70	John Landy 1950	Edwin Denovan 1964–66
C: Ian Hollick 1969–71	Daryl Reid 1969–71	Peter Rennick 1966–68
HF: Gary Beavis 1969–71	Jim Walduck 1968–70	Ken Pullen 1967–69
F: Rod Ackland 1967–69	Alex Slocombe 1948–49	Greg Kotschet 1967–69

Rucks: Frank Dunin 1954
Jim McColl 1953
Rover: Rex Pitman (Captain) 1968–70
Interchange: Tom Speedy 1962–64
Rod Whiteway 1966–68

(The diploma course at Dookie was a three-year course. Until the opening of the Melbourne University Mount Derrimut Field Station west of Melbourne in 1964, agricultural science degree students from Melbourne University spent the second year of their course studying at Dookie, hence some of those in the above team being shown as playing for the college for only one year.)

INTERLUDE B *A few kicks*

Team of the decade
(Selected in 1982 by radio station 3TR football commentators, Graeme Eddy and Richard Zachariah, as the best 20 Latrobe Valley League players from 1972–82.)

B: Peter Campbell (Traralgon)	Chris McRae	Len Petch (Moe)
HB: Jeff Gieschen (Maffra)	Rob Foster (Sale)	Tom Beveridge (Traralgon/Moe)
C: Stan Davidson (Sale)	Brian Hammond (Traralgon)	Brian Royal (Bairnsdale)
HF: Terry Hunter (Traralgon)	Ian Salmon (Leongatha)	Ray Stamp (Sale)
F: Bill Bennett (Maffra)	Kelvin Templeton (Traralgon)	Geoff Jennings (Traralgon)

Rucks: John Gallus (Moe/Warragul/Maffra/Bairnsdale)
Barry Rowlings (Moe)
Rover: George Brayshaw (Traralgon)
Interchange: Peter Hall (Morwell/Traralgon)
Ernie Hug (Maffra)

Best played-with team

(Composite side of the best footballers in each position from the six clubs I played with.)

B: Rod McLean (Uni Blacks)	Chris McRae	Chris Cordner (Uni Blacks)
HB: Col Boyd (Leongatha)	Simon Costello (Uni Blacks)	Des Thorson (Leongatha)
C: Dennis Hogan (Leongatha)	Russell Bellingham (Uni Blacks)	Tony King (Uni Blacks)
HF: Ian Cordner (Uni Blacks)	Kevin Coverdale (Captain, Bairnsdale)	Terry Kilday (Warragul)
F: Ian Salmon (Leongatha)	Tony Moffatt (Uni Blacks)	Peter Lynch (Leongatha)
Rucks:	John Gallus (Warragul)	
	Tim Maxwell (Leongatha)	
Rover:	Wayne Lynch (Leongatha)	
Interchange:	Clive Salmon (Leongatha)	
	Chas Dickens (Dookie College)	
Coach:	Peter O'Donohue (Uni Blacks)	

INTERLUDE B *A few kicks*

**Members of radio station 3TR's
'Latrobe Valley Football League Team of the Decade, 1972–1982'**

Standing: Graeme Eddy (3TR Selector), George Brayshaw, Kelvin Templeton, John Gallus, Chris McRae, Rob Foster, Ian Salmon, Stan Davidson, Richard Zachariah (3TR Selector)

Sitting: Barry Rowlings, Brian Royal, Jeff Gieschen, Terry Hunter, Peter Campbell, Brian Hammond, Tom Beveridge

INTERLUDE C

Faith

Christian faith has always been and continues to be important to me, albeit with changes over time in what I understand that faith to mean, and its implications for the way I live life.

I suspect my perspective on matters of God and faith is now quite different to that of many of my forebears whose conservative, literalist interpretation of the Bible and understanding of a personally interventionist God formed the basis for my early teaching and experiences. The McRae and Knox families were strong Scottish Presbyterians. For both, but particularly for the former, their relationship to God, church and faith was the central reality of their lives. This was certainly true for my parents and many of their generation and one only needs to read the obituaries of my great grandparents, Christopher and Margaret, and those of my grandparents, Alexander and Bessie McRae, to get a glimpse of the place Christian faith played in their lives and actions.

As generations have evolved, a greater range of views and understandings has emerged among family members. I perceive this to be not only as expected but also positive, although I can understand why some may view the developments and changes more cautiously.

I am mindful that describing the changes in my perspectives and understanding may seem to imply some disregard for, or criticism of, those who were instrumental in my early Christian life. That is not my intention at all. Despite the changes in the way in which I understand my faith now compared to previously, I am immensely thankful for the strong heritage I received in this regard and the examples of living that resulted from those in my family and beyond who were influential in my formative years. I have nothing but a deep and abiding regard for and love of those of my family who initiated and encouraged my faith journey.

In attempting to understand the formation of my faith, I need to take a perspective from today and apply it to what I recall as being the circumstances when I was younger, growing up in relatively small rural communities in Victoria in the 1950s and 1960s. I would describe the world view that I had presented to me, and which I grew up to initially accept, as being best illustrated as a series of four concentric circular bands, each fitting more or less neatly into each other.

Although there was some degree of variation within each of these bands, the clearest and most obvious demarcations were between them. They formed the basis on which I came to understand the implications of faith as a child and within which my world views began to be formed. It seemed important to have people placed into convenient categories, so they could be thought about or interacted with appropriately, and we naturally tended to interact most commonly with those who had similar outlooks to ourselves.

My immediate and wider family were part of the second innermost band, which I would describe as the Conservative Protestants. We were less strident and doctrinaire and more likely to be involved in community life than our brethren in the innermost band, the Fundamentalist Protestants, but thought of ourselves as being more faithful and correct in our expression of the Christian faith than the group immediately beyond us, the Nominal Protestants, many of whom only intermittently, if ever, attended church. We certainly saw ourselves as being very different to those in the outermost band, who would nowadays be referred to as the PINOs (Protestants In Name Only).

Despite the dubious regard held for the theological position of those in this fourth band, they at least fell within the realm of general acceptance in matters of religion. On the outer edge of the circumference of this ring was a very clear line of demarcation. Beyond this dwelt a whole range of groups who were considered to simply be wrong in matters of faith. Most obvious and locally visible of these were the Catholics, but the reaches beyond the fourth band also contained those of Other Faiths and those of No Faith. They were generally considered collectively as a job lot of Error.

It appears to be a peculiarly human tendency to identify and defend differences between ourselves and others in order to provide ourselves with reassurance regarding our worth. Even if we are not completely sure about our views or whether they are correct, so long as we can identify differences between ours and those held by others, which we see as wrong, things are more-or-less okay. The history of religion, including Christianity, unfortunately provides as many sorry examples of this approach and its negative impact on society as virtually any other aspect of life.

My experience of this as a child was more one of indifference to and general lack of engagement with those seen as different — a polite and cautious wariness rather than overt prejudice or sectarianism. It was nonetheless a real and pervasive way of thinking that I needed over time to move on from. The more recent, predominantly conservative, political cynicism of attempting to leverage electoral advantage from demonising those of different faiths or cultures is an unfortunate reminder of this. In all cases, the impact of such actions, not only on those targeted but on society more broadly, is decidedly negative.

My early faith was also characterised by a strong emphasis on and understanding of an unchanging God, which frequently led to a stated or presumed proposition that His followers also should be unchanging. Having arrived at a position on a matter of faith, openness to different points of view was not actively encouraged, presumably because this presented the risk of views forming that could be different to those prevailing in the group at that time. This approach occurred in parallel with support by many Conservative Protestants for the conservative side of politics — personified in East Gippsland by local politicians representing the Country Party — and the outcome was that faith and politics in my youth were heavily based on continuity and lack of change. The link between Christian faith, social conservatism and support for conservative politics was strong.

Personal understandings regarding God in this environment were also accompanied by a high degree of certainty. Positions were arrived at regarding what was correct in matters of faith or interpretation, and these were then held on to with great tenacity, to the exclusion of alternative views or even the possibility of there being any. Doubt was avoided or at least seldom admitted.

While a personal understanding of faith was perceived to be essential, in practice there were reasonably well-prescribed lines of belief within which this personal faith would be expected to fall for Conservative Protestants. Traversing too far from that subliminally understood norm would be resisted, and maybe even result in suspicions from others that one was moving towards the Nominal Protestant circle or even (heaven forbid!) beyond.

These norms were evidenced as much by practices or, more particularly their avoidance, as by beliefs. As well as adherence to what were seen as appropriate theological tenets, the evidence was frequently focused on what was *not* done — smoking, drinking, swearing, gambling, dancing, sex outside of marriage — rather than on what *was* done. Even though there was support given for some forms of 'doing', via social service activities, for example, for many Conservative Protestants these were given reduced prominence lest one be thought to overly emphasise the 'social gospel', which was seen as a pale and inferior imitation of the 'real gospel'.

Looking back from my current understanding of faith and life, these outlooks appear almost quaint, but they were nonetheless very real and strongly held at the time. They were also well defended. I recall the level of concern expressed by many in the Presbyterian Church at Bairnsdale when an 'It's Time' sticker appeared on the rear of the local minister's car in 1972. In 1975 I was at a church meeting in Warragul, just prior to the dismissal of the Whitlam government, when one of those present expressed the view that it was not possible to be both a Christian and to support the Labor Party. At the time this didn't cause any comment, probably because there were so few of us present who were going to have to make a call regarding our voting intentions if that observation was true.

Change is a constant and expected part of life, both in what we experience and how our personalities and perspectives develop over time. Despite this, we appear to find it much easier to deal with change in some aspects of our lives than we do in others. Although we may resent it and employ various means to lessen or stave off its impact, we accept as inevitable and normal that as we age our physical appearance and capabilities will change. We look back on earlier times probably with affection but accept, begrudgingly or otherwise, that physical changes we are experiencing are a natural part of life's journey. We view such changes in others with similar equanimity.

We seem not to be as sanguine about changes in the emotional, intellectual or spiritual understandings of ourselves or others. There appears to be an unstated expectation that these perspectives should be more immutable, less changeable and more constant in their expression than the physical characteristics of life. Admittedly, we have choice in how our outlook on life develops while our physical ageing is largely predetermined, but the comparison remains valid.

This resistance to change, or the perception that it is intrinsically something to be wary of, is probably more evident in established environments such as churches or other Christian organisations than in many others, but I believe this remains a generally accurate observation in many aspects of life. One needs only to observe the negative delight of opponents if a politician's opinion can be shown to have moved even marginally from one that they had expressed years earlier, often in quite different circumstances.

In considering my own journey in these areas, I have regularly discovered how much my outlook in many of them has modified over the years. I originally tended to feel mildly disquieted by this, perhaps even a degree of embarrassment when looking back that my views could have been as they were earlier in my life, or that they have evolved to what they are now.

Logically there is no reason for this of course, in the same way there is no need to feel in the least embarrassed or apologetic that my hair was once black rather than its current grey. Time and experience bring change and we should expect, celebrate and make the most of it. I believe life can only be led honestly in accord with the understanding and principles one has at that time, and I don't believe it is sensible to expect that this understanding should not change, nor to lament retrospectively if it does.

When I was younger, based on the general examples and experiences I had grown up with, I identified most strongly with the evangelical strand of Protestant Christianity. Over time I became less comfortable with this. I found that adherence to what I increasingly perceived as a limiting, constrained and formulaic view of life and faith to sit uneasily with me, to the point that I now find myself some way removed from that.

This trend has been driven by a range of factors, mostly relating to the differences I have found in my lived experiences compared to the rather static and partial perspective I believed was being presented. I have also grown to believe, based on experience and observation, that the politically conservative right is in many instances a malign influence in the democratic world. I regularly find the rhetoric and behaviour of those of this persuasion to be at odds with my understanding of Christianity and the alignment of, and support from, evangelical Christian groups with some of the more extreme of these perspectives has increased my inclination to distance myself from them.

INTERLUDE C Faith

Time and life's experiences have led me to having different views to those I previously held on numerous matters, including those related to faith. I expect this would be an experience common to many. My faith views are now generally less certain and more open to the possibility of alternative perspectives than they once were, and I am also less certain than I previously was that they will not evolve further in the future. But rather than seeing this as a problem as I once may have, I view it as a positive and an exciting aspect of whatever period of life I have ahead of me.

There are a number of matters which I could use to illustrate this, but one issue on which I formed a view and which led to particular actions was that of playing sport on Sunday. This may be perceived as a lower-order issue and may cause little concern today, but at the time I was playing sport I found it to be one that I needed to think through carefully and act on accordingly.

Initially it was not really an issue for me, as it was very rare for sporting matches to be played on Sunday while I was growing up. Life and its various activities were more set and compartmentalised than is now the case. Sport in country areas was almost exclusively played on Saturdays. Even Test cricket matches had a rest day on Sunday until well into the 1970s and VFL football did not begin to be regularly played on Sunday until the 1980s. However, as Sunday sport become more widely embraced and my sporting involvements increased, I found I needed to consider my approach to it.

The Conservative Protestant view was no doubt that Sunday was a day of rest and, although as I grew up my family were far less strict in observance of this than some, it was still a view that was broadly embraced. I therefore commenced my consideration of the issue from that base, and I have no doubt that this influenced my decision as much as any other factor.

As I began to form my own views on matters of faith and the practical impact of them for me, I became increasingly convinced that an important aspect was not simply the issue of what I *believed*, but more importantly what I *did* as a consequence of this belief. If faith was to mean anything to me, I believed it should be visible and observable, and it was also important to me personally that I should consistently live according to my views and principles. This obviously had impacts far more broadly than in my reaction to playing sport on Sunday, but because of the public nature of sport, particularly in smaller country communities, and the profile I developed because of my participation in it, this became the focus for a degree of attention.

Inevitably, as I began to consider this matter in my late teens and early twenties, I retained a hangover from my youthful experience and understandings, but I also came to the view that retaining Sunday as a day apart was one way in which I could demonstrate my faith and priorities, and that these principles meant something to me. I was actively involved in Christian activities, such as youth groups. I attended church on Sunday mornings, was involved in church governance, taught Sunday school, and on occasions had related involvements on Sunday afternoons. These were important to me, so I chose to make myself unavailable to play sport on Sundays.

I didn't attempt to convince anyone else of the position I had taken nor, I hope, did I portray it as a superior point of view or one that others should embrace. It was simply a choice I made in response to my understanding of my faith. In that sense it was one that I needed to remain comfortable with and to be consistent in its application, irrespective of the views of others.

My playing team sport meant it was not as simple as this, of course, and I was aware of the impact my personal decision had on others involved with the teams I played for, from players to supporters. I always made it clear to clubs that I joined what my approach was, and I obviously had to accept the response of the clubs regarding whether they selected me in various games or not.

Melbourne Herald, 2 August, 1980

My decision not to play on Sunday did have some impact on my sporting involvement which, given my keenness for football and cricket, naturally caused me some disappointment at the time. I was unavailable for selection for inter-league cricket, which was almost exclusively played on Sunday, or for inter-league football on the occasions these matches were played on Sunday. In a couple of seasons at Leongatha, I missed early football finals because they were played on a Sunday, then returned for later finals played on a Saturday. In cricket finals, played on both days of the weekend, I was most commonly selected but played only on Saturdays. On one occasion the choice was made not to select me for a cricket grand final, which I was disappointed with at the time but fully understood.

I can recall no occasion when I had negative views expressed directly to me by team-mates regarding my not playing on Sunday, although I would be surprised if it did not frustrate some. The same is true for officials and supporters. I had a number from all these groups over the years express to me the view that while they neither understood nor agreed with my position, they respected the fact that I remained consistent in it.

Understandably, because it was so uncommon, opposing teams and their supporters also came to know of my stance on this matter. I heard only occasional comments from them, either on the ground or over the fence, sometimes bemused — 'Ya wouldn't reckon that bastard went to church, wouldya?' sometimes derisory — 'Your religion won't do you any good now, McRae,' and sometimes humorous — 'Must be Sunday is it, McRae? You haven't had a kick!'

On one occasion I had loaned my sprigged cricket boots to fellow Nerrena fast bowler Brian 'Ernie' Salmon to wear on the Sunday of a final. As he delivered his first ball, he slipped and fell at the bowling crease. Watching from the boundary, another Nerrena club member, Paddy Cummins, always one for a pithy comment, yelled out, 'I told you not to use Tractor's boots, Ernie — they don't play on Sundays.'

Over time, following retirement from competitive sport, my opinion changed on this issue. I still maintain the view that faith should be evident primarily in actions arising from that faith, rather than simply from beliefs and tradition. I retain the view that it is important for an individual to demonstrate by the way they live the principles that are important to them, and for their interactions with others to reflect this. But I don't now see refraining from playing sport on Sunday as a way in which I would do that.

Given the scale of the issue at times when I was playing sport, this may appear as a belated admission of error, but I don't believe that is so. I don't regret the position I took at the time and am pleased that I remained true to it, but it is simply not one that I would take now with my current understanding of Christian faith.

INTERLUDE D

An amazing match

The following was written in the early 1980s, at a time when Australia's performances in world sport were going through a decidedly low period.

No cricket match I have been associated with has been as amazing as the one I played in December 1961.

Cricket at that time was back on the map, following the visit from the West Indies the season before and Australia's retention of the Ashes in England during the year. Perhaps it was this surge in enthusiasm for the game that led to a Saturday morning competition being organised for primary schools in the Bairnsdale area that year; whatever the reason, we boys were very excited at the prospect.

The instigator of the competition was Don McGregor. Don was a cricket-playing teacher from the central Bairnsdale Primary School, known locally as 'seven five four', its number on the register of Victorian primary schools. To a young boy attending the smaller Bairnsdale West school, he and the school at which he taught were both highly imposing. He was coach of the 754 tumbling and gymnastic team, the best in the district. He was coach of the 754

INTERLUDE D   *An amazing match*

football team, which beat us and everyone else they played during the year. He was pictured in the local paper following a particularly fine series of scores he had made in the local cricket competition that year. In short, Don McGregor appeared a cut above anybody we had at 'our' school.

Despite this, we boys were happy just to have a game of cricket, and reckoned Mr McGregor was a pretty good bloke for organising the competition. Besides, he was one of the best cricketers in the district — I knew that because I heard the barber I attended at the time tell the person in the chair next to me that he was — and it was always good to be involved with a local celebrity.

(Incidentally, have you ever pondered the damage done to the fabric of our society by unisex hair salons? They are a frail and insipid reflection of a more robust past, the endless anonymous muzak piped around their walls a sad commentary on their lack of individuality and character.

(Time was when a visit to have your hair cut resulted not only in the removal of some unwanted thatch, but also the gathering of information and opinions essential to the smooth running of the country. Barbers then were men with strongly-held and often-voiced opinions on all matters of substance and consequence — football, racing, cricket, tennis and boxing. For six bob you could have almost all your hair removed — short back and sides, or shorter, were the options — and receive the bonus of being informed on a whole range of important local and national matters.

(The relative numbers of New South Welshmen and Victorians in the Test side, the need to play so-and-so at centre half forward this year, or the absurdity of not selecting what's-his-name for the Davis Cup were all discussed comprehensively and with authority.

(Conversations were carried on above the carefully tonsured head of younger patrons. When they were considered old enough — roughly the time it first became necessary to shave the bum-fluff on their neck following the haircut — they may be drawn into the discussion. The proximity of the gleamingly sharp cut-throat razor invariably meant the opinions they expressed bore a striking resemblance to those already proffered by the barber.

(There can be little doubt that the slow decline in Australia's performances on the world sporting stage in recent years can be directly attributed to the decline in the number of barbers. How selectors could possibly pick a side capable of winning any important match in any sport without advice from a suitable barber is beyond me.)

However, I digress.

When this competition in Bairnsdale started, it soon became obvious to even the most hopeful participant just where the balance of power lay. Being one of the two largest schools in the district, we were required to field two sides, as were 754. The big difference was that we had around eight or nine 'good' cricketers, while 754 had seemingly 15 or 20. The other two sides — St Mary's ('the Catholics') and Lucknow/Paynesville — fielded one side each and, it transpired, had fewer 'good' cricketers than even we had.

Our chances of fielding a competitive Number 1 side appeared quite good, although we would never have been a match for 754's best side. These hopes were dealt quite a blow, however, when Bert Cliff, the teacher who took on the job of looking after our teams in the competition, decreed that one of our 'good' players had to play for our Number 2 side, to make them at least slightly respectable. No amount of reasoning or complaining on our part would dissuade him from this.

This decision was a severe and apparently fatal blow to our chances of success in the competition. The strength of the 754 Number 1 side was such that we needed all our 'good' players if we were to be even mildly competitive. The stupidity of the decision became even more obvious when we were allocated a fleet-of-foot, pleasant but limited cricketer, Les Howlett, to compensate for the 'good' player we were forced to concede to our Number 2 side.

Les was a good bloke, a good runner and footballer, and very keen on being part of the cricket competition. But cricket wasn't his game. Any fieldsman in the general area of the pitch was in grave danger when Les bowled. He was an acquisition when it came to chasing balls in the field and throwing them into the wicketkeeper but had serious deficiencies when it came to actually stopping a ball hit towards him. When he batted it was a rare occurrence for him to lay bat on ball. Had it been possible, he would not have been sent out to bat in a match — he was an ideal number-13 batsman.

Despite this handicap, our team could be described as reasonable. We had a few steady batsmen, a handy wicketkeeper and a fair attack. True, we fell away a bit in the later-order batting, and our attack was limited in number and variety, but for a primary school side we were alright. I had the considerable honour of being elected as captain of the side.

The 754 Number 1 team on the other hand were awesome. They were led by a bespectacled lad who was thought by us not to be the popular choice of the team he led. He was a good bowler, good batsman and good boy. He was by repute 'brainy', but he didn't play football during the winter, so was considered by some not to be a 'real' boy. All this was of small consequence, though. Such was the strength of the side that captaincy decisions and the ability to inspire the team to greater effort were immaterial.

The side's batting was tremendously strong. In many games only the top order was required and getting a good score on the board was never a problem for them. Scoring as many was always a problem for their opposition. Their bowling was magnificent, led by one of the local toughs who bowled at a frightening pace. Even if it had been possible to make runs against him, most opposing batsmen would have thought twice before doing so; the dangers of being 'got' in the future on some deserted street militated against any free-scoring heroism.

The early games went much as expected. We were trounced by 754 Number 1 first up, then won the next couple of matches; it was obvious we would make the finals. This realisation called for some ingenious activity. Perhaps if we could go to 'Old Cliffy' and get Les Howlett to say that he would prefer to play in our Number 2 side, we could then reasonably suggest that the best player in that side should move up to our team. This seemed like a brilliant idea, which would improve our chances considerably in the forthcoming finals.

The task of getting Les to consider the team's interests above his own was not easy, but was achieved with some backroom (behind the shelter sheds) negotiations that would have done any group proud. The number of marbles that changed hands has never been disclosed.

Our efforts were in vain, however, as the deputation sent to negotiate the deal met with a firm negative response. The lack of

INTERLUDE D *An amazing match*

absolute enthusiasm in Les's presentation of his request for demotion was thought to be at least partly responsible for this.

Our fate was therefore sealed. We finished second on the ladder, won our first final against the 754 Number 2 side, then faced the formality of defeat in the grand final against their undefeated Number 1 side.

The day of reckoning dawned. Boys in white shirts, shorts and sandshoes pedalled their way to the ground, where the respective camps set themselves up an appropriate distance apart. A good number of parents lined the perimeter of the ground in their cars.

Don McGregor came over to wish us well and toss the coin. I happened to win the toss and sent the opposition in. (There was no suggestion that there might have been something 'in' the malthoid strip, but at least batting second put off the task of facing their demon bowler for a bit longer.)

Fielding and bowling better than we had in any previous match, we restricted our opposition to just over sixty runs. This wasn't a bad effort, but the total was still more than twice what we could reasonably expect to make.

With resignation and a fair degree of trepidation, we began our innings. Time ticked away, our score rose slowly and, surprisingly, our wickets fell only occasionally. But then the inevitable happened: we lost two wickets in successive balls and a further wicket in the same over, to be left with half the side out, Les Howlett still to bat, and still needing over forty runs to win.

It was at this stage that 'Old Cliffy' came up with a suggestion. We had one batsman who had been in for a while, handling the job reasonably well. Why not send Les in now? You never know, he might happen to stay there for a short while.

This suggestion was greeted with disbelief and scepticism. However, as those of us who *knew* the game could all see that Les was unlikely to make any runs wherever he batted, the course of action was agreed to, on the basis that we didn't have anything to lose.

Thus, Les marched out to meet his fate.

The 754 demon was at his fastest, but Les managed to survive the over. The move had succeeded — any extra time he stayed there was a bonus!

Our batsman at the other end saw out the next over, so Les was now back in action. He had an unorthodox back-lift which went approximately towards point, following which he took his bat in an arc towards mid-wicket. His footwork usually took him in the direction of square leg, the speed of his retreat being directly proportional to the speed of the bowler.

Despite these apparent deficiencies in his technique, he somehow began to get his bat in the way of the ball. What's more, he started to make a few runs. He retreated quickly to square leg as the demon released the ball and drove the delivery with great assurance through the slips. He cringed in front of the stumps, held his bat hopefully forward, and glanced the ball to the fine leg boundary. He late cut a well-pitched-up delivery on his leg stump with the action of a person who had just discovered a snake on the ground at his feet.

As the runs mounted and the demon fumed, we looked on in astonishment. Les's previous batting achievements had been measured in terms of the number of times he hit the ball, not the number of runs he made. Yet here he was carving up the most feared bowler in the competition and carrying us towards an improbable victory.

INTERLUDE D *An amazing match*

As the on-field events unfolded, activity on the sidelines also mounted. Don McGregor rose from his seat and began to pace the boundary line. Parents from both parties increased the volume and frequency of their advice. Those of us who had been dismissed whooped with delight as every run was made.

Drinks were called for and advice passed on both to the batsmen and the fielding captain. The instructions to the fielding team had obviously been that the demon bowler be removed from the attack — what! He was dispatched, sulking, to the outfield. Realising his reputation, none of us greeted this move with the cheers it deserved.

Nothing the fielding side did had any effect, though. Les continued to get at least some portion of his bat to every ball he needed to. His partner was as solid as ever. Inexorably, our score rose, to the stage where we dared to believe we might even win the game.

Our recent efforts to rid the side of Les were forgotten. Protests made at the suggestion that he bat up the list were put from our minds as we prepared to acclaim him as our hero. This we did shortly afterwards, when the winning run was hit and Les walked from the ground, smiling with a mixture of embarrassment and self-satisfaction. He had 35 runs against his name in the exercise book that contained the score.

A most unlikely victory had been achieved largely through the efforts of a person whose lack of aptitude for the game was obvious to all. But was it?

Bert Cliff sat relatively quietly through all these events, although his pleasure at our victory was obvious. His guidance of us through the season, his refusal to bend in the face of protests regarding the make-up of our team, and his suggestion on altering the batting order in the grand final all had the mark of genius about them.

It was only in later years that I worked out the secret of his success.

Without wishing to be personal, it is fair to say that Bert had a rather broad part in the middle of his hair. Despite this, or maybe because of it, he kept the hair that he did have closely cropped and neatly combed. It was seldom allowed to show even a semblance of unruliness.

I have no doubt that before he told us to keep Les in the side and on the Friday night before the grand final, Bert had been along to his barber.

INTERLUDE E

Rolling the arm over

Having had the experience of playing competitive cricket at the end of Grade 6, I was keen to continue that the following year. Similar to football, there was no junior cricket competition in Bairnsdale at that time, but the Bairnsdale Cricket Association commenced a C Grade competition in 1962/63 which I believed I may be able to participate in.

I think probably because of next-door neighbour Eddie Edsall's involvement with Wy Yung, I decided to join that club. Wy Yung was not the closest club to home, and Eddie played for only a short while, but I soon settled into the club and the competition. The Technical School entered a club in C Grade a couple of years later, but by then I was well involved at Wy Yung and chose not to move.

At that stage the club's ground was behind the Wy Yung Pub. The malthoid pitch — a thin bituminous layer covering a concrete base — ran east/west along the highest point of a ridge, with the ground sloping down from the pitch on either side, particularly to the south. The curve in the ground was such that players on the northern boundary were visible only above the ankles to shorter players on the southern boundary. When I joined, Wy Yung fielded B and C Grade teams, but soon after began fielding a side in the A

Grade competition (not that this was of any consequence to me at that stage).

Practice was on Tuesday and Thursday evenings. Living in West Bairnsdale meant that I rode my bike down the Pound Swamp hill (unsealed at that stage), and then up the hill from the Mitchell River to the ground behind the pub. The task was done in reverse following training. Although not a great distance — only between two and three kilometres — the hills made it a task not to look forward to, particularly on the return journey. I was always keen for one of the senior players, John Goodman, to be along at training, as I was able to put my bike in the back of his ute and get a ride home from training whenever that occurred.

The C Grade competition commonly comprised teams with a majority of players from around 12 to 18 years of age, with a few older players, some of whom had been good cricketers in their younger days and others who had never 'troubled the scorers' in that regard. It was a good environment in which to learn.

The Woodwards were a prominent Wy Yung family and a number played with the cricket club at that time. Bill Woodward was the captain and mentor of the C Grade team for some seasons after I commenced playing, and I have very fond memories of his participation and guidance during that time. It was also well before the heightened focus on road safety and before seatbelts became a feature of vehicles. I am sure the number of young players crammed into his Mini for trips to places such as Paynesville, Fernbank, Glenaladale, Lakes Entrance and Bruthen went well beyond what was recommended even then.

At the time, almost all cricket gear used at practice and in matches was supplied by the club. There was a noticeable hierarchy and

INTERLUDE E *Rolling the arm over*

sequence to this, with newer gear going to the B Grade side, while C Grade used that which had been passed down from that side or continued to make do with existing gear. Usually, by the time it was discarded, it was in quite poor condition; gear for practice was often of a similar standard.

It was common not to have sufficient gear to fully equip three batsmen at the same time during a game — two batting and one ready to do so. Items such as helmets and thigh pads were unheard of, but even supplying the basics of bats, pads, gloves and protector ('box') was regularly a challenge. On many occasions a dismissed batsman would be waylaid on his way off the ground to pass over a bat or pad, a batting glove or two, or a box to his replacement. If you were the new batsman in such circumstances, it was always good if the dismissed batsman had not made too many runs and got the gear too sweaty, particularly for the latter two items.

In my earlier days in C grade, it was not uncommon to see players batting with a pad only on their front leg or batting without gloves and being apparently quite comfortable with this. If the opposing clubs were similar to ours in their access to gear, they probably looked at this as making a virtue out of necessity. I often reflect on this when I watch players in the lower levels of the suburban competition that my son Ewen plays in. To watch even some lower-order batsmen delve into their personal kit-bag, often larger than the club kit-bags I was originally familiar with, and array themselves with their own bat, helmet, box, sweat bands, inner and outer batting gloves, and thigh pads on both legs before going out to bat, emphasises the differences between the times.

I don't recall our C Grade team ever playing in the finals, but I certainly enjoyed getting into cricket in that way. I wasn't sure which aspect of the game I most enjoyed or should concentrate most on, so tried a number. As well as the obligatory batting, I can recall attempting to bowl both off and leg spin in matches, probably with limited success. I also spent a full season early on as a wicketkeeper, although not being requested to do the job the following season is adequate comment on the success of that effort.

By the time I reached around 15 years of age, I had settled on batting and medium-pace bowling as the focus of my endeavours. Both were done sufficiently well to maintain a place in the team, but it wasn't until I had a spurt of growth during my first year at Dookie College, when I was 16, that I began to find that I could bowl a bit quicker.

Dookie College at that stage fielded a team in the Lake Rowan and District Cricket Association (LRDCA), along with teams such as Devenish, Thoona, Glenrowan, St James, Bungeet and Lake Rowan. There was a good oval and facilities at the college along

Dookie Agricultural College, Premiers,
Lake Rowan and District Cricket Association, 1967/68
Back: Alastair Kensley, Tom Macdonald, Chris Otto, Nigel Smith,
Rob Knight, Chris McRae, Russell Allison Front: Greg Kotschet,
Ian McKenzie, Rod Ackland, Peter Howes (Captain)

with a turf pitch — the only one in the Association — and conditions for cricket were certainly an improvement on those I had experienced at Wy Yung.

The 1967/68 season was a successful one for Dookie College, who won their first ever premiership in the LRDCA, beating Devenish in the grand final. I played as a lower order batsman and didn't bowl.

There were sufficient numbers of students and staff in season 1968/69 to enable the college to form a second team, which was called Currawa. The Association was obviously able to accommodate this new team, as it played in the same competition as the college's senior team and was effectively a second eleven to it. It was the side that I became a part of and, for the first time, I began to bowl a reasonable amount in most matches.

Currawa had only moderate success during the season, but at least it meant that most students who wished to play could do so each week. The senior team was more successful, being defeated in the grand final. This was the year that I began to consistently open the bowling for clubs that I played with, a role that I continued largely until I retired from the game.

Most clubs we played against had malthoid pitches, but Bungeet used a pitch consisting of coir matting stretched over an anthill base. Prior to each game, the base would be scraped and smoothed using a steel tractor wheel turned on its side and pulled along the length of the pitch by a tractor or ute. Two coir mats would then be stretched over this base and held down with pegs driven into the ground along their edges. There was a small area of the base left uncovered in the middle where the two lengths of matting didn't quite meet.

The turf pitch at the college was generally in good condition and the ground almost always retained a better covering of grass than others in the Association. Bruno Serek, the groundsman, was very diligent in attempting to provide good conditions for a game and the college oval was certainly the highest standard ground on which we played.

I played two full seasons while at Dookie, in addition to the second half of 1966/67 and the first half of 1969/70 seasons. The cricket was of a reasonable standard, with most teams having some very good players but tailing away a bit after that. Opponents I particularly recall from my time there, were Bill and Ray Irvine, and Bill McLauchlan from Lake Rowan, the Lidgerwoods — Lockie, Peter and Rob — as well as Geoff Dalton from St James, and Bill Sammon from Bungeet.

In one of the last games I played on the college oval in late November 1969, I collected the only hat-trick of my career as part of a nine-wicket haul against St James, again the highest number of wickets I ever took in an innings. Along with the premiership from 1967/68, it was a good experience with which to remember my involvement in cricket at Dookie College.

Following my time at Dookie, I worked at Bairnsdale for a year and then spent three years at Melbourne University, returning to Bairnsdale during vacations. I therefore recommenced my association with Wy Yung and, given the university timetable, it was possible to play close to a full season of cricket at Wy Yung during the summer recess. The club by this stage had relocated to a ground on the flats near the Lind Bridge over the Mitchell River, a significantly improved facility compared to its previous home, and again with a malthoid pitch.

Over the four seasons I played during this stint with the club their A Grade teams were captained by Jim Baylis and then Laurie Woodward, both fine cricketers. I recall only one season of participation in finals, but we were always very competitive and worthy of our place in the highest grade of the competition.

As in the Lake Rowan Association, most pitches at that stage in the Bairnsdale Association were malthoid, with only Bairnsdale, West End and Lindenow having turf pitches. It was always good to play on these, and the one at Lindenow had a deserved reputation as being particularly good.

My game developed further during this period with Wy Yung, particularly with bowling but also to some extent with batting, culminating in me winning the only club A Grade batting average I ever managed, batting in the upper order. This has always been a point of grateful bemusement to me, because I didn't have a sound enough technique to succeed regularly as a batsman, and in most subsequent seasons my occasionally providing mid-or lower-order runs was the extent of my batting contributions.

My time with Wy Yung came to an end with the 1974/75 season. By that stage I was living and working at Warragul and joined St Andrew's Cricket Club (now known as Western Park). I spent two seasons with them, both of which were very enjoyable even though we didn't reach the finals in either. The standard of cricket was comparable with that at Bairnsdale. Those whom I recall particularly, and had keen tussles with over those two seasons, include Alan Rankin from Trafalgar; Bob Mason, Kevin Kilday and John Crofts from Yarragon; Tom Carroll and Laurie Rippon from Drouin; Phil McKenzie from Nilma Dusties; and Neil Boxshall from Jindivick.

I won the St Andrew's bowling average and was selected in the Warragul Association team for Melbourne Country Week in both seasons, as well as winning the Association's Best and Fairest award in the second season, so I have fond memories of my time playing at Warragul.

Newspaper article from Warragul Gazette, 2 March 1976

Country Week cricket in Melbourne in February was a great experience, with a game played against another association each day from Monday to Thursday, then the final on Friday for the top two teams in each grade. A promotion/relegation system was in place from year to year. I was fortunate to collectively attend around eight Country Weeks with Warragul and Leongatha over the years, playing largely in A Section (although in my first year at Leongatha — 1976/77 — we played in Provincial, the top section, with the Leongatha Association having won that grade the previous year).

The standard of cricket was high and games were played predominantly on the grounds of District (now Premier) or Sub-District clubs. Playing against teams from large centres such as Geelong, Ballarat, Bendigo, Warrnambool or Wangaratta was a big task for sides from smaller towns such as Warragul or Leongatha, but both acquitted themselves well and during that time remained in the upper grades at Melbourne Country Week.

Early in the winter of 1976, I received a call from Ron Christofferson, a dairy farmer from Nerrena, a district just east of Leongatha. I didn't know him and had never heard of Nerrena. Ron was President of Nerrena Cricket Club, which played in the Leongatha and District Cricket Association (LDCA) and said he was keen to come and visit me. He said he understood I may be moving to Leongatha in time for the next cricket season. (Although not certain at that stage the move was likely, so the 'bush telegraph' was pretty accurate.)

Ron came across to Warragul one evening shortly afterwards, accompanied by Frank Welsford, Nerrena's coach at the time, and Noel Clark, a long-time player. At the end of our discussions, Ron tentatively enquired whether I would be prepared to sign and agree to play with Nerrena when I arrived in Leongatha. I was certainly intending to play cricket, but had thought no further ahead than that, so I was pleased to take up his offer.

It began another wonderful involvement with a sporting club, which I remain tremendously grateful to have experienced. I am sure I would have enjoyed wherever I played, but can't imagine any other club providing such a positive cricketing and personal outcome as has the Nerrena club over the years I have been associated with it.

Nerrena Cricket Club had been formed in 1935/36. Although they had won a B Grade flag in 1968/69, they were yet to have similar success in A Grade and were naturally keen to redress this shortcoming. They had a strong base for the team, had some good young players coming through, and had been active in recruiting.

At the end of the 1976/77 season, we finished on top of the ladder and played in the grand final. After we batted on the first day, the second was completely washed out. Having finished on top, we were awarded the premiership. It was great for the club to have won their first A Grade flag, although there was understandable disappointment that the second day's play wasn't possible.

The Nerrena home ground at the time was in a paddock on the property of Tom and Margaret Kindellan, on the road between Leongatha and Dumbalk. In some ways it reminded me of the Wy Yung ground I had commenced my career on, in the sense that it was not a conventional, flat sports oval. Rather than being on a ridge, this ground sloped gently from north to south, and when not being used for cricket was used to graze the Kindellans' sheep flock. There was a small shed that served as a storeroom, built beneath a somewhat underwhelming tree on the western end of the ground adjacent to a rudimentary scoreboard.

Although occasionally the butt of jokes from opposition players, the ground served cricket in the area very effectively from 1966 until 1980. At that stage a new ground was developed near the Nerrena Hall, on the site of the disused Nerrena Primary School, with the addition of some extra land donated by the adjoining Christofferson family. The current ground is a wonderful location for cricket and must have one of the best views, across the farmland and hills to the north, of any ground in the state.

I spent 13 seasons playing with Nerrena from 1976/77 until we moved from Leongatha to Maffra in 1989. During that period, the club won six A Grade premierships and has since won two more. I concluded my time at Nerrena having moved down to B Grade, but was pleased to have won the A Grade bowling average

INTERLUDE E   *Rolling the arm over*

Nerrena Cricket Club, first 'A' Grade Premiership side, Leongatha and District Cricket Association, 1976/77
(photo: courtesy Leongatha Historical Society)
Back: Cameron Kindellan, Clive Salmon, Ian Salmon, Chris McRae,
Graeme Salmon (Captain), George Torcutti
Front: Rod Walker, Ron Adkins, Frank Welsford (Coach), Noel Clark,
Steve Lincoln, Russell Harrison

for the club on a few occasions and twice for the Association. The second of these — 37 wickets at an average of 5.4 in 1980/81 — was recognised at the 1994 centenary celebrations of the LDCA as the 'best season bowling average' for the Association over the previous 100 years.

It is interesting to reflect on what makes some country sporting clubs successful and enduring while others are less so. In the case of Nerrena, no other cricket club in the district, which played in the competition when Nerrena was formed, is still in existence. Some have disappeared entirely, while others have merged or

A bit of this and that

> PAGE 34 — "THE STAR", Tuesday, January 20, 1981
> • L.D.C.A. "A" GRADE
> # 'TRACTOR' POWER
> Tractor McRae had a field day against R.S.L. and finished the day with 7/7 as R.S.L. was slaughtered by Nerrena.
> They could only score a trifling thirty all-out in a display of ineptitude against the sheer pace and aggression of this mild mannered "quickie".

Newspaper article from Leongatha Star, 20 January 1981.

modified in some other way. The LDCA has changed considerably and now covers a far greater geographic area in South Gippsland than was previously the case, but still Nerrena continues and thrives after almost 90 years.

Even though it is impossible to be certain on the reasons for this, I suggest a few potential options. Being close to, but a little separate from, the town of Leongatha is an advantage — they can obtain most of the benefits of the town without having to directly compete with other clubs in it for support and profile.

They have very strong family affiliations, with names such as Clark, Christofferson, Salmon, Kindellan, Trease, Bolge, Riseley and Wightman being prominent. It would be impossible to quantify the respective range and cumulative contributions of these families to the success of the club during its history, but it means that the contributions of others are built on an already strong base.

Even something seemingly as mundane as the Nerrena Hall being available (when many similar district halls have closed), provides the opportunity for events to be held and a meeting place for people, all of which are fundamental to supporting any community of interest. Whilst functions associated with country sporting clubs may ostensibly be focussed on celebrating or commemorating activities of the teams themselves, their positive impacts are far broader than this.

The community benefits derived from locals gathering at such events are immeasurable, and I have many great memories of being present at country halls full of good people doing just that. This also enhances the support for the club and its functions from those in the surrounding district, even if they have no other direct association with it.

Doubtless there are numerous other factors, including a bit of good fortune involved as well, but this latter cause generally serves only as a bonus, rather than a driver of success. The heart of the club's fortunes has been the benefit it brings to many people and their willingness to support and contribute to it, and I certainly derived much more than I contributed during my time there. I expect many others would have had a similar experience.

In looking at my time at Nerrena, playing with the Salmon brothers — Graeme ('Grubby'), Brian ('Ernie'), Ian ('Curley') and Clive — was a highlight. All were tremendous all-round cricketers, they and their families were great people to have supporting the club, and they were a major factor in its success before, during and after my time there. I consider myself very fortunate to know and to have played sport with all of them, both at Nerrena and at the Leongatha Football Club.

Comparisons can be odious, but I assess my time playing in the LDCA as being the highest standard of club cricket that I experienced. It was during this time also that I encountered both Graham Challis, the best cricketer I played against, and Brian Salmon, the best I played with.

A QUIET CHAMPION

(by Malcolm Conn)

Chris McRae would never admit he is a champion sportsman.

The 30-year-old Nerrena cricketer and former Leongatha footballer plays for the love of the game; but he plays it tough.

"I'm a competitor, I like to get stuck into anything I do."

Chris a beef husbandary officer, has been a part of Leongatha Football Club's success since he moved from Warragul four seasons ago. He was a member of Leongatha's '79 premiership team and played in Leongatha's losing grand-final side last season.

He is captain-coach of Meeniyan-Dumbalk this season, a challenge he is looking forward to.

The country-week fast bowler won the Leongatha and District Cricket Association bowling average with 37 wickets at an incredible 5.4 average.

Newspaper article from
South Gippsland Sentinel Times, 31 March 1981[12]

We moved to Maffra in 1989 where I played B Grade cricket for a season, but I retired in 1990 when we moved to Moora in Western Australia. It suited my work and our family circumstances better to do this, so I took up tennis as a means of retaining some involvement in sport. Initially this was only social tennis, but after one season the lure of competition prevailed and I began playing B Grade pennant tennis with Moora. This continued with Chiltern Valley when we moved to Rutherglen in 1994. I was fortunate to

---

12   Malcolm Conn began as a journalist at the 'Sentinel Times', later becoming chief cricket writer for News Corp. In 1999 he won a Walkley Award for his coverage of the dealings of 'John the bookmaker' with cricketers Shane Warne and Mark Waugh.

play in a premiership at both locations and enjoyed the physical and social aspects of the game, even though I had no background and limited skill in it.

As with football, I include below a couple of teams for cricket.

The first is a team chosen in 2000 as the best to that stage for Nerrena Cricket Club.

The second team I have included is comprised of the best club cricketers I played with during my time playing the game. I have listed it in batting order, with the same general caveat regarding my inclusion as I gave regarding the 'best played with' football team I included previously.

Nerrena Cricket Club team of the century (1935–2000)

Brian Salmon (c)
Alan Christoffersen
Noel Clark
Terry Clark
Bruno Croatto
Steve Lincoln
Chris McRae
Norm Munro
Claude Salmon
Clive Salmon
Graeme Salmon
Ian Salmon
Murray Wightman

Best played with

(Composite side of the best cricketers from the four clubs I played with, in batting order.)

1. Terry Clark (Nerrena)
2. Murray Wightman (Nerrena)
3. Steve Lincoln (Nerrena)
4. Tom Macdonald (Dookie College)
5. Mick Herrald (c) (Nerrena)
6. Ian Salmon (Nerrena)
7. Barry Morphett (Nerrena)
8. Brian Salmon (Nerrena)
9. Clive Salmon (Nerrena)
10. Chris McRae
11. Laurie Woodward (Wy Yung)

12th man Graeme Salmon (Nerrena)

INTERLUDE F

Some more poems

I was introduced to and became interested in poetry at a young age. Don was keen on it and I recall readings or recitals of 'Banjo' Paterson as bedtime stories on occasions at the Basin. I found I enjoyed poetry as a form of literature and eventually developed an interest in attempting to write some myself, which I did for a number of years. The following are some examples, with brief explanations where necessary of the circumstances under which they were written.

INTERLUDE F   *Some more poems*

To Alex on his 50ᵗʰ birthday

In youthful days I used to pine to be as old as you,
So I would have the chance to do the things I saw you do.
But times have changed and when I think of ages now I find
I'm quite content to tag along some fourteen years behind.

I'll try my best to not be rude nor draw to your attention
Some painful points which, though they're true, perhaps I shouldn't mention.
But I'll present this poem here in hopes you won't reject it,
And cast my mind back on your life as I can recollect it.

It seemed to me, in days gone by, that Father Time and you
Would never have a falling out as others seem to do.
I thought perhaps you may have reached some keenly-sought position,
So you'd forever keep your youth in its unchanged position.

But then, alas, there came the signs I'd all along been fearing
As, surreptitiously at first, I saw your pate appearing.
And then, to add momentum to the trend that had been started,
The hair remaining turned to white and gradually departed.

Still, nature has a marvellous way of balancing its debits,
When losses in a certain field are matched by others' credits.
And so with you, as quickly as your hair was dissipated
I saw, as if to compensate, your girth became inflated.

I noted this with some alarm and heard the dire predictions
Regarding those who grow too large, and their diverse afflictions.
But happily, the strokes and gout I feared may have assailed you
Were kept at bay, for then at least, because your teeth had failed you.

But this was just a short-term cure, and still grave fears existed
In case these dangers to your life in future years persisted.
But luck again was on your side, because your eyes grew dimmer
Which meant you couldn't see to eat, so gradually grew slimmer.

This happening seemed to put to rest all fear and apprehension
About your premature demise from some severe condition.
'Til rumours started surfacing, and are this day prevailing,
That sundry joints are showing signs of some arthritic failing.

Still, fifty years is quite a feat, deserving celebrations,
So I herewith send off to you my warm congratulations.
I only hope that, as I close and send this off to greet you,
That lack of further parts to fail won't finally defeat you.
—**Chris McRae**

INTERLUDE F *Some more poems*

A petition on behalf of some spurned friends

Howard Stevens, as with most things he took on, was a very diligent amateur beekeeper. During the time he was courting his future wife Lucy — he in Leongatha and she in Melbourne — he spent few weekends in Leongatha and his bees were neglected to an extent that caused him considerable and regular concern. It turned out the concern was shared by his bees. These verses were 'written' and mailed to him (Mr H Stevens, Apiarist, c/o Leongatha High School) by one of them, on behalf of the others, attempting to obtain more favourable consideration.

Among the hordes you house in hives I'm but a single member,
I'm not distinguished from the rest by size or rank or gender.
But fate this day's decreed that I the things below should mention,
So now I seek your listening ear and beg your full attention.

No worth nor reason lifts me to this high, exulted station,
Save that to me the lot was cast to voice the consternation
Of myriad beings of my ilk, who've served you without failing,
But now who view, with growing fear, a care from you that's ailing.

We view askance our hard-earned spoil, untouched since its extraction;
We see with shame the unfilled tins, mute signs of your distraction.
As o'er us hangs a cloud of doubt, an air of dark foreboding,
And memories bright of cared-for days each dreary week's eroding.

Time was when winter held us in not fear nor trepidation,
As sheltered from the chilly blast we spend its bleak duration.
Then hale and hearty from its throes, foretelling coming pleasure,
We into spring with joy did wing, to fill our stores with treasure.

But now, alas, this year we feel that chilly, dread sensation,
As biting winds and sleet assail our dreary habitation.
Still stoically we face this time, cold winter's hungry hours,
And forward cast a longing eye for spring's content and flowers.

The beauty of fair Lucy's form it's not our place to question,
Nor do we doubt the rightful sway she holds on your attention.
Our only plea (and here with care I choose my words discreetly),
Is don't erase us from your mind, nor cast us off completely.

We seek no more of time nor care than we were once accorded,
But covet still the kindly hours in days gone past awarded
To us for all our honest toil, that saw our hives o'erflowing,
And drew from you those sought-for words, a tribute warm and glowing.

It's not with rage I bring to you this heartfelt, poor petition;
I simply seek your cognisance of our reduced position.
And if perchance, by willpower's might, you're found in this location
Some weekend hence, be pleased to grace us with a visitation.
  —*Chris McRae*

INTERLUDE F   *Some more poems*

The big match

Written as part of my best man's speech for the wedding of Howard and Lucy Stevens, being a description of a wedding as seen through the eyes of a particularly keen but somewhat 'ocker' football follower.

For past years without number I'd awaken from me slumber,
And I'd head off to the footy every Sat'dee.
Where I'd chew me sausage roll up behind the outer goal,
And I'd barrack and abuse me team to vict'ry.

So I'd go home feelin' hoarse, splattered with tomater sauce,
And I'd watch the replay as I et me tea.
And the missus used to say, "Can't you find a better way
Than this, to spend your time each Saturdee?"

Well, I'm a cultured sorta bloke, so I listened when she spoke
To me about the way I spend me leisure.
And I started lookin' 'round for some other sportin' ground
Where the players give a loftier sorta pleasure.

I soon found a game to go to that you'd wear a tie and coat to,
And they used the local churches as the oval.
Where for some peculiar reason there was no partic'lar season,
And the captains all had contracts, called betrothal.

I've got followin' this caper, 'cos the pace is much sedater,
(Which suits us cultured blokes, the missus reckons.)
And although the game is slower the admission price is lower,
Which must be because they never play the seconds.

When the crowd from all around arrive and file into the ground
Things are tense, you reckon anythin' could happen.
So they draft 'em at the door, depending who they barrack for,
And they separate 'em, so's they don't get scrappin'.

There's a buzz of expectation as the crowd just sits there waitin'
And yer feel the tension gettin' ever keener.
'Cos the fans are tense and jumpy, 'til at last you see the umpy
Lead a team of blokes out on to the arena.

Then a hush falls on the crowd as the music strikes up loud,
And yer jostle to be in a good position.
When from the back of the arena comes the message,
"Someone's seen 'er."
And yer know that means, "Here comes the opposition."

There's a point that's worth a mention as yer feel the risin' tension,
And yer know the game can't be far off beginnin'.
At every match that I've attended since me footy days has ended,
The last team on the ground's composed of women.

And the captain, aw she's cunnin', 'cos she never comes in runnin'
Like she reckons she's a cert to win the bacon.
No, she bungs on that she's ailin', that her sight is poor and failin',
And she gets this bloke to lead her out to where they're waitin'.

So she waddles down the aisle with a faint, allurin' smile,
And a net around her head to give protection
From the bites of flies and mozzies, and the gaze of busybodies
Who would comment on the state of her complexion.

You should see the ump's surprise at the way this tart arrives!
(I s'pose he reckons she's too crook to be competin'.)
So he asks the leader bloke about 'er, and the crowd there in the outer,
If they reckon she should be 'ere at this meetin'.

But they don't seem concerned at the way events have turned
Or the fact that one team seems a trifle stronger.
The game's been talked about for weeks, so they just sit there in their seats,
Hopin' that the start won't be put off much longer.

So the teams stand there together, you see 'em strainin' at the tether,
And the umpy's got the job to smooth things over.
So he just starts quietly yappin' before a single thing can happen,
'Til yer see the captains smilin' at each other.

Then the umpy sez to both, "Will youse each now plight yer troth?"
And they answer with a squeak of affirmation.
So the captain of the women heaves 'er net back and she's grinnin'
As she gives the bloke a kiss of consolation.

Next the teams that are the drawcard have to go and sign the scorecard
To show the game was played the way it shoulda been.
And while this is goin' on they get someone to sing a song,
Which must be the theme song of the winnin' team.

But it seems not all the fans who are crammed there in the stands,
Are 'appy when they see this quiet transaction.
'Cos ev'ry Sat'dee without failin' comes the muffled sound of wailin'
From the mob that's sittin' closest to the action.

After the match there's a 'do' that the crowd's invited to,
And the tucker at the clubroom's somethin' splendid.
So the fans go home delighted at the way them troths were plighted,
And they're hopin' that the season hasn't ended.
—*Chris McRae*

INTERLUDE F   *Some more poems*

Musings of a flaccid feline

I was taken for a drive quite recently,
Where some fellow did a little job on me.
Now my anatomy's depleted in my private, nether reaches
But the reason for the op I can't quite see.

'Cause it's not as if some part was causing strife
Which may have forced me to request the surgeon's knife.
And he should have realised that those items he excised
Had never caused a moment's pain in all my life.

I've heard it said that ignorance is bliss,
But I doubt that that will be the case with this,
For although I'm still bemused and don't know quite what's been removed
I've a feeling that they're something that I'll miss.

For some changes have occurred which couldn't fail
To cause concern to those who listen to this tale;
As I just can't work out how to drop the squeak from my meow,
Or why my purr's an octave higher up the scale.

And my feelings, too, seem now to be awry;
I can't recapture that bright twinkle in my eye.
While those flutters of desire to be a most prolific sire
Are somewhat faded and I can't explain just why.

Still, I hope that things improve as time goes past –
That this aura of despond will fail to last –
And that quintessential drive which made me glad to be alive
Will not have disappeared forever with those parts.
  —Chris McRae

Aerobics — the last gasp.

In the early 1980s a gymnasium opened across the road from the Department of Agriculture offices in Leongatha. Attendance at aerobics classes became quite regular and popular among some staff, a source of amusement among others, and a matter for considerable banter around the office. This poem purported to be the experience of one of the attendees.

I'd just had a look in the mirror,
And seen to my shock and surprise,
That the bulk of the sight was my width, not my height,
And the flabby expanse of my thighs.

So, struck with a burning ambition
To be trendy, terrific and trim,
I hoisted my weight from its somnolent state
And waddled along to the gym.

Strange feminine sights met my vision
As I cautiously looked through the door.
All shapes, weights and sizes in modish disguises
Cavorted around on the floor.

I didn't much like the sight of the dancing,
The wriggles, the kicks and the skips.
But alas, I could see it would help one like me
To again find the bones in my hips.

Still, the thought of it all was appalling –
The puffing and panting and writhing.
And I questioned the worth of a much-reduced girth
If it meant prolonged sessions of jiving.

But I'd failed when I first viewed aerobics,
To see what its benefits are.
Though I soon was to find that these weren't confined
To reduction of avoirdupois.

In fact, fitness can hardly be seen as
The ultimate fruit of the visit.
As its major appeal is the pleasure you feel
At being quite trendy and 'with it'.

It's the place to be seen in attendance
If you wish to be socially 'in'.
'Cause the theatre, the races and other such places
Have now been replaced by the gym.

A bit of this and that

I've bid farewell to societal evenings,
To gatherings for gossip and cards.
And my excess of fat is now decked out in black
In the form of my new leotards.

I'm so glad that I made the decision
As it's lifted my social estate.
For it's now highly chic to be lithesome and quick
And to be quite concerned with your weight.

The music is rhythmic and constant
And the bodily movements quite tiring,
But the aerobics 'set' are too cultured to sweat –
Though they do quite a bit of perspiring.

In photos, the saints of aerobics
Smile sweetly across at each other.
From one wall of the gym Jane Fonda looks in,
While Olivia graces another.

And such is the force of their presence
That I'm winning the fight to be slim,
And I now look askance at the very real chance
That I'll soon have no need for the gym.

That fact by itself's not a worry —
I can't say I'd miss it at all –
But I know I'd be stunned to be socially shunned
By those whose weight still has to fall.

INTERLUDE F   *Some more poems*

Just fancy the stigma and trauma,
After all the demands had been heeded,
To find once you're slim that you're no longer 'in'
'Cause aerobics is no longer needed.

So I now have a plan that I'll follow
To ensure my continued approval,
And to make sure my waist will be always encased
By bulges in need of removal.

I'll replace my abstemious habits
With a ploy quite cunning and clever;
I'll eat like a horse, which will make sure of course
That I'll need my aerobics forever!
   —Chris McRae

Some anonymous advice

Tricia and I were married on the Saturday between the cricket and football seasons. This note was written to Tricia by an anonymous advisor, providing some first-hand experience of the pitfalls of marrying someone with sporting interests.

'Tis many years since I have walked the path that you now tread,
But still I've recollections of the time that I was wed.
That happy day seems now long gone, its vision fading fast,
As it's driven from my mem'ry by events that since have passed.

I tried my best, when in my youth, to be demure and sweet,
And longed to meet some handsome bloke who'd sweep me off my feet.
I thought I'd found the answer to my planning and my schemes
When I met a man who seemed to be the husband of my dreams.

He told me how he loved me with a deep sincerity;
How he cared for no one other, how he'd only eyes for me.
With youthful joy and innocence I pledged to be his bride,
But alas, once we were married, I discovered how he'd lied.

No sooner had we settled in our modest first abode
That out onto the cricket field my bold deceiver strode.
Despite our promised mutual love, fidelity and such,
I soon found out that these for him just didn't count for much.

INTERLUDE F *Some more poems*

The first day he arrived back home with news that left me cold –
He was bragging, unrepentantly, of maidens he had bowled.
Then with a quite disdainful air and smile upon his lips,
He told, without a trace of shame, how he'd performed in slips.

My broken heart and wounded pride had scarcely time to mend,
When a week had flown past me and I faced the next weekend.
But hopes of contrite penitence from him were sore misplaced
As again into another's arms my brazen husband raced.

Now I think her name was Bertha, but I couldn't vouch for that.
She quite plainly wasn't pretty; in fact, he said she was a bat.
But his air of feigned indifference made a very rapid switch
As he told of how he'd held her and gone waltzing down the pitch.

He informed me of an orgy that went on without respite,
How caresses through the covers caused him unrestrained delight;
While his tickles down the leg had been the best he'd felt about,
'Til at last he had to stop because some bloke had caught him out.

So I viewed the end of summer with considerable relief,
But I found the winter season simply added to my grief.
For the football field was now the spot he went to have a play,
And I followed his philandering in the papers of the day.

There were dreary little items of the way each game had gone,
How the locals would have won if their opponents weren't so strong.
But the news that I found galling and which left me quite dismayed
Were the regular descriptions of the way my husband played.

My suspicions rose abruptly, as you well may understand,
When they said that he was nifty, with a lovely pair of hands.
But I blanched in outright horror at his brash, audacious pranks
When reports were printed praising his performance 'round the flanks.

He showed scant regard for morals right throughout his football days,
'Til the years brought on retirement and a mending of his ways.
Then one day as he was chatting to some kindred sporting souls,
They enquired if he'd be int'rested to go along to bowls.

I was not at all concerned when he agreed to play this game,
As I thought that he'd have little chance of adding to my shame.
But again he took up antics quite devoid of care or pity
As he openly discussed his skill at lying close to kitty.

And so, my dear, as you embark upon your married course,
I sincerely hope your husband doesn't cause you such remorse.
But I urge you to be careful, if you find he's keen on sport,
As it's often not as innocent as first you may have thought.
—Chris McRae

INTERLUDE F *Some more poems*

On information to incoming batsmen

Not-out batsmen regularly pass on tips to an incoming batsman about what the bowlers are doing, and any other information they deem potentially useful to assist the new batsman. Sometimes this advice is useful, but it can never overcome the impact of the skill, or otherwise, of the batsman receiving it.

"Allow not for the swing," he said, "don't worry at the speed;
A steady eye and steady head is really all you'll need.
You'll find the bowling's mainly trash, there's not a cause for worry,
Just play your game and plug along and don't be in a hurry."

I took my stance with confidence, surveyed the situation,
And viewed the bowler's feeble looks with very great elation.
I thought then as I settled down, "It's very plain to see,
That on this day I've every chance to make a century."

I worried not about the swing, his speed was no concern,
But of the art of bowling straight he'd little more to learn.
And so I left the battle front, a duck against my name,
And never will I listen to that other gent again.
—Chris McRae

A bit of this and that

Nerrena Cricket Ground

Written regarding the cricket ground in Tom and Margaret Kindellan's paddock on the Leongatha–Dumbalk Road, prior to Nerrena moving to their new ground in 1980.

In a paddock at Nerrena there's a slab laid down with care,
Which holds mem'ries for a number here around.
And the times that they remember are the days they've spent out there,
Locked in combat on Nerrena Cricket Ground.

The ground has been donated by a philanthropic squire,
So it's used throughout the season, every round.
While those energetic hopefuls who to greatness all aspire,
Parade their talents on Nerrena Cricket Ground.

The ground is on an incline somewhat like the one at Lord's,
Though the pitch itself's devoid of ridge or mound.
So conditions for the contest which that famous ground affords,
Are slightly bettered at Nerrena Cricket Ground.

The grass is kept in order by a large curator's staff –
(On whose presence some misguided folk have frowned) –
But they mow with dedication and they cut down costs by half,
Because they fertilise Nerrena Cricket Ground.

INTERLUDE F *Some more poems*

There's a Members' stand and scoreboard just outside the boundary line,
Which on many other ovals can't be found,
While the tree along the outer comes in handy every time,
Shading patrons at Nerrena Cricket Ground.

If you happen to be passing and decide to pay a call,
Like as not you'll hear that soft melodic sound,
As an opponent's stumps go crashing and another wicket falls,
To the locals on Nerrena Cricket Ground.

Some folk in tones unfriendly sometimes ridicule the site,
But their whinging voice of protest soon is drowned,
For there's few who have an oval they can call their own by right,
Like the one we call Nerrena Cricket Ground.

And it doesn't seem to matter, if they're successful in their quest,
And their heads with victor's wreaths are duly crowned,
If the conflict they've engaged in where they proved themselves the best
Was conducted on Nerrena Cricket Ground.

For the place has got a character, a tone you can't define,
And an aura 'round which legends can be wound.
So long after many players have just quietly slipped from mind,
We'll still remember the Nerrena Cricket Ground.
   —*Chris McRae*

The bowler's lament

I happened one day, when the weather was wet, and play for a time was suspended,
To find myself sitting beside an old gent whose vigour and youth was expended.
But although on the path winding down to old age, he had keen and alert observation,
And we passed the time well, until play recommenced, with a pleasant half hour's conversation.

"I see that you bowl," said the wizened old sage, as a smile of despair creased his features.
"I've contended for years that bowlers are most to be pitied of all cricket's creatures.
For there isn't a doubt that those folk in control, who decree how the game is conducted,
Have batsmen in mind when they're forming the rules, and again when those rules are enacted.

"The pitches are made of the same lifeless stuff that you'd find in a soft feather pillow.
The batsmen are padded, protected and armed with a slab of resilient willow.
But see the poor bowler with sweat on his brow, with nought to assist him at all,
In his striving for vict'ry against these big odds but a five-and-a-half-ounce red ball.

"Yet that's just the start of the poor trundler's ills, in his quest for athletic survival,
For many's the obstacle placed in his way in his duel with his much-favoured rival.
The umpires, the rules and, often as not, the fieldsmen with whom he is playing,
Conspire to oppose him, whatever he does, and add weight to these truths I am saying.

"The umpires stand there, aloof and unmoved, considering the points of contention
Which appeals from the bowler will force them to note, as has been the time-honoured convention.
But should there arise in the mind of a judge just the slightest suggestion of doubt,
The case of the batsman's considered supreme and always he's ruled as 'not out'.

"If the bowler decides that his cause would be helped if he pitched a few in a bit shorter
And a batsman is hit, then up go the cries denouncing the imminent slaughter.
But if he is cut, or hooked to the fence, it's acclaimed as a shot of distinction,
While the bowler's admonished for bowling too short, or lack of control and direction.

"Perchance he'll send down a venomous ball, and leap when he sees his foe snick it,

Then watch with delight as it heads for the slips, convinced that he'll now have a wicket.
But many's the hope in the poor bowler's heart that's dashed on the rocks of despair
As the ball hits the hands, then drops to the ground at the feet of the man fielding there.

"So the bowler then, naturally, changes his ploy and when his next over commences,
He sends down a ball that swings from the leg and breaks through the batsman's defences.
But the batsman is struck on the pad, and although he was sure to be bowled middle peg
If his pad wasn't there, he's ruled as 'not out', as the ball was pitched outside the leg.

"Now bowlers are generally calm and serene, and few things arouse them to anger;
But faced with oppression as blatant as this it occasionally kindles their dander.
But if they then bowl a bumper or two, to release all their pent-up frustration,
As likely as not they'll be pulled into line by the umpires, for 'intimidation'.

"So don't expect plaudits," concluded the gent, as I left to again begin playing;
"Though as some consolation I should make a point just to balance what I have been saying.

INTERLUDE F   *Some more poems*

If you can approach the job that you face, and give all you've got to the task,
You'll find you're re-payed much more than you give, and that's all any person can ask."
—Chris McRae

The recruit

All community sporting clubs are constantly on the lookout for new players. It is common for the capabilities of potential new arrivals to be widely discussed, and possibly embellished, before they arrive at a club. Most clubs have people associated with them who seem particularly adept at gathering and spreading this information, irrespective of its veracity. Sometimes the reputation of these new arrivals turns out to be well deserved, but other times not. With cricket, nothing stirs the emotions more than the rumoured impending arrival of a demon fast bowler.

The season was quickly approaching,
Each club was assembling their side;
The talk was of who would be coaching,
And youngsters who ought to be tried.

But new blood was what we were needing,
An infusion of strength from without;
Yet despite all our watching and pleading,
There seemed to be no one about.

Now, Bert followed our opposition;
He was keen and, some said, quite astute;
He just laughed when he heard our position,
And told us about *their* recruit.

"He comes from up north, that's the story,
They say he's the quickest they've seen.
He's preceded by tales fierce and gory,
And they reckon he's hard, and he's mean.

"They say he's got no sense of humour,
That he's never been known to smile;
And although this may only be rumour,
They reckon he's easy to rile.

"Ooh, they reckon he's mad if you stir him,
Or get on his nerves in some way.
Pools of blood on the pitch won't deter him,
He'll bowl bumpers and beamers all day.

"They say he once hit this bloke with a bumper
A most fearful clout on the chin,
Then wiped the blood from the ball on his jumper
And straight away did it again!

"He'd as soon kill a batsman as bowl him,
And if you happen to cart him at all
Not a captain around can control him –
He'll be after your head the next ball.

"All the batsmen from where this bloke hails –
I'm only going on what has been said –
Go out padded from shoulders to toenails,
With a helmet protecting their head.

"He's so fast they say wood will splinter
If it's struck by a ball he's propelled –
They kept widows in kindling last winter
Using stumps that this fellow had felled.

"And, though this may be slightly fictitious
I'll repeat it, 'cause I've heard it's been said,
They don't use wooden bats he's so vicious,
They use great slabs of metal instead!

"I hear we play you first game of the season;
He'll be down here by then, so I'm told.
You'll be first to face up to the demon
And see for yourself how he bowls.

"Still, I guess there's some small consolation,
To assuage your most passionate fear,
If you're the victim of decapitation,
At least there's a hospital near."

So we went to our first game that season
Making sure that our wills were complete.
We were nervous, with every good reason,
As we didn't know what we would meet.

This big bloke strolled in from the covers
And marked out his run with aplomb;
Then a hush fell on all of us others
As he sent down the first of his bombs.

He'd told the men in the slips to go deeper,
So you can quite understand our surprise –
As the ball dribbled through to the 'keeper,
The batsmen completed two byes.

He was no great deterrent to scoring,
He was belted all over the place;
Then when adding up runs became boring,
We tried to agree on his pace.

If you said he was fast you'd be lying;
Then again, he was faster than slow,
So at last we just gave up our trying
And decided we didn't quite know.

We ran into Bert that same evening
And told him of this bloke's debut.
We said, "Though he's somewhat deceiving
He bowls not much quicker than you!"

But Bert's not the type to be worried
When things don't transpire as he'd wish;
So he whipped out this letter he carried
And told us, "Just listen to this.

INTERLUDE F   *Some more poems*

"It's from a bloke who once played for our seconds
 Who's living up east now, it seems.
 He's a big shot up there, so he reckons,
 And he's captain of one of their teams.

"He tells me, for some obscure reason,
 The best bat in the comp up that way
 Has decided to move here for next season,
 And he's wanting to know where to play.

"If we get him — talks have already started —
 We'll be set for the flag, we're a cert!"
 Then we smiled as he turned and departed,
 "Just like you are this year, eh Bert?"
   —**Chris McRae**

Ode to the watchers

For everyone who has a go there's many others who
Are quite prepared to sit and tell the players what to do.
These non-participators set a standard hard to match,
And they'll treat you with derision if you don't come up to scratch.

You might see them on the sidelines, always eager to expound
Their theory on the way things should be done out on the ground.
They're a source of endless wisdom on the skills of all the sports,
And they're always quite forthcoming in expression of their thoughts.

If you find you're having trouble with some aspect of your game;
If your search for form and fitness proves to largely be in vain;
When you find you're in the doldrums, quite devoid of any hope,
These are just the circumstances that fall within their scope.

They will pass on their suggestions in a condescending tone,
Just to reinforce the fact of how their skills surpass your own.
Though they've never had occasion to participate themselves,
They can give you the directions that will help you to excel.

They never seem to manage any speed above a walk,
But this proves of little hindrance when it comes their turn to talk.
For they've always got the answer to any topic that you name,
And they show a keen commitment to the fine points of the game.

They seldom seem to have the time to go and watch a game,
Though their frequent non-attendance is quite simple to explain.
As they find it quite demanding to know what the basics are,
They find it more rewarding to be experts from afar.

They pontificate in leisure from the comfort of their chair;
They can pass on gems of wisdom anytime and anywhere.
For there's really only one thing that will send them to their shells,
And that's any faint suggestion that they have a go themselves.

So when next you find your ears assailed by charlatans like this,
Just confess you have a phobia you're struggling to suppress.
Then tell them that it really is the chief among your fears,
That someday you'll be as sedentary as they have been for years.
  —*Chris McRae*

CHAPTER 10

On the move

In mid 1989 I applied for and was appointed as manager of the Department of Agriculture office in Maffra, a town of around 4,000 people, 130 kilometres north east of Leongatha. The office had around 15 staff, similar in size to Leongatha, and I knew most of those working there. At the time it was part of the East Gippsland Agriculture Centre managed from Bairnsdale by Bob Pitman. We sold our house in Fairbank and moved to Maffra late in the year.

The Maffra office provided services to the Macalister Irrigation District, largely dairy farming and some vegetable production, as well as to grazing industries in surrounding dryland areas. The focus of programs was very similar to those I had been involved in at Leongatha, although there was a developing concern regarding salinity in both the irrigation and some dryland areas, which resulted in projects addressing 'sustainability' being more prominent than I had experienced previously.

The role required me to be less involved with direct producer contact and to spend more time in coordination and management tasks. This took a little time to come to terms with, but progressively I found I was able to switch to the modified demands and that I quite enjoyed doing so. The 'vibe' in the office was very collegiate, and collaboration with other entities such as the local milk factory, herd-improvement centre and veterinary practice was close and productive.

During 1990 there was a departmental initiative implemented which resulted in employment of many new staff throughout Victoria, and we were successful in having three appointed to Maffra. As well as expanding our capacity, it resulted in the arrival of new personalities, energy and ideas to the office.

In April of that year, the upper Mitchell River and the Avon River experienced one of the largest floods ever recorded in those reaches, with the Macalister and Thomson Rivers also seriously affected. Particularly on the Avon River flats around Boisdale, Stratford and Airly there was significant damage to farms and many houses were flooded. It was my first experience of being involved in the response to and recovery from a natural disaster.

Our immediate task was largely to catalogue the extent of animal, fencing and other losses from farms to assist the government in determining the type and level of assistance required. This involved visiting as many individual farms as quickly as possible, collating the information we gathered, and passing on to other relevant organisations the details of individual needs that they were more suitable to respond to. Staff from department offices throughout Gippsland arrived in Maffra to assist us, and for many days this was virtually an around-the-clock activity.

The response from the community and emergency organisations was tremendous. While the immediate trauma was widespread and significant, in a comparatively short period of time arrangements were in place for the necessary support to be provided. Farm organisations from elsewhere in Victoria and beyond worked with the local Victorian Farmers Federation members to provide fodder, fencing supplies and labour. Personal support by way of accommodation, food, clothing and other supplies for families both on farms and in towns was obtained and distributed. Counselling and personal support services were offered and coordinated, government financial assistance was provided, and donations of money from the community throughout Gippsland began to be arranged.

Soon after the floodwaters subsided and recovery action commenced, a public meeting was held at Maffra. Large numbers of affected individuals attended along with local, state and federal politicians and representatives of all major response and recovery organisations. Anger was palpable, spleens were vented and tears were shed. The perceived deficiencies of numerous agencies, largely government, were highlighted and blame was apportioned by various speakers from the floor of the meeting. Gradually though, guided by the skilful and respected chairing of Shire President Don Sunderman, the mood of the meeting shifted and became one of looking forward. The long task of recovery was embraced in earnest.

This was obviously a challenge for many. In some cases I suspect full recovery to pre-flood circumstances took many years or wasn't achieved at all. But it was impossible not to be impressed by the professionalism and personal commitment shown by those involved, nor by the positive and supportive approach to the future shown by most of those impacted.

I have a number of recollections of that experience, some of which have been confirmed or added to by subsequent involvement in matters such as drought or disasters like bushfires. Responding to these events brings out the best in most people, as well as occasionally revealing the less attractive side of some.

On the first visits to farms immediately following the flood, it was not uncommon to have some who were very greatly impacted advising staff not to worry about them, but to visit a neighbour because of concerns they had about how they may have fared. Conversely, sometimes those who had been impacted only slightly would quantify in great detail all that they had lost (and sometimes more) and seek information on what type and level of support they may be eligible for, and when.

I was reminded of this experience many years later when I was involved to a small degree in fire response. If water from a farm dam was accessed to successfully defend a property, the impacted landholder would usually express gratitude for the efforts of firefighters in protecting their property — yet occasionally some complained about the loss of water.

A final observation coming from that experience is the fine line politicians need to tread, both in timing and approach, when visiting areas impacted by natural disasters. Most communities impacted by disasters are grateful for these visits, usually from the responsible minister. The visits are predominantly to provide moral support and to assure the community that the government is actively concerned about their situation. Ideally, those visiting should also be broadly aware of the extent of damage and trauma suffered to enable them to effectively empathise and be able to provide some details of government support that is available or soon will be. Communities are adept at discerning when the focus of these visits is not on them.

If ministers visit too early, they may appear opportunistic or too eager to project themselves into the action, details of community needs and government support may not yet be available, and visits at that time can also distract response agencies dealing with the disaster. If a visit is delayed too long during what is inevitably a time of high emotion, locals may feel that the government is not responding as quickly and vigorously as they believe is reasonable, or become cynical that the visit is finally being made simply to save face rather than as a sign of genuine concern.

The soundest principle for these visits is that 'less is more', not always an approach that comes naturally to politicians who have risen to become ministers. They should ideally spend a good proportion of time being publicly visible, listening and being empathetic. Some understand and are more adept at this than others.

At the time of the Maffra floods, Barry Rowe was the Minister for Agriculture in the state Labor government. It was his first ministerial role and one that he had been in only since the previous year. He was understandably keen to be visible in an event which was so clearly within his portfolio of responsibilities, but unfortunately misjudged the form of his involvement.

Concerns were raised initially when he and his office made early and unrealistic demands for detailed information on the extent of agricultural losses, despite communications to farms still being down in some areas, and access to others impossible because of floodwaters. Best endeavours were made, but it was fortunate that many of the resultant 'guesstimates' provided under duress and with limited data turned out to be reasonable.

Very soon after the flood receded and mopping up and recovery planning began, the minister advised he would visit the area. This was welcome, but the form of the proposed visit appeared ill-advised. He didn't wish to publicly meet with any groups, nor those involved with recovery activities, but could we arrange for him to meet with some individuals who had been severely impacted?

This was a request of locals that we were reluctant to make, largely because the focus both of impacted landholders and departmental staff was still very much on the day-to-day practicalities of discovering the extent of losses and beginning recovery. Despite this, we managed to organise a small number of visits to farm families who were prepared to host him.

The minister duly arrived, flying in to the Sale airstrip. I accompanied him on his visit, and it soon became obvious his highest priority for the trip was to obtain a photograph of himself with enough impact to warrant publication on the front or near to the front of a metropolitan newspaper. It was his stated desire and he had brought a well-known photographer along to help him.

Bruce Postle was a long-time photographer with *The Age* newspaper in Melbourne. Among many iconic images he had captured over the years, those of Prime Minister Malcolm Fraser in bed reading the paper on the Sunday morning following his 1980 federal election victory, and of trainer Tommy Woodcock, former strapper of Phar Lap, laying down in a stall with his racehorse Reckless before the 1977 Melbourne Cup, were among the best known.

While we did sit and chat with a couple of severely impacted families in kitchens through which water had been flowing a few days earlier, this was never allowed to curtail the time available for photo shoots. Some of these we had to travel some distance for, or took seemingly inordinate amounts of time to arrange, and the meetings with locals were clearly relegated in importance.

There were photos taken of the minister in gumboots opening a gate on a track with water still flowing over it. There were photos taken of him in front of a tree with a drowned sheep in its lower branches. Other photos were taken of the minister beside a line of flattened fencing, and still others of him beside deep erosion gullies caused by the floods. It became quite a tedious process. I don't recall any of the photos having the prominence or impact obviously hoped for. Although the locals who participated were nothing but gracious, it was a good example of what to avoid in ministerial visits to disaster areas.

CHAPTER 11

Time in the west

Around the same time as the floods, I applied for a job with the Western Australian Department of Agriculture at Moora. Having seen the position of Officer-in-Charge (OIC) at the local department office advertised, my first move was to find an atlas to see where the town was! It was approximately 200 kilometres north of Perth and 100 kilometres in from the coast.

Although Tricia and I had only recently moved to Maffra with our two children, we had not settled into the town to the extent that a further move would have been too disruptive, but it was still a significant decision to contemplate a move to the other side of the country. I had no great expectation of being offered the role but following an interview I was. We both travelled to WA to visit the town, check out housing and schooling and meet some WA department folk, prior to being required to decide whether to accept the job.

While we had discussed and agreed that I would apply for the role and that we were prepared to move if it was offered, when the time came to actually do so, it became obvious that I was more at ease with this than was Tricia. This led to some indecision — accepting the role, then declining it before again accepting it (and the WA department being prepared to continue to offer it to me, despite this indecision!) In September of 1990 I resigned from the Victorian public service and our family of four moved to Moora.

At the time Moora had a population of around 1,800 people. The town was the centre of the West Midlands area and the agricultural district surrounding it was large and diverse, bounded on the east by the pastoral region and on the west by the coast. In the east of the district, large cereal and lupin cropping operations predominated, some running no livestock at all. In the centre of the district, mixed cropping and sheep operations were most common, while to the west the soils became increasingly sandy so sheep predominated, with some beef cattle, and cropping was less important. In the south-west of the district, horticultural operations using groundwater were increasing in number and scale.

The OIC role was to manage the operations of the district office of around 25 staff, as well as those on two research stations, one to the east at Wongan Hills focused largely on cropping, and another to the west at Badgingarra focused on livestock. The district was part of the Northern Agricultural Region managed from Geraldton by Regional Manager Charlie Thorn.

We lived in a small government house around 500 metres from the office. I recall walking to the office on the morning I commenced working there and reflecting that I knew no one in the office, only one other person in WA (and he was at Katanning, over 400 kilometres south of Moora), knew nothing of agriculture in the district, nor of cropping, its major enterprise, and yet was

CHAPTER 11   *Time in the west*

beginning a role managing the department's operations in the area. The realisation was both daunting and exciting.

Despite beginning from this uncertain base, our time at Moora was a wonderful experience. We made many close friends and found the experience of living and working in an environment very different to what we had been used to enjoyable and stimulating.

The industries and issues being dealt with were quite different to those I had experienced in Victoria, but the fundamental approach to service provision was not. I valued highly (and relied on) the technical expertise and local knowledge of others, but found no difficulty in becoming familiar enough with both to manage delivery of district and regional programs, and to contribute to developing the strategies needed in planning them. My experience in the beef industry was beneficial as this industry became more important in the district, based on developing and utilising tagasaste or 'tree lucerne' on the deep sands in the west of the district.

Western Australian agriculture had followed the usual development pathway of agricultural industries, but a number of decades later than Victoria. By the early 1990s the unashamedly pro-production period for the state marked by 'a million acres a year' release of new land for agriculture, trumpeted in the 1960s, had given way to that of prioritising the management and repair of damage resulting from some of the excesses of this approach. The extensive scalds throughout the WA wheatbelt, many caused by dryland salinity resulting from over-clearing, were some of the most visible reminders of the need for this action.

In a further stark example of how quickly priorities can change, there were producers in the west of the Moora district who had first settled on their land when it was initially released for agriculture. They had moved from broadscale clearing of vegetation when they commenced their farming careers to implementing strategic revegetation programs towards the end of them.

The salinity impacts were more obvious in some districts other than Moora, but there were staff positions in Moora and most department districts funded by state and federal governments under the National Landcare Program. These staff were employed to work with groups in Land Conservation Districts to implement wide-scale responses to salinity and other land degradation challenges farmers faced.

The focus on sustainability programs was thus greater and more overt than I had experienced in southern Victoria. There was still a heavy focus on productivity and marketing programs for both livestock and grains, however, with wool quality and production of wheat for specific markets a major feature of advisory effort. Annual information on the latest crop varieties, herbicide and fertiliser regimes, quality demands of specific grain and wool markets, and crop rotations were expected and keenly sought, as were updates from longer term agronomic or livestock experiments. In particular, the annual field day at the Wongan Hills Research Station attracted large crowds.

There was a more extensive network of private agricultural consultants operating in the state than was the case in Victoria, and many of the larger agricultural supply firms also employed advisors. The industry was thus well supported by advisory services, and there was a broad desire from many farmers to seek and expect the latest technical and marketing information.

CHAPTER 11 *Time in the west*

The value of agricultural production in WA was significantly less than in Victoria, but the industry made up a greater proportion of WA's economy. It had more prominence in the consciousness of the wider community than had been my recent experience in Victoria, and I found the department to be a very positive and encouraging organisation to work in.

Being new to the state and department, I was initially unknown. My actions and contributions at the time were therefore the basis for opinions formed of me, not those — positive or negative — which had been built up over many years and which had inevitably become attached to me in Victoria. While I did not feel at all constrained by the latter before we moved to WA, I did feel a degree of professional freedom and renewal, which I doubt would have been possible had I remained in Victoria.

Disenchantment with the operation of the agriculture department in Victoria had not been a factor in our decision to move to WA, despite there being a general sense of malaise and economic fragility in Victoria in 1990. This mood of uncertainty and negativity had permeated the department as well, and the organisation I moved to in WA was a far more positive environment in which to work.

Our time in WA coincided with a period of major upheaval in the public service in Victoria, following the election of the Kennett government in 1992. Along with closures of schools and hospitals across the state and some country rail services, major public-sector reform resulted in thousands of public servants losing their jobs. Some whom I knew from the agriculture department in Victoria lost their job. A small number of those displaced from roles in Victoria applied for jobs in WA and some relocated. It was certainly preferable to observe this disruption from a distance, rather than being directly impacted, quite apart from the debates occurring on the merits of the direction and scale of the government's actions.

When we moved to WA, we intended to remain there for at least two years irrespective of how well we settled in. That time came and went and the longer we stayed, the more settled and positive we became. Tricia had quickly obtained work at the Moora hospital, and Ellen, our youngest child, was born there in 1992. We became involved in a range of activities associated with childcare, school, church, tennis and other interests, and our two older children began their primary schooling there.

It was common for government and other professional people to come to the town and move on within a few years, and the local community had become used to this; we came to understand that short-term mobility through country towns was far more common in WA than in Victoria. This seemed to make the task of becoming involved in social networks easier. 'Eastern staters' were often viewed with some real or confected caution — particularly Victorians, with long-term interstate rivalry from the days of the Victorian Football League probably a major basis for this — but we found our origins to usually be the grounds for good-natured banter, rather than an impediment. (I could never work out why WA football supporters were so negative about their better players moving to play in Victoria, though; surely they could accept they would need to go *somewhere* to get a decent game of football?!)

There was a generally more vibrant feeling abroad in WA than in Victoria at that time. The impression gained was of endeavour and positivity, although the boundary between appropriate state pride and parochialism was often only casually observed. There was a sense given by some that they genuinely believed WA carried the rest of the country, and the economic and other troubles that were besetting Victoria at the time were viewed by these folk with undisguised schadenfreude.

At a farmers' meeting in the district in 1994, a questioner asked the Minister for Agriculture, Monty House, what the government's current attitude was to secession. The minister gave no indication that the government was keen to free the state from the constraints imposed by being part of Australia, but I found it intriguing that the question was prominent enough in the inquisitor's consciousness for it to be asked in a public forum.

CHAPTER 12

Back to Victoria

In mid 1994 the position of Regional Manager North East with the Victorian Department of Agriculture, based at Rutherglen Research Institute, was advertised. Although we were very happy in WA, this job had the twin benefits of being both an attractive role and enabling us to move back closer to family in Victoria. After being interviewed and offered the role, I had no hesitation in accepting and we were on the move again.

In October 1994 I returned to a department vastly different in both structure and morale to the one I had left four years earlier. Mike Taylor was now secretary and Ras Lawson was responsible for regional services. The leadership of the organisation was strong, its strategic direction clear and a sense of collegiality among senior leaders was apparent. Strong relationships with agricultural industry bodies had been forged and were prioritised. There remained occasional references to the bruising experiences of the previous couple of years, but the organisation was clearly moving on from that, despite the individual challenges or personnel changes that had been experienced.

Matrix management was in vogue in many parts of the department at the time, evident both in the structure of many research institutes and in the operation of industry programs across the organisation. In this latter case, most regional managers, as well as having responsibility for staff management and service delivery in a geographic region, also had state-wide responsibilities as the program leader for a specific industry. In my case I was initially responsible for the small New and Emerging Industries Program, then the much larger Meat Program.

The programs of the department reflected government priorities and were based on formally agreed plans developed in close consultation with respective industry sectors in Victoria and national Rural Industry Research Corporations (RIRCs), which also involved regular funding support from the latter. These RIRCs were in part funded by levies paid by all farmers on the sale of their produce. The funding of research and development projects supporting producers was thus a means of providing benefit back to the industry in return for these levies.

Strategies for wool, meat, dairy, grains, horticulture and other industries guided the investment of state government funds into the programs. Integration between research and advisory programs was strongly sought, as was collaboration between the industry sectors in any areas of common interest such as soils, pastures, economics, marketing, farm management and sustainability. Large projects were commonly developed, often conducted across more than one state, and variously involved department staff from Victoria and interstate, researchers and advisors, universities and private consultants. Delivery was almost exclusively through groups and frequently contracted to private consultants to lead.

*Hannah, Ellen and Ewen — the only year (1997)
they all attended the same school, Rutherglen Primary School*

The evolution in the form, focus, funding and delivery of farm advisory work with the Department of Agriculture in the period between 1970, when I commenced my involvement, and the mid 1990s had been immense. A young staff member beginning work in a district office in 1995 required a far more expansive and integrated perspective on their work than I had needed, not to mention paying attention to government and industry priorities. Training and technology enabled most to meet these new demands to a high level, and it was gratifying as regional manager and program leader to participate in these activities as the evolution of agricultural industries and the means of providing advisory services to them continued to change.

The impact of this could be seen across all regions and industries, as all agricultural industries were impacted by the economic and social changes affecting the sector. In addition, change in some industries was driven by additional forces specific to them.

The tobacco industry in Victoria had commenced in the river valleys of the north-east in the 1850s, then grew through the 20th century to become a major local industry, particularly in the Ovens and King River valleys. The Victorian government had set up a Tobacco Research Station at Ovens, east of Myrtleford, in the mid 1950s, as one component of its support for the industry. According to the 1961 census, there were over 1,000 tobacco growers in Victoria at that time, the majority Italian-born.

By the mid 1990s, however, the industry was undergoing major change, with only around 200 producers remaining in Victoria, and another small group of producers around Mareeba on the Atherton Tablelands in Queensland. The health implications of smoking were by then overwhelmingly accepted, and the industry was increasingly becoming socially and politically isolated. Governments were supporting anti-smoking campaigns and not keen to appear to support the tobacco industry in any way, apart from efforts to assist with winding it up and for growers to move to other forms of agriculture. The Victorian government had

CHAPTER 12 *Back to Victoria*

rebranded the Tobacco Research Station as Ovens Research Station, projects there were now predominantly focused on researching and supporting alternative crops for the area, and government buy-back of tobacco production quotas had begun.

During my time in the region, I had quite a bit of involvement with the tobacco industry and with attempts to encourage alternative industries. The industry was fortunate to have respected and astute local leaders who understood and accepted the situation in the industry, but who were also determined to ensure the best was done for the growers as tobacco was phased out. They were capable and positive people with whom to work. Meetings with them were seldom held at Ovens, though, as by that stage it was a 'no smoking' environment, in keeping with all government and most other facilities.

An abiding memory is of attending a national tobacco industry conference at the Savoy Club in Myrtleford late in 1995. By that stage smoke-free meetings and events were virtually ubiquitous in public places, but certainly not so at the Savoy.

Many conference speakers, both farmers and industry representatives, prefaced their presentation with a defence of tobacco and suggestions that the scientific evidence regarding its health impacts was not as clear-cut as the public had been led to believe. The term 'nanny state' received more than one mention. Attendees sat through the various sessions enveloped by wraiths of smoke, with the unmistakable sound of cigarette lighters regularly being flicked into action around the room. It was an experience reminiscent of perhaps two decades earlier, and one I have been glad not to have had repeated since.

During my time in the north-east and subsequently, the restructuring of the industry continued. Production quotas were bought from more marginal growers with government assistance and tariffs on imported tobacco were reduced to zero. A sales and processing facility was relocated from Melbourne to Myrtleford early in 1996, where it operated until the industry closed. In 2006 growers at Mareeba accepted a buy-out of the industry in their state, and when the majority of north-east growers did the same late in the same year, the tobacco-growing industry in Australia had closed down.

One of the associated impacts of these changes in the tobacco industry was the opportunity to commence a broader agribusiness support group in the region. Both federal and state governments had funding available for such initiatives, particularly those attempting to provide support to regions impacted by industry restructure. At the time all municipalities in Victoria were being run by commissioners, as part of the Kennett government reforms to local government in the state. In 1995 I met individually with commissioners from six of the municipalities in the north-east — Delatite (as it then was), Wangaratta, Indigo, Alpine, Towong and Wodonga — and worked subsequently with groups and individuals to develop a coordinated approach to sustainable agribusiness growth in the region.

A consensus on the form and focus of the initiative developed. At a meeting in Wangaratta in 1997, attended by representatives from all these municipalities, relevant local industries and bureaucrats from both state and federal governments, agreement was reached to form the Australian Alpine Valleys Agribusiness Forum. It was recognised by both Commonwealth and state governments and funded under the Rural Partnership Program.

The forum officially commenced in 1998, with John Brown from Brown Brothers Wines at Milawa as chair. I became deputy chair

CHAPTER 12   *Back to Victoria*

and the forum became active in running projects supported by funding from the three tiers of government. It became the forerunner of similar groups in other regions of the state such as Gippsland, the Wimmera and Yarra Valley, many of which continue today, and helped to promote the establishment of an ongoing agribusiness network in the state.

While government and municipalities were instrumental in the initial formation and support of the forum, it progressively became more producer-driven over time and was active and influential in a range of marketing, industry development, sustainability and leadership development initiatives. It was a clear example of the evolution over many years of the balance of effort from the Department of Agriculture moving from on-farm production to industry development and marketing.

My time in the north-east region also coincided with the implementation of a series of actions in the public sector change agenda of the Kennett government, some of which impacted our department only slightly, but some of which caused significant change. Consolidation of government departments, the formation of statutory authorities, and the transfer of some responsibilities formerly delivered by departments to these agencies were among the changes that occurred.

The policy of the government to form fewer, larger departments first impacted the Department of Agriculture early in 1995, when the Department of Agriculture, Energy and Minerals was formed by the amalgamation of the Department of Agriculture with the Department of Energy and Minerals. This had little impact in the north-east region as there were few staff from the latter department based there.

One of the more historic aspects of this change was that it marked the first time that a stand-alone Department of Agriculture had not existed as a formal entity in Victoria since the original department was formed in 1872 (even though 'Rural Affairs' had been part of its title between 1985 and 1991, and 'Food' in 1991 and 1992). This change passed largely unremarked at the time. It was probably fortunate that it was implemented by a conservative government of which the Nationals were a part — I expect there would have been a more vocal and negative response from rural areas and politicians had a Labor government been responsible for the change.

Following the state election in 1996, the amalgamation of the Department of Agriculture, Energy and Minerals with Conservation and Natural Resources occurred, forming the Department of Natural Resources and Environment (NRE). This was a far more major change and had a significant impact across all of Victoria, bringing together the functions of agriculture, energy and minerals with those of forestry, catchment and land management, fire management, parks, flora and fauna, Crown land management and land administration. It was an amalgamation justified, at least in part, by the aspiration of the government to have cross-sectoral policy development and debates involving the public lands, conservation and primary industries sectors 'in house', rather than publicly aired between departments. Mike Taylor became secretary of the new department and, Ras Lawson having retired, Bruce Muir and then Ken King became responsible for regional services.

In the north-east region over 500 staff were initially part of this new department, more than three times the number in the previous Department of Agriculture, Energy and Minerals. There were now over 20 towns in the region where the new department had

CHAPTER 12 *Back to Victoria*

an office or depot, compared to six for the department for which I previously worked.

The regional office for NRE was located at Benalla, around 90 kilometres south of Rutherglen. After I was appointed Regional Manager North East for the new department, Tricia and I decided that we would continue to live in Rutherglen and I commuted to Benalla daily.

Over the next few years, as well as continuing and consolidating the regional work programs of the expanded department, there was considerable time spent both regionally and across the state in implementing new structures and operating arrangements. This is the unseen and regularly unaccounted for cost of machinery of government changes. While they can bring about greater alignment and efficiencies — and I believe the formation of NRE did this — they are not without cost either financially or in terms of staff morale and performance.

In the 20 years following this initial amalgamation of primary industry and environmental functions, and the setting up of regional arrangements to deliver their services, there have been seemingly constant iterations implemented by successive governments and secretaries. Primary industry and environment functions have been together in one department during one term of government, separated in a subsequent one, brought together again and then separated again. Strongly regionally based structures have been implemented, changed to a statewide-delivery approach and then re-formed into altered regional structures. It has been difficult to keep up with the changes and no doubt challenging for both staff and clients impacted by them.

As NRE was being formed, the government also continued

implementing changes to the governance of natural resource and waterway management functions across the state. Catchment and Land Protection Boards were formed initially, followed by their consolidation with waterway management responsibilities of local River Management Trusts in 1997. The resulting 10 Catchment Management Authorities (CMAs) were established as statutory authorities with responsibility for integrated planning for land, water and biodiversity management in their region.

Most state and federal natural resource funding from then on was provided to regions according to the strategies developed by these bodies. When they were first formed, regional managers from NRE had a place on their boards, and I served for some time on the board of both the North East and Goulburn Broken CMAs.

The period from the mid to late 1990s was a time of fundamental structural and organisational change for government primary production and conservation services in the state. While there have been subsequent iterations and modifications, they have largely occurred within, or built on, the framework set up during those years.

The changes caused significant disruption at the time and occurred despite vocal opposition from some quarters. This was usually portrayed as a concern that the benefit of local knowledge would be lost in the consolidated arrangements for whatever function was being considered. While there was doubtless some basis for these concerns in certain cases, in most they owed more to those expressing them fearing the loss of their local influence that they had developed over a long period. There is little doubt that the outcome overall has been significantly positive, and a return to the more *ad hoc*, disparate and less strategic arrangements common prior to that period is unthinkable.

CHAPTER 12   *Back to Victoria*

During 1999 an opportunity to move to head office in Melbourne arose. Although there was no imperative for this to occur and despite very much enjoying my regional role, I was quite positive about such a move and appreciated the support of Mike Taylor and others in bringing it about. For our family, particularly given our children's stage of schooling, it was also a satisfactory time for us to move if we chose to. At the beginning of 2000 we moved to Melbourne after five very positive years in Rutherglen and the north-east region.

The following poem was written by David Donehue, NRE staff member from Benalla, and presented as part of a farewell to us from the North East Region.

Farewell Chris McRae

Thanks for your memory
Planners and scholars and all working folk,
We are all gathered right here today,
To say Bon Voyage
From this region so large
To the bloke that they call Chris McRae.

I didn't know much 'bout this bloke from the north,
And I felt a bit left out alone.
So I called on assistance,
Some close and some distant –
You can blame all this info on Joan[13].

---

13   Joan Fenwick, my Executive Assistant at Benalla.

Well, Chris I found out has a story to tell,
And his learnings he may like to boast.
He's got "B" things and "C" things
And bells that might ring,
From the bush to the edge of the coast.

He's been "everywhere, man" across this great land,
With his studies and his working life.
Through these long years
He's built quite a career,
And moulded three kids and a wife.

He's been overseas to the Pommies and Yanks,
Through Canada in late '98.
To study their farming –
I hope the French girls were charming –
Anything you'd like to tell us there, mate?

I was given a list of committees and things,
But to mention them just seemed too much.
Officer in charge,
Or manager at large,
Chairperson and leader and such.

Saleyards committees and industry liaison,
Agri-business in this place and that.
Wool industry downturn
And flood works concern,
With records and flowcharts and graphs.

CHAPTER 12 *Back to Victoria*

Well, Chris I found out is a Collingwood man,
And Malthouse has turned up to reign.
If you work near the "G"
Make a coupl'a hours free –
You may need to get there and train.

To those who don't know, Chris has a nickname,
He's been known as Tractor for years.
For the origins I'm lost,
Well, McRae has me tossed,
You're not a Fordson, David Brown or John Deere.

I was talking to a bloke who's working down south,
And he cleared up a bit of a mystery;
On the cool and tough factor –
We were talking of Tractor –
He advised of a bit of McRae history.

Apparently one day came a bloke from the city,
A thug who had played VFL.
He was running around
Sniping blokes to the ground,
Generally giving the local boys hell.

In one passage of play Chris got fed up with this,
And burst his way up through the pack.
With good old persuasion
Chris fixed the occasion,
And had this bloke watching his back.

I understand Chris is the McEnroe of Rutherglen,
And regularly serves up a storm.
Or is seen working out
For the local young scouts,
Serving hot dogs I hear is the norm.

I once spent some time on a car trip with Chris,
It's amazing what secrets are within.
And wouldn't you know it
That Chris is a poet,
Which is just like his father before him.

Thanks for your drive behind OH&S,
Your commitment to this is first rate.
The Region's progress
Has been a success –
The North East is leading the state.

One thing we'll remember about this Regional Manager,
A thing which has not been the same.
How he can converse
Whether funny or terse,
And how he can remember your name.

CHAPTER 12   *Back to Victoria*

Good luck in the city while we're in the bush,
We'll endeavour to work on and try.
We'll battle the smoke
And help country folk,
The anthrax, the drought and the fruit fly.

So when you look back on your extensive career,
And the smog has you coughin' and wheezin',
Kick back in your chair
And think country air;
Goodbye from the state's North East Region.
  — **David Donehue**

CHAPTER 13
More change

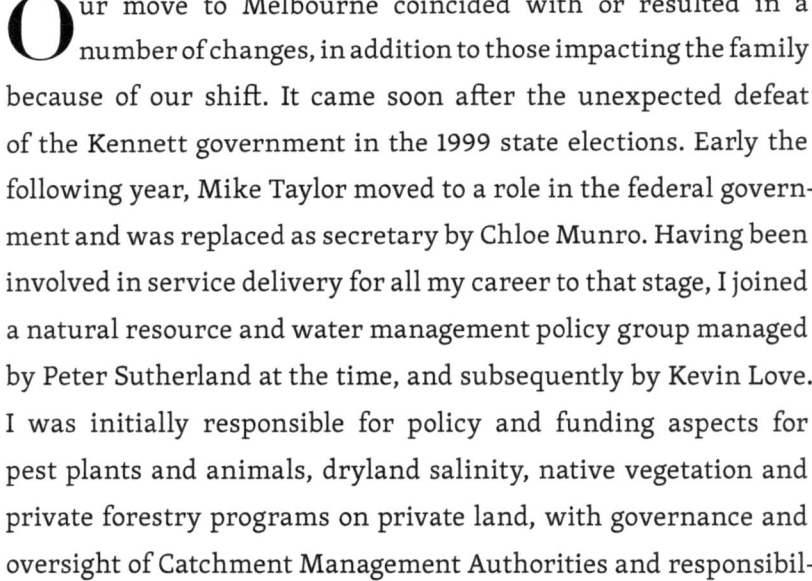

Our move to Melbourne coincided with or resulted in a number of changes, in addition to those impacting the family because of our shift. It came soon after the unexpected defeat of the Kennett government in the 1999 state elections. Early the following year, Mike Taylor moved to a role in the federal government and was replaced as secretary by Chloe Munro. Having been involved in service delivery for all my career to that stage, I joined a natural resource and water management policy group managed by Peter Sutherland at the time, and subsequently by Kevin Love. I was initially responsible for policy and funding aspects for pest plants and animals, dryland salinity, native vegetation and private forestry programs on private land, with governance and oversight of Catchment Management Authorities and responsibility for co-ordination of state and federal funding programs delivered through them subsequently added.

Following the 2002 state election, a further machinery of government change occurred, with the splitting of NRE into the Department of Primary Industry (DPI) and Department of

CHAPTER 13   *More change*

Sustainability and Environment (DSE). It was not quite a reversion to the structure that had prevailed prior to the formation of NRE in 1996 but did result in the splitting of agriculture and conservation responsibilities once more, and further changes to regional service-delivery arrangements. Chloe Munro became secretary of DPI and Professor Lyndsay Neilson secretary of DSE. Being involved in natural resource management, I became part of DSE, the first time since I commenced work in 1970 that I had not been a part of an agriculture department.

As had been the case in agriculture, natural resource management programs were becoming increasingly strategic, involving greater levels of engagement across jurisdictions, agencies and levels of government, and being delivered in accord with regional catchment strategies developed by CMAs. Victoria collaborated with other jurisdictions in national initiatives for weeds and pest animals, dryland and irrigation salinity, native vegetation and the implementation of approaches to enable auditing of progress in natural resource management initiatives across Australia. I spent six years in this policy role, becoming a member of numerous inter-jurisdictional groups responsible for development of national strategies, as well as a board member of a Cooperative Research Centre focused on plant-based management of dryland salinity.

During this time updated Victorian government policies on pest plants and animals, dryland salinity and native vegetation management were developed and released. As with all such documents, they were completed following consultation with and spirited representations from individuals and interest groups with a range of perspectives, from industry (most prominently represented by the Victorian Farmers Federation) through to a range of conservation-related bodies. All were naturally convinced of the worth of their views and many asserted the primacy they believed theirs deserved in the final strategy. Once completed and endorsed by the government, the policies were influential in determining the direction and focus of future government investment in each area.

This investment occurred through policy, research, advisory and regulatory services provided directly by the government, or through provision of funding to regional Landcare or other groups to plan and undertake agreed projects. Virtually all investment was aligned with regional, state and national strategies developed for the issue being targeted.

Governments have a role in promoting behaviour from individual land managers to protect or enhance landscape-level natural resource values — to encourage behaviour that achieves this and discourage that which is contrary to doing so. It is effectively a task of supporting and influencing the behaviour of individual landholders to achieve both an individual and collective benefit, or at least to avoid private gain being achieved by individuals transferring the cost of achieving this to other landholders or the broader community. They do this predominantly through investing in either *education* — providing research, information and advisory services to enable private individuals to make better informed decisions — or by *encouragement* through the provision of grants to promote specific beneficial actions from individuals, or by *enforcement* that ensures compliance with legislated standards in matters such as weed and pest, native vegetation or salinity management.

All components of this approach are required and need to be

available, but most funding goes to education and encouragement, and the least to enforcement. Almost all landholders understand that long-term private benefit and public good are largely achieved by the same practices and act accordingly. There is certainly a need for compliance efforts with those who don't but, despite the publicity garnered by some who face enforcement actions, their numbers are comparatively small.

The balance of expenditure was sometimes questioned by those who favoured a more heavy-handed regulatory approach (the 'lock-'em-up' approach), although support for a more punitive approach to changing producers' behaviour was often not consistently applied. For example, producer organisations were commonly more supportive of this approach being used against those failing to meet weed and pest control responsibilities, than they were for those transgressing against native vegetation regulations.

While they have a place and were used, compliance activities were never the major focus of investment. Experience suggests that positive approaches are more cost-effective, and often the only ones necessary in encouraging long-term behaviour change by individuals. The actual split of investment could be, and was, questioned, but I have no doubt the order of it was appropriate.

For natural resource management programs on private land, government funds — both state and federal — are an important but relatively minor component of total investment. They act largely to influence, encourage and help coordinate programs, with most funding, time and effort being contributed by private landholders. This is entirely appropriate given the private benefits which landholders derive, but there is little doubt that the increased alignment of effort made possible by development of state and regional strategies, and initiatives such as regional planning and Landcare, have increased the effectiveness of overall investment in natural resource management.

Even with defined strategies in place, criticism often remained regarding the focus of funding allocations to issues, the balance of investment between competing priorities, or what was variously seen as being a too-lenient or too-punitive approach to policing regulations (depending on the issue and the perspective of the interest group expressing the opinion). By far the most common criticism though was that the government should simply invest more in particular programs.

It was impossible to argue that additional funding for most programs would not have been useful. However, faced with a virtually limitless demand for expenditure at the same time as ongoing expectations of careful budget management and prudence in spending, governments understandably need to make choices on the direction and level of funding for the programs they support.

Almost all interest groups believe governments should spend more money on the issues they are passionate about or on which they represent members. My experience both in service delivery and policy roles, though, was that many stakeholders saw government money as being in some way different to 'real' money and didn't appreciate, or chose not to, that an increase in funding to one area inevitably reduced that in another unless additional funds were made available. There appeared in many cases to be an expectation that additional government money could be miraculously conjured up almost at will in response to a perceived need, without this impacting either other funded programs or government budgets.

CHAPTER 13 *More change*

I had a stark example of this during my time in the north-east. Immediately prior to an election, intense community and political pressure resulted in increased funding being made available from the region's budget to the local wild dog program, one of the more high-profile and emotive programs we were responsible for. When this increased investment was reported to the committee advising the region on resource allocation (some of whom had been urging — and probably lobbying politically! — for additional funds to be spent on wild dogs), it was very positively received. This positivity disappeared when it was discovered that the local weed and rabbit programs had been reduced by a commensurate amount, because no additional funding was available to the region.

One of the projects to garner some public prominence, during my time involved in natural resource management, was a fox bounty trial conducted in 2002 and 2003.

Bounties are frequently touted as an effective means of encouraging pest-animal control. Virtually all studies conducted have shown that they are not cost-effective in providing long-term control however, except perhaps in rare situations where small populations are targeted in constrained areas. Alternative methods such as ongoing, coordinated baiting programs have been shown to be more cost-effective in controlling the impact of pest animals across large areas, particularly when used in conjunction with other tactical control methods. They suffer in popular opinion, though, because there is usually no physical evidence of a dead pest to 'demonstrate' their effectiveness.

In circumstances of constrained resources (almost always the case), diverting funds to pay bounties for destruction of pest animals, many of which will be controlled as part of regular farm and recreational activities anyway, is not justified. It effectively results in the government providing some of their limited funds direct to landholders or shooters who have existing economic or recreational incentives for destroying pests and do so irrespective of receiving government support. Introduction of a bounty may encourage some extra activity in both cases, but a positive long-term benefit from doing so has seldom, if ever, been demonstrated. Despite this, they continue to have strong support, particularly among shooters and many farmers, and there is no doubting their political attractiveness.

In mid 2002 the government surprisingly announced that a trial of a fox bounty would be conducted in Victoria, with $10 to be paid for each fox killed. It is unlikely to be coincidental that this announcement was made in the lead-up to a state election.

Prior to the announcement, there had been a low level of correspondence to Minister Sherryl Garbutt, requesting the introduction of a fox bounty. She provided responses resisting these calls, based on evidence widely accepted by pest-control specialists of the greater cost-benefit of alternative approaches. A degree of embarrassment arose for her when some of these replies were publicised following her announcement of the trial.

The trial was set up to run for 12 months from July 2002, after which its effectiveness was to be analysed and a decision on its continuation made. Conveniently, this analysis and decision were timed to occur after the forthcoming election. Collection points were set up at departmental offices and depots across the state to enable presentation of fox tails, which had been decided as being the required evidence prior to a bounty payment being made.

Those submitting tails were required to provide details of where foxes had been destroyed to enable spatial depiction and subsequent analysis of the impact of the bounty. Though beneficial, even this did not provide certainty about the benefit of the bounty, because those analysing the trial had to use historical estimates of fox populations and there was no way of knowing how many foxes would have been controlled without it. Despite this, it did provide a reasonable basis for drawing conclusions on the likely long-term impact of the removal of foxes on which bounties were paid.

During the trial there was criticism that conclusions from it would not be valid because those receiving bounty payments would not be honest about where they had killed the foxes, and it was even possible that, in the north of the state, Victorian funds may be paid on 'interstate' foxes (what a scandal!) The trial was attacked by at least one skin buyer because of its negative impact on his business. In another case 1,000 fox tails were stolen from a depot following payment of the bounty but prior to their destruction by departmental staff. They were presumably re-presented and paid for again at a different depot or depots subsequently and, as a result, protocols around collection and destruction of tails were tightened. Overall though, the trial went remarkably smoothly and was well received by many stakeholders.

At its conclusion, bounties had been paid on 198,000 foxes, but analysis showed that there would be 'little long-term impact on fox populations' in any area of the state. In August of 2003 the minister responsible, by then John Thwaites, and the government determined that the bounty would be discontinued. Available resources were to be focused on programs likely to be more cost-effective, such as broad-scale baiting.

If the decision to introduce it owed much to its political

attractiveness, that of discontinuing it relied heavily on lack of evidence, either from this or prior examinations, of it being likely to provide long-term control. It probably qualified as one of Sir Humphrey Appleby's (*Yes, Minister*) 'courageous decisions', but it was also undoubtedly principled.

At the time the decision was described in one newspaper article as being 'about as popular in rural Victoria as a fox in a hen house'. Criticism came from Opposition and independent politicians, recreational shooting groups and farmers. This did not result in any change in the decision at the time, but it was no surprise when, a few years later, bounties applying to both foxes and wild dogs were re-introduced in Victoria.

The divergent views on the effectiveness of bounties are unlikely to disappear, nor will their political attractiveness. Of themselves they do no harm, perhaps even encouraging a degree of additional effort and social cohesion in dealing with a common challenge, but they also result in less government funding being available for more effective control methods. They are a classic example of governments having to balance the importance they place on these competing interests.

Competing interests inevitably lead to differences in opinion on how many matters should be managed. One consequence of this is that the responsible minister receives a large amount of correspondence advocating for particular views, and that was certainly the case for natural resource management. It was the area of government in which managing ministerial correspondence became a greater component of my role than on any occasion before or after.

Letters to the minister initially go to the relevant section of

CHAPTER 13 *More change*

the department to draft a response and an accompanying brief. If required, letters are modified by the minister's office prior to them being signed and despatched.

Most letters from the general public are 'one off' and, after responses are provided, nothing further is heard from the correspondent, whether or not the response they receive is deemed satisfactory. Some individuals become regular correspondents, often on obscure or unusual topics, and memorable because of doing so. Responses tend to repeat the same or similar information to the same or similar question received every year or so, sometimes to the extent that incessant writers are listed and handled as 'vexatious correspondents'.

Most ministerial correspondence is genuine, though, and high priority is placed on providing timely and appropriate responses to it, whatever the topic. A small number of the hundreds of ministerial letters I dealt with over the years have remained in my memory, either because of the topic involved or the aftermath to it.

One concerned a letter to the minister on wild dogs, a perennial source of agitation for many sheep producers in the high country of the north-east and Gippsland. Despite significant effort, co-ordination and expenditure by both private landholders and government, losses caused by wild dogs in these areas are a continuing and apparently intractable problem. In this case the female correspondent was from East Gippsland and had written two previous and similar letters shortly before, for which we had prepared ministerial responses. As there were no further initiatives or action able to be offered in response to this third enquiry, it fell to me to write in response to it. My letter effectively provided the same information that had previously been sent under the minister's signature, prefaced with the comment that was standard in such circumstances, '... as this matter falls within my area of responsibility, the minister has asked me to respond on his behalf.' As the minister's responses had not been deemed satisfactory, it was unlikely that mine would be either, and this proved to be the case.

A few days after the third letter was sent, I received a phone call from the correspondent. I had an idea of what was likely to come, what the tone of the interaction was likely to be and was braced for a challenging encounter. I was therefore surprised by the way in which the conversation began. 'Mr McRae,' she said, 'you recently sent me a letter and I don't believe a word of it. I'm going to let you off, though, because I know your mother.' We then proceeded to have a very amicable discussion, despite the gap between her expectations and what the government was offering on wild dog control.

Another letter which caused me some wry amusement several years later, concerned a property valuation matter soon after I arrived at Land Victoria. It was from a couple who had purchased a semi-rural property to the north-west of Melbourne in the late 1980s for around $400,000. It was low-quality agricultural land and over subsequent years the property's value had risen only slowly. In the early 2000s this had changed, initially with speculation and eventually the reality of the property's inclusion within the Urban Growth Boundary and rezoning for residential use.

In the 2006 municipal valuation, the property had been valued at around $17 million. The owners had effectively become multi-millionaires as a result of a land rezoning decision by the government. Rather than rejoicing in their significant new wealth, they wrote to the minister to complain about the increased rates they were now required to pay!

CHAPTER 14

Dry times

In 2002 I was appointed to the National Rural Advisory Council (NRAC), a body that advises the federal Minister for Agriculture on issues of rural adjustment, regional development and drought. Given the weather conditions across Australia at the time, during what became known as the Millennium Drought (2001 — 2009), during the four years of my membership of the council its focusced was very heavily on drought. Warren Truss and Peter McGauran were the ministers to whom we provided advice during this time.

NRAC was comprised of eight appointees with experience and expertise in areas relevant to its advisory role, one drawn from each of the federal government, state governments (collectively) and the National Farmers' Federation (NFF), and a further five from the rural industry across Australia. During my initial term, the council was chaired by Dr Wendy Craik, a former chief executive of the NFF and subsequently of the Murray-Darling Basin Commission. Keith Perrett, a grain grower from NSW and former chair of the Grains Council of Australia, chaired the council in my final year of membership.

Farmers manage a wide range of business influences, among them being the vagaries of weather and climate in the areas in which they farm. Many are successful although, as with any area of business, some are more so than others, for reasons not always directly related to the impact of weather.

The specific issue of drought — and how governments should assist individuals, the industry and local communities to respond to it — is difficult, emotive and politically sensitive. It can be deemed harsh and unfeeling to query the appropriateness of some forms of assistance, particularly if these opinions come from non-farmers or politicians, or are made during a time of high stress such as a drought. They are an easy target for attack or misrepresentation by the media or other politicians. There are few areas of agriculture where a clear, long-term and agreed national strategy is more important than for drought.

There is a view among most policymakers that drought should be viewed as an example of one extreme of the normal variation of weather conditions under which farmers operate. In other words, it should be treated as a testing but normal part of the business environment in which farming is carried out, not as a natural disaster, nor something which governments should respond to at the time by providing direct business support.

Over time there is a regular movement of farmers in and out of an industry for a range of reasons — economic and market conditions, changed technology or personal choice being among the most common. As any industry evolves, consolidation of businesses and movement of people in and out will inevitably occur. The changes in Victorian agriculture mentioned in Chapter 7 reflect this; the industry is undoubtedly more efficient and productive

CHAPTER 14 *Dry times*

now than it was 50 years ago, despite there now being less than half the number of farmers.

While this may be true, it is still the case that for many farmers and their families a drought may be the final issue which precipitates their departure from the farm and district. This personal stress remains difficult no matter how 'normal' this may be or whether it impacts the efficiency and production of the broader industry.

Governments provide a range of programs that support individual farmers and communities in dealing with both the normal business challenges of farming, as well as those specifically caused by drought. These latter programs vary to some extent, depending on the location and duration of the drought, but are usually aimed at supporting farmers to be self-sufficient and to manage their own business and personal needs through both good times and bad, underpinned by access to Australia's broader social-welfare provisions. Direct business support — such as subsidies for stock or fodder transport, fodder purchase or interest on farm loans — has been increasingly accepted as being inconsistent with this goal.

Drought does present specific challenges, however, particularly because the demarcation between business and personal is often difficult to make in the case of farms and farmers. Meeting a policy goal of providing access to social-welfare support while resisting provision of direct business support can be challenging and administratively difficult.

For governments there is often significant media pressure during a drought for them to act by providing direct business assistance at the time, even though the most effective long-term benefit from their assistance comes from them supporting individual businesses to plan and prepare for drought when it is *not* occurring.

Australians also appear to consider differently the worthiness of farmers compared to others who receive government assistance. Many farmers are also wary of how their acceptance of it may be perceived, particularly if there is a possibility it may be viewed as welfare. The politics around drought response and how it is portrayed becomes fraught because of the broader expectation of what governments should do balanced against the desire of both politicians and farmers to avoid links being drawn between the personal/household aspects of this support and similar assistance provided to the community more generally.

Some politicians also occasionally make derogatory inferences towards those in the broader community who legitimately receive welfare payments for a time to support themselves and their families. These same politicians may later attempt to explain that farmers legitimately receiving similar assistance to enable them to support themselves and their families during drought are *not* receiving welfare payments. Their amnesia regarding their prior statements and the verbal gymnastics necessary to explain the distinction between these and their support for farmers receiving such assistance can be interesting to observe.

For many years the overall policy direction of governments has been to focus support on individual businesses to help them develop greater self-sufficiency. However, politicians of all persuasions have found it difficult to completely move away from programs which provide direct business support to farmers in times of drought, even if they have been philosophically inclined to do so.

CHAPTER 14 *Dry times*

The tension between long-term principle and short-term expediency is constantly faced, and acquiescence to the latter during periods of political pressure is common.

As droughts develop, public awareness increases, lobbying intensifies and the political imperative for governments to be 'seen to be doing something' becomes strong. By the time the prime minister has donned elastic-sided boots, a chambray shirt and Akubra, and met the media in a bare paddock beside a near-empty dam somewhere in rural Australia, all bets are off.

During my time on NRAC the National Drought Policy (NDP) was in place. This was a joint agreement between all Australian governments implemented in 1992, with most of the funding for programs supported under it provided by the federal government. Various iterations of the NDP had occurred since it was originally introduced, with access to direct business subsidies in the time of drought gradually being removed. These were replaced by initiatives such as the Rural Financial Counselling Service and business-training programs for farmers. The major form of business support made available was the Farm Management Deposit scheme, which enabled individual producers to tax-effectively set aside income in good years, then withdraw these funds in times of drought or other challenges.

Even with the nationally agreed approach, some states continued to run jurisdictional programs in addition to those supported under the NDP, and these most commonly provided access to direct business subsidies to those in drought-declared areas.

Under the NDP there was a requirement for clearly defined geographic areas to be declared by the federal minister to be facing what was termed Exceptional Circumstances (EC) prior to farmers in those areas being able to access business or household support. This inevitably led to the much-despised 'lines on a map' where farmers inside a declared EC area were eligible to apply for assistance, while those outside the area were not.

Although problematic, under the arrangements in place at the time there was no alternative to this situation. It meant that jurisdictions pushed for the boundaries of the EC areas to be as expansive as thought feasible without compromising the chances of their application being successful.

Nationally agreed criteria were in place that had to be satisfied prior to the minister declaring an area as being in EC, and NRAC was required to provide advice on every application prior to a decision being made. The process required a formal application from the relevant state, which was also required to provide a small component of the funding and support if the application was successful.

Applications were typically made with the support of the state's farmer organisation(s) and, on occasion, local municipalities. They were carefully documented and included detailed statistical and anecdotal information supporting the claim that the area was eligible for declaration and assistance. They were required to accurately define the geographic area that an EC declaration was being sought for.

Most applications from states were well presented and consistent with the spirit of the NDP, although there were differences between states as to how early in the drought this support was sought. There appeared to be quite a strong relationship between the political strength of the National Party in a state and the earliness with which applications were submitted, although the

CHAPTER 14 *Dry times*

eventual success rate of applications depended on the degree to which criteria were met, irrespective of the jurisdiction the application came from.

All applications were forwarded by the federal minister to NRAC for consideration and advice, accompanied by an analysis from the federal agriculture department of the economic, agronomic, social and meteorological conditions in the application area. An inspection of the area by NRAC — including consultation with people such as local producers, rural counsellors, bank managers, stock agents or machinery dealers — was then arranged.

During my time earlier as State Drought Coordinator in Victoria, from 1998 to 2000, there were only a couple of EC applications made for parts of the Mallee and East Gippsland. There was also only a small number of applications during that time in other areas of Australia. For the applications during that time, all or most NRAC members visited each application area, an approach that had been in place for some time.

In the Millennium Drought, given its geographic scale across much of Australia and the number of applications being made for assistance, an approach of only two NRAC members going to each area, accompanied by a couple of federal agriculture department officials, was implemented. Over my four years of membership, I participated in around 25 EC inspections across Queensland, New South Wales, South Australia and Western Australia. As with all NRAC members, I avoided participating in inspections in my home state. Other council members had a similar level of activity, with around 70 applications being handled during that time.

Visits to each area typically involved inspections of selected properties and discussions with farmers and others in small or larger groups in venues, such as around kitchen tables or in farm lounge rooms, on verandas, on back lawns, in machinery, shearing or packing sheds, pubs, local halls or municipal offices. They all involved considerable distances travelled by car or light plane. At the conclusion of each visit, a report and recommendation was prepared by those undertaking the inspection, which was discussed with NRAC as a whole before being provided to the minister.

All visits involved seeing individuals or regions in difficult circumstances which would benefit from external assistance, but not all of these met the threshold for NRAC to recommend that EC be declared for them. Assessments were made according to well-defined criteria, as leniently as thought reasonable, but ultimately within the constraints of the agreed policy. Because of the severity of the drought, the majority of applications were supported, and those that weren't were sometimes later re-submitted for modified areas. I expect there were few, if any, areas of the country that were eligible for assistance under the criteria at the time which did not receive it, despite the level of criticism directed towards NRAC from some areas where applications were not supported.

Various reviews of the NDP have been conducted and governments have now agreed that drought support based on EC is no longer appropriate. It has been replaced by a National Drought Agreement, which emphasises the need for farming families and communities to plan and prepare for climate change and variability, and provides measures to bolster risk management, long-term preparedness and resilience. Despite this, the need and demands for a comprehensive and agreed national strategy for assisting farmers and rural communities to manage drought remains. The

CHAPTER 14 *Dry times*

history of policy contention around this topic makes it likely that this will continue, particularly given the additional challenges resulting from the increasingly apparent impacts of climate change.

I particularly recall a few situations from my time on NRAC for different reasons. In 2002 we flew into a meeting at a sheep station west of Ivanhoe, in the Western Division of NSW. The area has a long and rich history in Australia's rural life based almost exclusively on wool production. The financial strength of that industry in the decades following the Second World War was very positive for the region in particular and for Australia more generally. Early in the 1950s, for example, wool made up around half of both the value of agricultural production in Australia and of the country's export earnings.

In 2002, however, the long-term decline in the fortunes of the wool industry and the current seasonal conditions were putting considerable pressure on producers in the division. The meeting followed the general format of numerous presentations from locals and then a period of general questions and discussion between those attending and NRAC members.

Following the meeting, held on the back lawn of the homestead at the sheep station, we broke for a cup of tea where individual locals and NRAC members had a chance to chat. Among those whom I met with was a family group from a nearby property who provided a poignant snapshot of the evolving fortunes of producers in the area.

The grandparents I estimated to be in their eighties, smartly and conservatively dressed, if a little more formally than necessary for the occasion. Their son appeared mid to late forties and his wife a bit younger, both more casually dressed in shorts, tee-shirts and thongs; both they and the grandparents were living on the property, but the younger members were obtaining whatever off-farm work they could, which was not easy in the area. The younger couple's son, around 12 or 14, was there as well.

In the short discussion I had, they indicated they were close to being forced into a decision on what to do with their property; it was increasingly difficult for it to provide the returns necessary to adequately support those seeking a living from it. There was limited opportunity to diversify from wool production, limited options for work off the property, and the current weather conditions had placed significantly greater pressure on the business. The desire of the grandson to continue on the property or not was still a few years away from being clear.

Despite the relative remoteness of the area and often difficult weather conditions, I could envisage the grandparents having lived comfortably for much of their lives, very satisfactorily supported by a buoyant and remunerative wool industry. But changing economic conditions in that industry had progressively squeezed the situation for them, their children and grandchildren, until the continuation of a once-viable business in a major Australian industry was under question. It is a situation repeated in virtually all agricultural industries and districts, but that family group brought the situation into particularly clear focus for me.

On another trip we arrived at Gympie in Queensland just prior to lunch. The tour of the surrounding area was to commence in the early afternoon, with a meeting at the local municipal offices, so we gathered there with perhaps 20 or 30 locals and were briefly welcomed by the mayor.

CHAPTER 14   *Dry times*

There had been a recent history of strong conservative sentiment around Gympie. It had been a focus of vocal opposition to John Howard's successful efforts to introduce national gun laws in the late 1990s. One Nation, after polling well in the area in the 1998 Queensland elections, had won the local seat in the 2001 state elections. We had been advised that the current mayor was aligned with One Nation and that support for the party was quite strong among members of the local council. In his pre-lunch welcome, the mayor made it clear that he saw our (NRAC's) role as little more than quickly doing the right thing by supporting the EC application so the government assistance that the area was obviously entitled to could quickly commence flowing. (Following our visit the application was not supported.)

Over a sandwich lunch, I chatted briefly with numerous small groups and individuals. I became aware of one gentleman who for most of the time stood apart from others in the room and went to have a chat with him. It soon became clear he was not a conversationalist. He also had the capacity to see a problem in almost any topic raised, had a decidedly negative outlook on life, and could easily have been a direct descendant of P.J. Hartigan's *Hanrahan*. He appeared to hold the view that the world owed him a living on his terms but that for some time, particularly recently, it hadn't been keeping up its end of the bargain.

After limited success in getting into a discussion, I asked him what his circumstances were and how he came to be along at the day's meeting.

'Aw,' he said, 'I don't really believe in all this bullshit, but you've gotta get into it otherwise the government just gives all the money to the greenies and the poofters.'

Late in my time on NRAC, I participated in a visit to western Queensland, largely based around Richmond but also including areas around Winton and Longreach. It was common on NRAC tours — and probably to be expected — that the same information or point of emphasis would be repeated multiple times by different groups, given that the experiences of many people in the areas would be quite similar. That was certainly the case on this tour, with the mention of dead Mitchell grass featuring strongly and regularly at virtually every inspection we made.

Mitchell grass is a widespread, persistent and important perennial grass in the area, and the fact that it was struggling under the conditions was certainly very relevant information. No one was necessarily at fault in the repetition of information, but I lost track of the number of paddocks we drove over, looked over, had pointed out to us, or took short diversions to inspect, to reiterate the fact that the conditions had been so harsh that a lot of the Mitchell grass had died. It became a point of amused comment amongst the NRAC group as the tour proceeded.

After our final stop in Longreach — and a *further* examination at the local Department of Primary Industries offices of dead Mitchell grass and another fulsome description of the implications of this — I purchased a copy of the local paper to read on our small chartered plane on the trip back home. Glancing at the personal notices, I was intrigued to discover that the single death notice in the paper for that week was for a gentleman by the name of Mitchell. We had decided to recommend that the area receive EC assistance, but that seemed to confirm it!

Despite visiting areas and people under considerable stress, irrespective of whether the applications were ultimately supported, virtually all of those whom I met with on these visits were nothing but genuine individuals. Even when local, state or industry politicians participated in meetings, it was rare for anything other than an honest and open approach to presenting a case in support of applications to occur.

While I and others were obviously outsiders and would be in the areas for only a short time, most of those with whom we dealt seemed to understand that this was the process currently in place for obtaining additional government support for the area and its farmers, and participated on that basis, largely without rancour. I have numerous very positive recollections of those inspection trips, despite the difficult circumstances under which they occurred.

CHAPTER 15

An unexpected move

At the beginning of 2006, I transferred to the role of Executive Director Land Victoria, the division responsible for the state's land titles register, the Office of Surveyor-General Victoria and Valuer-General Victoria. At the time an external review of the division was being conducted, and I expected to remain there for only a few months — the time necessary for the review to be completed and recommendations implemented — before returning to a natural resource management role. I eventually remained at Land Victoria for 12 years, prior to retiring from the public service at the end of 2017.

Lyndsay Neilson was Departmental secretary at the time I moved to Land Victoria, followed by Peter Harris, Greg Wilson, Dean Yates, Adam Fennessy and John Bradley. Genevieve Overell was deputy secretary of the group that Land Victoria was part of for the first year I worked there, and Terry Garwood for the last four.

Apart from the operational aspects of my time at Land Victoria, it was also something of a case study in the experience of many in the public service of changes to name, structure and

CHAPTER 15   An unexpected move

responsibilities of the departments in which they operate. While the functions of the division continued to be carried out, and initiatives implemented to deliver these more effectively and efficiently, there were regular changes in the environment in which we operated and the scope of our responsibilities.

There were changes of government from Labor to Coalition and back to Labor. We operated as part of the Department of Sustainability and Environment (DSE) until mid 2013, Transport, Planning and Local Infrastructure (DTPLI) for the next 18 months, and finally Environment, Land, Water and Planning (DELWP). We were initially part of the Built Environment Group within DSE, ran as a stand-alone entity within DSE for the next six years, then became part of the Local Infrastructure Group within DTPLI and DELWP.

The Spatial Services section of the division had been removed from Land Victoria and located elsewhere in DSE shortly before I arrived (a strategically poor decision), but was returned when Land Victoria had other government land responsibilities added to its role, along with a name change late in 2016 to Land Use Victoria. Then in 2017 the government announced a process to examine privatising the land registry functions of the division, which led to this occurring in a transaction worth almost $2.9 billion the following year.

It is easy to understand why some both within and outside the public service can find the frequency and extent of changes in government departments difficult to keep up with.

The division was responsible for both service delivery and policy across all the areas they were involved with. In this sense it was an amalgam of my previous roles covering both these functions.

There were many similarities between commencing at Land

Victoria and my earlier experience in moving to Western Australia. In this case the technical aspects of the division's role were quite different from those I had previously been involved with, and I was heavily dependent on the knowledge and skills of managers and staff across the division, as I had been in WA. I needed to develop virtually new industry and inter-jurisdictional networks from those I had in agriculture and natural resource management, where there had been at least some degree of commonality between the two. All of that was part of the challenge and enjoyment of the role that for many reasons proved to be among the most stimulating and fulfilling of my career.

The change of divisions also highlighted differences in the way government services interact with industry, the variation in how these actions are delivered, and the place of government services in the structure of the industry they support.

In natural resource management at that time, annual programs for state and Commonwealth funding worth around $150 million supporting local Landcare grants, advisory work, research projects, policy initiatives, compliance, reporting, evaluation and other activities were developed. Consultation and iteration occurred involving landholders, Catchment Management Authorities and state and Commonwealth public servants in developing the programs, which were finally signed-off by state and federal ministers. Both levels of government ensured they maximised favourable publicity around the range and level of support they were each providing, with even relatively small amounts of funding being accompanied by press releases or local launches to publicise them. There was a high level of time and effort involved from the community and governments prior to the expenditure

CHAPTER 15 An unexpected move

occurring, even though in most cases it made up only a minority of investment eventually made by farmers and others in the initiatives being supported.

At Land Victoria title registration was one of the main services provided and was depended on by the property industry of the state and the associated financial, legal and conveyancing industries. Each day this government service handled around 3,500 transactions on property worth around $400–500 million and did so without any fanfare and minimal political input. It just continued to happen day by day and was a central aspect of business dealings for all property transactors. I am sure there were many staff who worked in other sections of the department who were totally unaware of the central role their organisation played in the property industry, one of the largest contributors to the economy of the state. I certainly was until I went to work at Land Victoria.

Some positions included in the division were among the earliest public administration positions in Victoria: appointment to the role of Surveyor-General was first made in 1850, to that of Registrar-General in 1853, and Registrar of Titles in 1862. Since 1868, the latter two roles have been held by the one person concurrently. There was thus a long history of supporting various aspects of the property industry, and the specialist functions required meant there were many long-serving staff.

Despite the extensive history and precedence associated with much of the division's work, it was at the forefront of government agencies in deploying information technology (IT) to support its operations. It was also remarkably successful in doing so, experiencing few of the performance problems and cost over-runs that regularly appeared to accompany other government IT projects.

Many of the operational efficiencies the division was able to take advantage of, as well as to offer to its industry customers and the public, arose from this success.

An impressive measure of the cumulative impact of this came in 2015. An external review of the costs of registration operations revealed them to be less in nominal terms, and around 50 per cent less in real terms, of what they had been 10 years previously. Fees charged to the community for many of these services were reduced as a result. These efficiency gains resulted largely from the increased use of IT in the delivery of services and the capability of the Land Victoria Systems Branch in delivering them.

Most of the work of Land Victoria involves issues on which there is broad agreement between political parties. Victoria has one of the most advanced and efficient property administration systems in the world, based on the Torrens system of title registration, first introduced in South Australia in 1858 and now used in all Australian and many other Commonwealth jurisdictions. There is a focus across the political spectrum on maintaining and enhancing this, rather than indulging in political disputation around it. As a result there is little overt political dispute around much of the work done by Land Victoria and public contention around it is not common.

Even when legislation developed by Land Victoria was debated in parliament, which occurred reasonably regularly and during periods of both Labor and Coalition governments, bi-partisan support was almost always experienced. This didn't preclude Opposition speeches decrying the fact that the proposed legislation 'doesn't go far enough' or 'doesn't deal with xyz' (xyz often being only tangentially related to the legislation being considered),

CHAPTER 15 An unexpected move

Registry officials from Australian states and Commonwealth countries at Adelaide Oval, October 2008, at an event celebrating South Australia being the first jurisdiction in the world to introduce the Torrens titling system for property registration.
Victorian officials — Jane Allan, Richard Jefferson and Chris McRae — are second to fourth, respectively, from the right in the front row

but this rhetoric was almost always accompanied by full support for the proposed Bill.

Assisting governments to enact legislation to implement their policies is a key role for policy sections of government departments, and the relatively benign experience in achieving this at Land Victoria was a positive aspect of my time there. We were also impacted on a couple of occasions by another feature of governments — the 'machinery of government' change or 'MOG' — in which the experiences were more mixed.

MOGs are a reorganisation of structural and reporting arrangements for government departments and entities, and range in impact from relatively minor to far more significant. They are a common feature of public service life; anyone who has been involved in the sector for any period experiences them and becomes reasonably adept in responding to and implementing them. All initially cause at least some degree of disruption to service delivery, although at their best this disruption is short-lived and longer-term benefits are achieved. In others the disruption to service delivery or the functioning of departments is longer term and can call into question the benefits of the changes.

MOG changes usually have little impact beyond the public service but are commonly announced by governments as though they will, frequently accompanied by expansive rhetoric on their strategic sense and the benefits that will flow to the community from them. At their most effusive, these announcements can lead one to wonder why such an obvious and sensible leap forward in public-sector structure had not been put in place previously.

The reality is usually much more prosaic. As often as not, MOGs simply reflect the philosophy of the government of the day on what functions they wish to prioritise or to attempt to integrate the delivery of. They may reflect the need to highlight (either by structure or naming of a department) the political priorities of the government. For governments in their second term or beyond, they may be used to respond to political pressures that have arisen in an earlier term by appearing to 'do something'. On other occasions they appear to owe as much as anything to the need to provide individual ministers with adequate responsibility or profile to meet their real or perceived importance.

Whatever the reason, in my experience structure is a component of effectiveness, but usually not a major one. Most functions

CHAPTER 15   An unexpected move

can be equally well delivered under a range of organisational arrangements, although there are some which are more logically aligned with each other. Keeping natural resource management functions together is an example of this.

The only MOG I experienced that had an indisputably negative impact on the division I was a part of at the time was implemented in 2013, following the resignation of Ted Baillieu as premier and his replacement by Dr Denis Napthine.

The changes impacting us at Land Victoria were part of a broader reorganisation involving the land administration, planning, transport, recreation, local government and regional development components of the bureaucracy. As the area responsible for land administration, we were separated from other land-related functions of government and placed in a new Department of Transport, Planning and Local Infrastructure (DTPLI). Responsibility for the legislation we operated under was transferred from the Minister for Environment Ryan Smith to Minister for Planning Matthew Guy.

The changes had a deleterious effect on Land Victoria because of the poor alignment of functions within the new department, the poor corporate systems and support provided by that area of the new department, and an unwillingness of those responsible to attempt to improve them. In this sense it was a rare 'perfect storm' of negatives, but not one which I experienced in other MOG changes.

The experience was challenging, particularly for senior Land Victoria managers who were required to ensure enthusiasm and engagement of staff was maintained along with the delivery of business functions, despite the difficulties they had in doing so. It was the starkest example during my career of the negative impact on a department of non-aligned effort and of the impact poor support in one area can have on the work of another.

Shortly after commencing as Executive Director at Land Victoria, I was also appointed as Registrar of Titles. This is a statutory role under the *Transfer of Land* Act responsible for the operations of the Office of Titles and for carrying out the functions of the Registrar set out in the Act. In practice most of these functions — such as registering property transfers, mortgages or discharges of mortgages, and many others — are carried out under delegation by deputy or assistant registrars employed in the office, but the statutory responsibility remains with the Registrar.

There is an interesting and almost entirely academic nuance arising from an individual filling both a statutory and line management role. The formal 'chain of command' for those filling statutory roles differs from that of line management because courts are the final arbiters of disputes arising from statutory decisions, while managers higher up in the organisation fulfil this role in line management matters. This tension is unavoidable as those filling statutory roles need to be employed somewhere in the public service, and thus inevitably report to someone. In practice it virtually never causes concern, and I recall only three occasions during almost 12 years in both roles that I needed to consider it, and only one in which I finally deemed it necessary to adjust my actions because of these competing responsibilities.

One of the formal roles of the Registrar is responsibility for boundaries of properties registered in the state's title register. Late in 2013, as Registrar I approved an application to vary the seaward boundary of a property on Port Phillip Bay. I was required to respond to the application and made the decision following advice

CHAPTER 15   An unexpected move

from the state's Solicitor-General and Surveyor-General, as well as other professionals. Given the location of the property, the land impacted by the variation (a beach) and the public profile of the applicant, it was inevitable that there would eventually be significant publicity and contention regarding the decision.

Contention between parties with competing points of view is usually resolved more effectively if not done in public, and senior public servants are regularly involved in attempting to achieve this. It is not always possible, however, and in circumstances where executive directors become aware that public comment or dispute on a matter relevant to them is likely, they are expected to ensure that the secretary and minister are alerted to this, if possible prior to it eventuating.

Victorian Registrars of Title with Governor Alex Chernov and Mrs Elizabeth Chernov at a dinner celebrating 150 years of Torrens title in Victoria, October 2012 (Photo: courtesy of Land Use Victoria)

(Left to right) Tony Lyons (Registrar 1979–1992), Anne Astin (1999–2000), Governor and Mrs Chernov, Chris McRae (2006–2017), Ros Hunt (1996–1999), Barbara Flett (2002–2006), John Hartigan (2000–2002)

In this case I was making a decision in my role as a statutory officer. It was this action which would actually lead to any publicity. I took the view, though, that it was essential there was no possibility of the decision being seen by anyone as having been influenced either by those above me in the department or politically. If it was to be challenged, I believed this should be done on the basis of legal argument in a court. It was untenable that there be any sense that boundaries to private property in Victoria (more than 3 million titles) could be subject to anything other than interpretation of the laws of the state, despite the particular circumstances of this case. Accordingly, I arranged for advice to go to the secretary and minister immediately *after* formalising my decision and advising the applicant's lawyers of it.

This delayed notification turned out not to be an issue as it took almost two months for the decision to become public. When it did, it was front-page news and for a few days it was widely covered in the media and generated intense debate. Almost all commentary was critical of the decision made, some stridently so, as well as frequently being more emotional than informed.

The minister was reported to have made some statements on reversing the decision which, had he sought advice, he would have been encouraged not to make. Prominent newspaper reports that ministers were variously 'furious', 'incensed' or 'not happy' and believed that the titles office 'had questions to answer' didn't make for comfortable reading. For a few days I was unsure how the situation would evolve, while we at Land Victoria were heavily involved in dealing with media enquiries.

After a few days the public furore subsided and debates on how to respond to the decision continued within the bureaucracy,

CHAPTER 15   An unexpected move

principally those areas responsible for planning and Crown land, and related ministerial offices. These became intense on occasion and various responses were contemplated, but eventually a change to a planning regulation was introduced and activity within the bureaucracy and government subsided.

Interestingly, despite the intensity of much of the commentary and of ministerial reactions at the time, no legal challenge to the Registrar's decision has yet been made either by the government or private individuals.

Other responsibilities of the role can also involve contention — adverse possession claims, for example. Adverse possession claims can be made by a landholder who has had uninterrupted and exclusive occupation of land for 15 years or more. Successful claims enable that landholder to obtain ownership of the claimed land. Claims are often complex and, given they may result in land being included in a title when it previously was not, and therefore being removed from another, can cause significant disputation.

There is a detailed legislated process under which adverse possession claims are made, and claimants are required to provide statutory declarations attesting to the veracity of their claims. The Registrar is responsible for ensuring all aspects of the process are adhered to, and to allow or disallow claims based on them meeting this process. Virtually all are managed by registration officers under delegation, rather than by the Registrar personally.

While the Registrar is responsible for ensuring all aspects of the process are carried out as required, any disputation on the validity of the claim needs to be resolved by a relevant court. This can cause cost and frustration for those defending a claim. Although on average more than 100 adverse possession claims are made in

Victoria each year not all are concluded, because they don't meet one or more of the criteria. Surprisingly few result in disputes involving the Registrar or courts.

One such case I became personally involved with concerned a couple who had a claim made by neighbours for a sliver of land along the common boundary of their adjoining properties on which both had built holiday houses. For many years there had been an intermittent but entirely polite relationship between the parties. For a variety of reasons, I met with the couple shortly before a formal determination was to be given by the Registrar, or court action initiated if they wished to challenge the claim.

The meeting was civil but occasionally emotional, and it was obvious that the couple felt severely aggrieved by the position they found themselves in. They were disappointed that those who they considered at least close acquaintances should make such a claim, surreptitiously as they saw it, but most particularly because from their perspective they believed key aspects of it were factually incorrect.

The evidence presented to the Registrar and the process undertaken all appeared in order, however, which meant that the couple would need to go to court if they wished to contest it. They believed it was unjust that they were faced with the cost and effort of this, or of taking their case to the police if they believed (as they did) that some of the claims made, and on which a statutory declaration had been sworn, were fraudulent. Despite their strong belief that they were victims of an unfair system, they were disinclined to go down either path.

The couple worked at different businesses and for a few days following our meeting a series of 'reply all' emails were

CHAPTER 15   An unexpected move

exchanged between the three of us. After considering all options and having the relevant file checked and re-checked, including by our legal area, I eventually decided there were no further options to canvass, that the claim should be agreed to, and that the couple would need to decide what their response was to be. I composed and sent a final 'reply all' email to that effect.

Very soon afterwards I received an email from the wife, which was not 'reply all' and was obviously not intended to come to me. It read 'YEAH! YEAH! YEAH! DON'T LET THE TURKEY GET YOU DOWN! XXX.' It was the last correspondence I had on the matter.

Public servants also regularly become involved in attempting to resolve issues that have the capacity to reflect on either the department or, by extension, the minister or government. Most are resolved quickly and with varying degrees of satisfaction to those raising them, while some have amusing aspects as well. One of these I recall concerned a dispute over a postal address in north-east Victoria.

Accurate and comprehensive naming of locations, geographic features and roads, and consequent addressing of properties, is essential for all manner of reasons — postal deliveries, emergency services and general navigation being some of the more important. The Office of Geographic Names (OGN), a group within the Surveyor-General's area of Land Victoria, has policy responsibility for this in Victoria, although the actions to implement the policy are largely devolved to local municipalities.

In the early 2000s an audit process was run to confirm and, where necessary, adjust the geographic definition and naming of all locations across the state. Accurate addressing could then be applied based on these agreed locations. This was effectively a confirmation and stocktake in most cases. Only a few adjustments to existing addresses were made, but it did serve as a means of setting an agreed base from which all future naming and addressing could proceed.

In keeping with the policy for naming, the process was overseen by OGN but implemented by each municipality. A clearly defined program of local advertising and public consultation was conducted, with each municipality having discretion in how they chose to do this in their area. At the end of the process, each council was required to formally agree at a council meeting to the outcome for their municipality. These results were then forwarded to OGN who arranged for updating of statewide databases and maps, following which the updated information was used by whoever required it.

By the time results from across the state were finalised, the process ran for well over 12 months, but virtually all contentious issues were raised, debated and agreed locally before the municipality forwarded their results to OGN. Not all, though.

A few months after the work had been completed in the Shire of Towong, a farmer in the Tallangatta area realised that his long-held postal address had changed, and in his view was now incorrect. Understandably, he wanted this rectified. After some fruitless attempts to achieve this through approaching the likes of Australia Post — who were users of the information, but not responsible for it — he went public with his complaint.

The media and local politicians then became involved and for a couple of days there was a burst of activity between us at Land Victoria and Labor Planning minister Justin Madden's office attempting to resolve the complaint.

The local state Member of Parliament was Liberal Tony

CHAPTER 15 An unexpected move

Plowman, with whom I had previously had many dealings during my time as Regional Manager in the north-east. He was a fine person and an effective local politician.

All matters can be viewed through a political lens, though, and Tony was reported in the local *Border Mail* and the *Weekly Times* as sympathising with his constituent's plight, but more particularly seeing it as the unfortunate and inevitable result of there being a city-centric Labor government in power.

The local mayor was quoted as being similarly concerned about the situation, agreeing that it needed to be rectified, but being more inclined to see distant and out-of-touch bureaucrats as its cause.

When following up questions such as this, the over-riding requirement is to achieve a quick and successful resolution, but there is also a degree of subconscious self-interest in hoping that the cause has not been an administrative action or omission by the area you are responsible for, even if it occurred sometime previously.

In this case OGN had kept very complete files for each municipality on the entire process, including comprehensive maps, details of consultations carried out, and copies of the minutes from council meetings when agreement to the naming outcome was reached. These proved invaluable in getting to the bottom of the dispute.

On inspecting the Towong file, we found that the address in question was exactly as had been approved by the municipality. Even more enlightening was the discovery that approval of the location boundaries for the area under dispute had occurred following a motion at council which was seconded by the current mayor!

Following the 2014 state election, Land Victoria became part of the Department of Environment, Land, Water and Planning. Almost immediately the government announced an intention to focus on improving the use of government land (both Crown and government-owned freehold land), which led to additions and modifications being made to the responsibilities of Land Victoria. The Spatial Services function returned, a new government land-analysis group was formed and responsibility for the Government Land Monitor, a group which provides government with assurance of transparency and integrity in their land transactions, was transferred from the Planning Group. The revised entity was named Land Use Victoria. I was appointed Chief Executive when it was formed in 2016, a position I held until retiring from full-time work in December 2017.

Following retirement from the public service I continued as a board member of Property Exchange Australia Limited (see next chapter) and commenced a role as Executive Advisor in the Centre for Spatial Data Infrastructure and Land Administration. This Centre operates within the Infrastructure Engineering department at the University of Melbourne. It and Land Victoria had for many years enjoyed a mutually beneficial relationship researching and implementing enhancements to land administration systems and in training practitioners skilled in the development and introduction of technologies enabling this. For a number of years I had worked with the Centre's Director and Head of Department, Professor Abbas Rajabifard, as a member and chair of the department's Industry Advisory Group and welcomed the opportunity to continue this involvement in a part time advisory and mentoring role.

CHAPTER 15   *An unexpected move*

I had spent all my professional career in the Victorian or Western Australian public service. It was initially not a career choice I consciously made, but arose as a result of having attended Dookie College on a Department of Agriculture cadetship that required me to work in the department for five years after graduating. I then chose to remain in the public sector following this period and have no regrets on the career it led to. The changes in locations and roles, as well as the major adjustments occurring in the operation of state bureaucracies during that time, resulted in it being a varied and entirely fulfilling career. In addition, the opportunity to be involved in the development of policy or the

Family, December 2017
L to R: Ewen, Tricia, Chris, Ellen,
Hannah's husband Joel Vinicombe, and Hannah

implementation of changes impacting society that are brought about by governments, brings a degree of satisfaction to public service not available elsewhere.

The form of the public service, the functions it carries out, and the manner in which it operates have all changed markedly over the years, and the requirement to adjust, modernise and become more efficient has consequently fallen on it, as it has on private enterprise. The forces driving change — economic and commercial pressures, evolving community expectations and political responses — have been felt across both sectors, even though the impact of each may have varied between them.

When I commenced work in 1970 at Bairnsdale with the Department of Agriculture, district offices of that organisation consisted almost entirely of men. All or most offices had females in lower paid administrative/receptionist roles, but all technical positions were filled by men. It was not until 1980 that the state's first female extension officer, Judy Franklin (later Judy Backhouse), was appointed, to the Sheep Branch at Warrnambool. It was such a momentous event that it was remarked on in the department's quarterly newsletter and featured in *Stock and Land*, one of the state's rural newspapers.

Inevitably, the ethos and operational mores of the organisation reflected this staffing make-up, and it was not perceived as being anything other than normal and appropriate. Similarly, we regarded our clientele as farmers, and farmers as being almost exclusively male. Maybe more by repute and legend rather than actuality, some sections of the organisation were known (and perceived positively) as much by the ability of their leaders to thump tables and verbally dominate as by their undoubted technical capacity.

CHAPTER 15   *An unexpected move*

Government departments and services, the industries to which they are directed, and their manner of delivery are all quite different now. Changes in society and the consequent impact on employment conditions and expectations have had major impacts on these departments and their management, virtually entirely positive. More can and should be achieved, but the level of diversity, inclusivity and flexibility in current employment is vastly changed from that of my initial experience.

Major changes have also occurred in the services expected from and provided by governments and the manner in which this occurs. For example, the farm advisory services I began my career providing are no longer supplied by government and have not been for many years. The land administration services I managed at the end of my career are provided in vastly changed formats now compared to how they were in 1970. Governments and these industries have both transitioned from the former to the latter with varying degrees of difficulty or ease, and there are many similar examples of this across all industry sectors. In almost all cases an observer from 1970 looking at either a government or private-sector entity today would find both largely unrecognisable.

Although they have many similarities, government and private-sector businesses also operate with some different drivers and constraints, and it can be tempting to assume that these differences are also universally reflected in their respective performances. It is not uncommon to encounter reference to stereotypes, such as inefficiency and sloth (government) versus competence and enterprise (private sector).

In practice, even though objective comparisons between public- and private-sector industries are difficult to obtain, there is probably a similar range in performance in most characteristics across both. Personal experience and observation on one hand, through to public examples such as court cases and Royal Commissions on the other, make it clear that neither sector has a mortgage on either competence or principle. Many of the imperatives for success are common between the two, not least that they both ultimately depend for their success or otherwise on the character and capability of the people involved in them, and the degree to which this is harnessed in the provision of services to those expecting them.

CHAPTER 16
A national initiative

Most of my professional life was focused on encouraging and assisting others in the agricultural, natural resource management or land administration industries to make improvements and change, either through personally providing advice or assisting to develop policy, or by management of groups providing research, advisory, regulatory or policy services.

Change in industries is almost always slow and incremental; relatively rarely is there a rapid shift in the manner in which an industry operates or practices associated with it are carried out. While it is possible in retrospect to perceive large changes accruing over a period of years, the annual increments of this are frequently difficult or impossible to discern.

Productivity gains usually follow a similar trend, with annual changes of between, say, zero and one to two percent, producing gradual improvement over time. Labour-saving devices, automation of some functions, use of larger machinery, genetic improvement of crops and livestock, and other such items are all common drivers of this.

Over time, though, the cumulative impact of annual improvements from innovations or from practice-change adds up, and those implementing them reap the benefits of having done so. Those such as researchers, policy developers and advisors who have been researching, assisting or encouraging change also see the impact of their efforts reflected in these incremental improvements.

During the 50 years of my career, there were very few changes in each of the industries I was involved with — agriculture, natural resource management and property administration — which could be viewed as being a fundamental paradigm shift in how that industry operates or how a practice is carried out, rather than a progressive modification or improvement of an existing practice. In some cases there have been major changes in the way some individual enterprises operate, but rarely has a change impacted the way virtually all enterprises within an industry carry out their business.

Conservation tillage/direct drilling in cropping is one change in agricultural practice that has been adopted virtually across-the-board. The direct sowing of subsequent crops into the residue of prior crops, without numerous cultivations being carried out to prepare for the subsequent crop, enabled much improved soil conservation outcomes and improved economic performance for farmers. In Australia it began to be widely adopted in the 1980s, and is now standard practice for the vast majority of producers in Australia's cropping regions.

For natural resource management, the development of Landcare, with its marrying of nature conservation with production agriculture, was a quantum leap from former more

CHAPTER 16 A national initiative

individual-based conservation efforts. This movement was shaped by initiatives from a number of states and commenced under the Landcare banner in Victoria in 1986. Landcare now operates across Australia as well as in numerous jurisdictions overseas. It is the basis for community involvement in natural resource management and for government, private and corporate support for its practice. A further reason for it being included as a transformational initiative is that it depends on, and in turn enhances, social connection in rural areas where population decline has made maintaining such connections increasingly challenging.

In the case of land administration, the introduction of a national electronic conveyancing system in Australia is a fundamental change, which I believe will have at least as big an impact in that industry as the other two transformations have had in theirs. It is also one that I was fortunate to be a part of in my roles as Registrar of Titles for Victoria and as a board member of the company formed to implement the system.

Each of the major industry sectors involved in developing a national electronic conveyancing system — land registries, State Revenue Offices, financial institutions, legal practices and non-lawyer conveyancers — had for many years and to varying degrees embraced and implemented electronic approaches in their businesses. All had experienced the efficiency and service-delivery improvements resulting from transforming largely paper-based systems into electronic ones, as well as the challenges and potential pitfalls in doing so. In the case of Victoria's land registry, for example, by the early 2000s almost all registry records were held electronically rather than in paper form, and virtually all information, such as title searches provided *to* the public and businesses, was done electronically. Business coming *from* the public, however, such as property transfer documents, mortgages or discharges of mortgages still did so in paper form.

While industry sectors had systems that allowed each to carry out much of their own business operations electronically, connecting these systems to enable property conveyancing transactions to be carried out from commencement through to financial settlement in a consolidated national approach had been envisioned but never achieved.

Late in the 1990s Australia's Registrars of Title began a formal process to develop such a system. This initiative was soon expanded to involve, as was essential, representatives of relevant industry groups. In its 2002 budget, the Victorian government funded the development of the IT component of an electronic conveyancing system, along with three other projects aimed at expanding the use of electronic business systems in the state's property industry. The SPEAR system (Surveying and Planning through Electronic Applications and Referrals), now universally used in Victoria's property subdivision industry, was one of the projects supported by this funding.

The technical challenges of agreeing on and developing an IT system were considerable, but it was not these which proved the most difficult to overcome. The work to implement a national business approach was being carried out by a national committee supported by New South Wales at the same time as the electronic system to enable it was being developed by Victoria. Whilst ostensibly there was close coordination and interaction between the two processes, there were no governance arrangements in place

CHAPTER 16 *A national initiative*

with the capacity to resolve differences of opinion or approach which inevitably developed. Personalities were often more prominent than progress, and although there continued to be a strong desire from all sectors for the venture to succeed, the means of achieving this became increasingly uncertain.

Maintaining momentum became an issue, and the challenges to Victoria of continuing to fund and defend the development of an electronic system while participating in debates on how to implement a national approach increased. Victoria was perceived by some as paying only lip-service to the aim of a national system, and its *bona fides* regarding support for this, rather than its own state-based scheme, was publicly questioned, most notably and commonly in *The Australian* newspaper. Questions critical of Victoria's approach were raised in the Victorian parliament and in Senate Estimates hearings in Canberra. It became the most public and intense inter-jurisdictional tussle I had been involved in.

The task of developing and implementing a national approach to revolutionise conveyancing could not be achieved quickly, because of the scale and complexity of the changes required and the range of interests which had to be catered for. Achieving this within a single jurisdiction would be challenging; doing so across Australia greatly magnified the difficulties.

With no possibility of an operational or political 'win' in the short term, irrespective of how successful the system build or development of national business arrangements were, political and bureaucratic support to withstand the attacks on Victoria became essential, but were not necessarily guaranteed. Gavin Jennings was the responsible minister at the height of tensions, and Peter Harris the departmental secretary. Thankfully, both provided strong backing throughout, which their successors in these roles continued in subsequent years, and this proved to be pivotal in the final achievement of the goal.

A major breakthrough occurred late in 2008 when development of a national electronic conveyancing scheme was included as a priority in the Council of Australian Government's (COAG) *Seamless National Economy* initiative. This resulted in the Queensland, New South Wales and Victorian governments jointly agreeing to fund the establishment of a company to build a national system, a mandate subsequently expanded into being responsible for operating the system following its development.

In January 2010 the company National E-Conveyancing Development Limited (NECDL) was formed, with the three states each initially providing funds of $1.67 million. Alan Cameron, a Sydney lawyer and company director was appointed chair, I became a member of the initial board, and Marcus Price was appointed as Chief Executive Officer soon after the company's formation.

Over subsequent years the company changed its form and name to become Property Exchange Australia Limited (PEXA). It sought and received investments from the Western Australian government, Australia's four major banks and a small number of other major investors, which was collectively to prove central to achieving its goal. It purchased intellectual property developed to that stage by Victoria and other states, and vigorously pursued the goal of making a national electronic conveyancing system a reality. In 2013 this was achieved when a single-party mortgage transaction was carried out in Victoria; in 2014 a more complex two-party transfer transaction was conducted in New South Wales.

These public achievements were the first of many by the company,

CHAPTER 16   A national initiative

which progressively expanded the geographic spread and range of services it offered. Not all proceeded smoothly and there were regular internal and sectoral challenges that needed to be negotiated or overcome. A small number of public missteps also needed to be responded to and managed, including some which were not directly the responsibility of PEXA. This was to be expected, as the company was the public face of the change occurring in the industry and the project involved development of major IT infrastructure, as well as significant modification of practices to enable this.

PEXA could be proud of the limited controversy or technical problems that accompanied their success in achieving such a major change to a business process across jurisdictions and sectors, which in aggregate involved many thousands of transactions worth billions of dollars each week. They were the pioneers on a path that none had previously travelled.

All sectors involved were necessary to achieve the outcome and share in the credit for doing so, but PEXA and the state registries were undoubtedly the pivotal players in managing the collective interests of industry groups and enabling the transformation of the property conveyancing industry in Australia. A major reason for this success was the ability of PEXA and the registries to engage all the parties that needed to be aligned, then ensuring they collaborated effectively to contribute to the transformation being realised.

PEXA was sold late in 2018 to a consortium, which included one of its shareholders, Link Market Services, for just over $1.6 billion, a far cry from the approximately $5 million initially contributed by the three states to commence this venture. I left the board at that stage, after one of the more satisfying involvements of my career.

There were numerous lessons to be drawn and observations to be made regarding the introduction of a national electronic conveyancing scheme. The first is the fundamental importance of appropriate governance in achieving success. The initial approaches of inter-jurisdictional and industry committees and working groups, however well-intentioned, and despite containing all relevant interest groups, were useful but insufficient to do so. The lack of a formally constituted body ultimately accountable for making and defending decisions was a fatal flaw which the formation of NECDL/PEXA finally overcame.

Another is the central importance of so-called 'soft' skills in enabling success, when multiple (powerful) groups are required to come together to achieve even a seemingly 'hard' technical outcome. Throughout the process, respective sectors of the industry, while remaining supportive of the overall goal, tended to prioritise different aspects necessary to achieve the goal and the benefits flowing from it.

Individual financial institutions and the Australian Bankers' Association were keen to ensure the national scheme enabled them to achieve the financial efficiencies and benefits they believed it offered. (Various independent studies identified greater financial institution efficiency as the largest component of the potential $250 million to $300 million annual benefit enabled by the scheme.) The legal fraternity focused heavily on matters of risk. The non-lawyer conveyancers had a keen eye on the business benefits the system could enable for their members and, at least in Victoria, were the most consistently supportive industry group throughout the process. Registries and jurisdictional treasuries concentrated heavily on the legislative and regulatory regime

CHAPTER 16   A national initiative

necessary to implement and maintain the system, as well as ensuring no increased liability was transferred to them in their role of guaranteeing property transactions under the Torrens system. All had an ideal version of how they would prefer the system to develop, broadly aligned but differing in detail according to their specific viewpoint.

Periods of change provide interest groups with the greatest opportunities to institutionalise features most favourable to them in any modified system, and understandably each attempted to exert that influence in this case. All interests were legitimate and necessary, and ultimately each sector needed to ensure adequate attention was being given to their priorities as the scheme developed, to enable them to accede to the compromises inevitably required. While far less obvious than the technical IT system developed and the final business transformation it enabled, the skill of PEXA and state registries in managing this process of consultation and agreement was fundamental to the success of the overall venture.

Another feature was the positive alignment of different primary goals of government and business interests among the company's shareholders, and the way in which these disparate interests were finally satisfied by the success of PEXA. It was another of the less visible but nonetheless positive features of the initiative that representatives of each party developed an enhanced understanding and respect for the other as the work progressed.

In broad terms, governments invested in PEXA to achieve micro-economic reform (a more efficient and cost-effective conveyancing system for Australian business and the public), and companies invested to enable this and to make money from doing so. Financial institutions (companies) and land registries (governments) also sought benefits-in-use from implementation of the system in their businesses. Though possible, it was unlikely in practice that one group of investors could achieve their goal without the other doing so as well, and each would share in the success of the other.

To achieve their aims, governments were prepared to invest in the riskier initial stages of the venture. As it developed and began to demonstrate success, companies invested funds to enable development to continue and governments reduced or ceased further investment. Over time the portion of PEXA owned by states moved from 100 per cent of a company worth a small amount to around 30 per cent of one worth considerably more.

When PEXA was sold in 2018, its operational success meant that it sold for a price that provided all investors with solid returns on their investment. It was operating in five jurisdictions with plans to do so in all eight. Its use was mandated in some jurisdictions, and others had plans to do so. The goal of some registries, including Victoria's, was for 100 per cent of transactions to come to the registry electronically via PEXA's or any other company's electronic system within a few years. There was no doubt that the goal of governments in originally supporting the development of a national electronic conveyancing system was well on the way to being met, and all initial investors in it had achieved at least reasonable returns from this being so.

POSTLUDE

This volume is focused on the past, but as it is primarily for my children it would not be complete without some brief consideration of my hopes for the country they will most likely live their future lives in.

The nexus between the society we live in, the politics which shape it and personal perspectives means that one cannot speak about personal hopes for the future without reflecting to some extent on the political forces which will help to shape that future.

Defining a political, social or moral outlook of a country is arguably impossible, and a single expression of such things doesn't exist. At the very least, the conclusion one individual comes to is likely to differ from that of others' simply because of the varying experiences and life perspectives of the observers. Despite this, it is possible for each of us to give a personal perspective on these matters, and to carefully consider how our own outlooks compare with those that past and current leaders of our country have championed or are currently attempting to implement.

For most of my adult life, my personal philosophy and outlook have been more aligned with those of the progressive side of politics, despite the conservative view being more prevalent in the experiences of my youth. By the time I came to participate in elections (21 years old in those days), I judged the social, environmental, economic and equity goals of progressive policies to be better aligned with my developing views on these matters. I assessed the philosophy of parties promoting them to be more focussed on seeking betterment for society as a whole, and to being open to promoting the change which may be necessary to achieve this.

It is important that we acknowledge and celebrate our heritage both personally and as a country. In doing so, we need to reflect on both the positive and negative aspects of it, because it will always be possible to identify both in any honest appraisal. Celebrating and maintaining the former while acknowledging, learning from and, if necessary or possible, working to redress the latter is the most effective way to honour the personal and broader influences which have formed us. All these actions should be undertaken, not just those that result in us not changing from past practices or opinions. Even though this latter is commonly presented in some political discourse as being the most appropriate way of 'honouring what has brought us to this point', celebrating our heritage more fully requires broader consideration.

Accordingly, we should not be reticent or apologetic about making changes to past perspectives or approaches, whether these changes arise in response to a contemporary assessment of these perspectives or simply in response to changing circumstances. Being shackled to past approaches because of a lack of desire or vision to conceive of a better future, because change is psychologically or emotionally difficult, or simply because it may appear in some way disrespectful of former generations, is an unduly limiting and timid approach. Yesterday should not, *prima facie*, be viewed more positively than tomorrow.

The policy leadership and political courage necessary to

envision, champion and implement positive change for society is far greater than that required to simply manage evolutionary change in existing circumstances. The former is far less common and, because by its nature it involves disruption, it is supported electorally for shorter periods. It is undoubtedly necessary, though, if society seeks to positively manage its future rather than largely react to it emerging.

The challenges to achieving this appear to be increasing, however. Absolute opposition to any initiative of another party is now common. Division is engendered as a primary means of deriving political benefit. Policy initiatives are now commonly framed and implemented in a manner that emphasises division or cultural bias. It is inevitable that differing political views result in differing perspectives on many matters, but the active search for division and the fomenting of it as a primary political tactic appears to have become far more prevalent in recent years than previously. It frequently occurs as an end in itself without a positive alternative vision for the issue being tackled being articulated.

This has led to political and leadership success too often being framed around highlighting differences between opposing views or groups holding them, and seeking to gain political advantage based on this, rather than prioritising and arguing for alternative visions for a positive long-term future. In Australia's case, it has led to an environment marked by recent leaders who have too frequently prioritised political cynicism, inward-looking nationalism, timidity towards a changing future and reduced regard for human rights.

Success has been measured less by the impact of implemented policies but more by incumbency and the cultivation of a polarised and indignant electorate. It has been accompanied by approaches such as discrediting or disregarding expert opinion that does not suit the political narrative being pursued, denigration or marginalising of minority groups within Australia, and the sophistry of pretending that choices regarding increasingly complex long-term issues can be reduced to simple and mutually exclusive alternatives. It has created a political environment in which compromise and nuance is anathema, contrary to so much of the practical experience of life.

Recent governments have effectively lived off and drawn down on the benefits generated by the political courage and policy vision of some prior governments. As much as anything, they have shown that an ability to count numbers, work angles and apply wedges is a very poor indicator of leadership capacity.

Life essentially distils down to multitudinous interactions between individuals or groups of human beings. Some of these interactions change the world, some impact governments, businesses, communities or organisations, while most are essentially inconsequential to all except the individuals or groups directly involved. All coalesce eventually, largely unknowingly, and with their various tones and impacts, to make up the world in which we live.

If the leaders of a country choose to prioritise a tone marked by suspicion, rejection, exploitation of difference and denigration of expertise, even if this forms only a part of their political approach, we cannot expect it will not have a negative impact on the broader life of a country. We are all negatively impacted and coarsened by it.

Conversely, if leaders choose a positive and embracing approach to tackling difficult issues, we can all be uplifted by this and become positive rather than suspicious of the future. It is a choice that leaders have the responsibility to make, and their choice often sets the direction for a country for many years into the future.

In sporting parlance I am now in the equivalent of the final quarter or post-tea session of my life. Despite some disappointment around the national tone of recent years and the perceived failure of many of our leaders during that time to appropriately respond to the challenges and opportunities we face, this is a wonderful country in which to live. I have been immensely fortunate to have lived my life in the circumstances I have. I am a member of a demographic — white, male, healthy, educated, baby-boomer, Australian, ... the list goes on — which could be argued to be among the most fortunate and privileged ever to have lived. I believe this needs to be acknowledged in the outlook I have on life, the manner in which I lead it and the contributions I make to it, irrespective of how narrowly or broadly influential these may be.

I have no reason to expect that the rest of my life will be any less positive than I have experienced to this stage and am certainly intending to pursue it on this basis. But I also have hopes regarding the society that my children will experience for the duration of their lives and on the characteristics of a polity I believe would best deliver this.

My hope is that the Australia of my children and theirs will be an open and positive country, as it makes the most of the present and looks forward expectantly to a changing future. I hope that its future leaders, whether progressive or conservative, demonstrate a capacity to provide leadership in promoting cohesion and equity in our society, in encouraging economic activity always in conjunction with sound environmental stewardship and active social concern, and in accepting that responses to challenges such as displacement of people by conflict, and climate change, are national and international priorities, not simply matters useful to foment political division.

As well as celebrating the marvellous legacies that have brought us to our current position, I hope also that we can embrace the far more difficult but necessary task of accepting both the deficiencies in our journey to this point and the failure of some of our current approaches.

In the case of the former, we have much to do in acknowledging, accepting and addressing the actions and impacts of colonisation on the original inhabitants of this land and in adequately including their ambitions in planning for its future.

In the latter, responding to the legitimate needs of those who come to this country through necessity, rather than planning, is a challenge to which we must respond far more humanely and effectively than we currently do. Similarly, we must get to a point where a national response to the challenges of climate change can be made by our politicians with a vision beyond three years, and prioritising science rather than ideology or protection of vested interests.

I would be delighted if we could collectively develop the assurance and self-confidence to decide to have an Australian as our head of state, not as a denunciation or repudiation of our past, but as a natural and mature embrace of our future.

We retain a choice in deciding how we respond to these and other challenges, but we do not have a choice in having to live with the impacts and consequences of the decisions we make regarding them.

As we respond to challenges and opportunities, I hope that we can accept that raising the status of one part of society does not need to diminish the circumstances of another, and that promoting division is not a road to genuine, long-term national progress.

The future rate of change in Australia's society, environment and economy is likely to be far greater than that which I have experienced, irrespective of whether this is welcomed or not. The extent that this can be positively managed will determine the degree to which our society will remain strong and resilient during these changes.

Australia will also be more diverse in almost every way in the future — ethnically, racially, religiously and other — than it is now. Despite the 'pulling up of the drawbridges' against this that is promoted by some in Australia, and the temporary slowing of the trend in some cases, it is unlikely to stop.

I hope that Australia in the future can find leaders who are equal to the task of engaging and guiding society as it navigates these and other changes, as an opportunity to be welcomed, responded to, managed and made the most of. I hope that these leaders can engage and inspire the community of the country to respond in the same way far more effectively than has been the case over recent years.

If that were to happen, while their circumstances will undoubtedly be different, there is no reason why the lives of my children and theirs will not be as positive as mine.

> Adieu, dear, amiable youth!
> Your heart can ne'er be wanting!
> May prudence, fortitude, and truth,
> Erect your brow undaunting!

In ploughman phrase, "God send you speed,"
Still daily to grow wiser;
And may ye better reck the rede,[14]
Than ever did th' adviser!

Final stanza of 'Epistle to a young friend' — Robert Burns

---

14 Heed the advice

ACKNOWLEDGEMENTS

I am grateful for the assistance of many people who have helped with this publication, and without whose contribution it would not have been possible. I obviously retain responsibility for any omissions, errors that remain or opinions expressed, but want to acknowledge the efforts of those who have helped in its development.

Former work colleagues David Wille and Rosco McJames assisted in searching early property details and George Mifsud produced the map contained in the book.

I am grateful for the contributions of those who have read and commented on sections of the draft document. Colleagues from many of the times covered in it have either corrected, expanded or improved the respective sections and I appreciate their efforts in doing so. Thanks are due to Rob Stafford, Kevin Love, Garry McDonald, Mark Dunn and Ian Ireson in this regard.

A number of others have supplied information or recollections on specific circumstances or events, and I am grateful to Rob Knight, Steve Walsh, Neil Hodge and Rhonda Coates for their willingness to do this.

I enjoyed working with and appreciated the skills of Euan Mitchell as editor.

I particularly thank Luke Harris for his advice and assistance in all matters related to the production of this book; it would not have been possible without his professional guidance.

Many members of my family have contributed wonderfully. My sisters Elizabeth Lee and Alison McRae, and cousins Alex McRae and Alice Mills were sources of either documented history, personal recollections or both and I thank them for the help they provided. Nieces Rebecca McCaig (Graphic Design) and Megan Lee (Plumtree Photography) are respectively responsible for the wonderful cover design, and the photographs of Vere Moon's paintings. Son in law Joel Vinicombe helped in finalising the map.

Finally, my wife Tricia has been a constant encourager, guide and prompter during this venture, which would not have occurred without such support. As in all things, I am indebted to her for this and for her ongoing love and support.

BIBLIOGRAPHY

A ton of cricket. A celebration of 100 years of cricket in Leongatha and District. 1893 — 1993. Leongatha and District Cricket Association

Adams, John, *The Tambo Shire centenary history*, Tambo Shire Council, 1981.

Birtles, Terry, *Contested places for Australia's capital city*, 11th Annual Planning History Conference, 2004

Blake, Jim, *Official history — Commemorating the centenary of the Stawell Athletic Club, 1877-1977*, Stawell Athletic Club, 1977.

Buchan 1905 School centenary 1877-1977: A brief history of Buchan district and schools, 1977.

Bukan Mungie: 150 years of settlement in the Buchan District 1839-1989, Buchan Sesquicentenary Committee, 1989.

Cameron, Rod, *Victory through harmony — a history of the first 100 years of the Leongatha Football Club 1894 — 1994*. Leongatha Football Club Centenary Committee

Coates, Rhonda, *John Flynn postcards from Buchan, 1905-1906*, Buchan John Flynn Centenary Committee and Buchan Heritage Group, 2006.

Cordner, John, *Black & blue: the story of football at the University of Melbourne*, Melbourne University Football Club, 2007

Early days at Murrindal and 4067, Back to Murrindal Committee, 1986.

Gador-Whyte, Rev. Peter (compiler/editor), *Pioneers and pilgrims — A history of the Presbyterian and Methodist churches in Orbost and East Gippsland*, 1986.

Gardner, P.D., *Gippsland massacres*, 3rd edition, Ngarak Press, Ensay, 2001.

Ginnane, Christine (compiler), *Drumanure and District — changing times*, self-published, 1999.

Grow, Robin, *Safe as houses — the history of the Victorian land titles office*, Victorian government, 2012.

Lucknow Primary School No. 1231 — 125 years of memories, Lucknow Primary School, 1998.

McRae, Chris (ed.), *Land to pasture — environment, land use and primary production in East Gippsland*, James Yeates and Sons, 1976.

Moon, Vere, *Cut lunch commando*, Estate of Vere Moon, 2010.

Murphy, John, *Nerrena — A pattern of progress*, Leongatha Historical Society, 1981.

Russell, H.M.J., Bardsley, J. B. and Lawson, R.A.S. (eds.), *Reminiscences from the inside — bringing science to agriculture: A history of the Department of Agriculture, Victoria, 1946-1996*, 2014.

Squatters — The Kings at Snake Ridge, Rosedale, www.theminters.co.uk

Youl, Rob, Marriott, Sue and Nabben, Theo, *Landcare in Australia - founded on local action*. Secretariat for International Landcare (SILC) and Rob Youl Consulting Pty Ltd, 2006

www.ingramcontent.com/pod-product-compliance
Lightning Source LLC
Chambersburg PA
CBHW051534010526
44107CB00064B/2720